Praise for

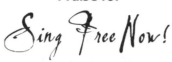

"Finally, a comprehensive, straightforward 'learn how to sing book' that hits the MARK! *Sing Free Now!* could be the game changer in the lives of those with a passion to sing. Five stars, Mark!"
—Dick Peterson, member of The Kingsmen of "Louie Louie" fame

"If you want to sing with more freedom, no matter what your relationship with your voice, this is the book for you."
—Valerie Day, voice teacher and lead singer of Nu Shooz who recorded the mega hit "I Can't Wait"

"For singers of all genres *Sing Free Now!* contains very accessible exercises and explains fundamental concepts that will help you improve your vocal instrument."
—Frizzi-Lilian Link, MM, MS, CCC-SLP voice consultant, speech language pathologist

"In *Sing Free Now!* Mark has coined an effective approach to singing that will have broad appeal and application for a wide variety of singers. With a jovial tone and bold conviction born from years of experience, this book is a compelling combination of a technical manual about singing, a thoroughly convincing pep talk, and an inspirational provocation to get at the source for why any of us sing—to know and express our authentic selves more fully. It's a great book with insights to be mined by professionals and amateurs alike. Enjoy and grow!"
—David York, PhD, voice teacher, choral director and composer

"Whether you attend his singing seminars, take a singing lesson from him, or read this book, to work with Mark Bosnian is to be in the presence of a master. Treat yourself . . . and set yourself free. I LOVE this book!"
—Jody Stevenson, author, coach, speaker and minister of the Center for Spiritual Living in Colorado Springs, CO

"*Sing Free Now!* is a masterpiece of detail and concise awareness of all the subtleties that a singer must consider. Bosnian has stepped into the breach beautifully with words that illuminate and uplift that invisible process of singing. I look forward to the continued support for my singing that this book offers. Thank you, Mark!"
—Charley Thweatt, touring singer-songwriter who has performed with Ram Dass, Tony Robbins, Deepak Chopra, Michael Beckwith and Wayne Dyer

"The very first time I met Mark Bosnian, I absolutely knew I wanted to work with him. His profound passion, as well as refreshing authenticity, radiates joy throughout everything he touches! And as his new vocal student, I can tell you that *Sing Free Now!* is a powerful book that brings Mark's encouragement, faith and unconditional love to anyone who wants to sing from their soul. Can you tell he is one of my most favorite people?"
—Rev. Debbie Taylor, senior minister, Unity of Beaverton

"In *Sing Free Now!*, Mark tells the real story of your voice, free of wishy-washy simplifications or hand-waving. His fascination with the mechanics of singing is infectious, and his teaching style fosters hope and confidence as he demystifies our own bodies' inherent and amazing capabilities. Mark's knowledge and practical methods make for an approachable and empowering book that I'll be recommending for years to come!"
—Scott Simon, President and Founder, Voicebox Karaoke Lounge

In *Sing Free Now!*, Mark Bosnian is giving us roots to grow our voices from, and sound foundational principles to enhance and restore singing health. Mark brings basic singing principles alive with stories, exercises and much experience. I highly recommend this work for any level of expertise.
—Vickie Dodd, Sound Therapist, Director Sacred Sound Work

Sing Free Now!

3 Steps to Power, Passion and Confidence

MARK BOSNIAN

**ARMENOID
PUBLISHING**

Portland, Oregon

Armenoid Publishing
2123 SE 37th Avenue
Portland, OR 97214
www.SingFreeNow.com

Cover design and illustrations: Keith Buckley, www.zapgraphics.com
Cartoons: Edwin Coleman III
Interior design: Jennifer Omner, www.allpublications.com

Paperback ISBN: 978-0-9748840-0-4
E-book ePub ISBN: 978-0-9748840-1-1
Library of Congress Control Number: 2011907345

Printed in the United States of America
10 9 8 7 6 5 4 3 2 1

For Arthur Bosna, my dad, who first showed me the power of vocal dynamics simply by raising and lowering his voice. He modeled the importance of a strong work ethic and taught me my first dirty word—discipline (it wasn't until I grew up that I realized the value of daily practice). And he could tell a story like no one else.

And for Tracy Bosnian, my wife. As a voice teacher, I am privileged to witness the flowering of singers as they work through vulnerable feelings and learn to own their power. I can't tell you how much joy I've experienced proudly watching my wife, Tracy, conquer her lifelong fear of singing and, in the process, discover her beautiful voice—literally and figuratively. She reminds me how blessed I am to do the work I do.

Contents

Step 1: Power—Make Friends with Your Belly

Contents

Contents

Step 2: Passion—Make It Your Own

Step 3: Confidence—Make a Move, Make a Connection

Contents

Acknowledgments

For their help in making this book a reality, I would like to thank:

Tracy Bosnian, for being a sounding board for ideas and an editor of awkward sentences—and for being my best friend;

My mom, Carolyn Merrifield, for making me feel supported from an early age on;

Wayne Bosna, my brother, and Christie Switzer, my sister, for having to listen to me sing throughout our childhoods and for loving me anyway;

Tom Blaylock, for turning my voice around and turning me into a voice teacher;

Jody Stevenson, for being my Master Mind partner for 20 years and for helping me to birth this book;

Joanne McCall, for pointing me in the right direction and showing me what to do once I got there;

Sharon Castlen, for knowing the details;

Keith Buckley, for asking the right questions and for stellar graphics;

Jennifer Omner, for being a steady influence and for creating a beautiful interior design;

Linda Gray, for being an editor extraordinaire—this book really became a book when she got her hands on it;

Robert Pater, for his down-to-earth ideas and suggestions and for his stunning "Aloha" shirts;

Steve Blackman, for his wonderful insights, suggestions, and questions;

Acknowledgments

Sandy Bly, for being the "it's" gal;

Wynter Byrnes, for being a "model" student;

Edwin Coleman III, for your creative cartoons;

And all of my students, for the laughs and tears they've shared with me and for the courage and incredible growth they've given me the honor of witnessing.

Introduction

The greatest secret in singing is that you have choices. Many of you have heard that, when it comes to singing, there is one "right" sound and that there is one particular genre or style of music that is best suited to your voice. Nothing could be further from the truth. You can sing whatever calls to you or moves you, and you can sing any genre of music that you like. In fact, singing with power, passion, and confidence—with joy, from the heart and soul—requires that you bring the music from a place inside yourself.

This is much more difficult if you are singing something that *someone else* thinks you should sing. *Sing Free Now!* will teach you how to sing what *you* want to sing the way you want to sing it. The principles of singing with power, passion, and confidence apply to all styles—from gospel to opera; from heavy metal to bluegrass. If you can hear it, you can learn to sing it.

Using an easy-to-follow, step-by-step system, this book shows you how to overcome the biggest issues that plague all singers, from projection, tone, and singing in tune to hitting high and low notes, breathing correctly, having a unique sound, and—most important—singing with confidence. The system is composed of 3 steps, which I call the 3 Steps to Power, Passion and Confidence.

Step 1: Power—Make Friends With Your Belly. The first step involves learning to correctly employ the mechanics of singing in order to sing in tune, project, hit high and low notes, eliminate your "break," and master many of the other physical elements of singing.

Step 2: Passion—Make It Your Own. In this section, you'll learn how to use the artistry of singing to create dynamics, evoke emotion, and put your unique stamp on everything you sing.

Step 3: Confidence—Make a Move, Make a Connection. The last step teaches you everything you need to know to create a stage presence that will connect you, the song, and the audience and that will have your listeners rooting for you.

These 3 steps will put you on the fast track to learning the options you have in singing, understanding them, and knowing how and when to use them. By following the guidance offered in this book and the exercises and audio tracks on my website, you will become an intentional singer instead of a hopeful one.

 ## Three-Legged Stool

If you picture the 3 Steps to Power, Passion and Confidence as the three legs of a stool, you'll realize just how important each step is to singing with confidence and experiencing joy with your voice. If one leg is weak, the stool can fall over. Similarly, if you haven't mastered each of the 3 Steps, your instrument—and your performance—can easily break down. I've heard singers who had great technique (Step 1: Power—Make Friends with Your Belly) but very little stage presence (Step 3: Confidence—Make a Move, Make a Connection). Their singing sounded mechanical, and their performances showed no sign of personality that could have touched the audience. I have also heard many singers whose mastery of mechanics was less than perfect but who connected with an audience by allowing their creative selves to come through (Step 2: Passion—Make It Your Own).

Throughout this book you'll come across this icon of a three-legged stool. It is used to alert you to important points and tips throughout the book and to remind you that you need to master all 3 steps in order to sing with power, passion, and confidence.

Why Sing?

Singing is not only about how well our instrument works; it is also about how willing we are to let what is on the inside of us be experienced on the outside—in other words, how willing we are to reveal our authentic selves to the world. I call this "turning yourself inside out." To many, if not most, singers, that sounds frightening. Why would anyone want to gamble on standing up in front of someone else and singing his or her heart out when there is a possibility that the performance will be harshly judged or criticized? *Because of the payoff.* It feels good to make sound with your body—it's liberating and exciting. And, when you sing a song and really connect with the audience, you can feel the exchange of energy. There is nothing like it in the world. When you trust enough to open your heart and soul by singing with power, passion, and confidence, you experience the true joy of singing and of being yourself.

Regardless of where you are on the path of singing or what your relationship with your voice may be at the moment, this system will help you to create and express power, passion, and confidence when you sing.

I created this book for:

- Those singers who have already been "onstage." You've sung with a band, at a karaoke club or party, as a featured singer at church, in a talent show, or at a competition. You've performed solo and you know you want to sing with more power, passion, and confidence. You want to experience more of the joy of singing.

- Singers in groups such as choirs, musical theater choruses, quartets, gatherings of carolers, and karaoke "gangs." You enjoy the camaraderie of singing with others and you'd like to improve your skills. You may be thinking about singing a solo. You might be anxious about the idea of singing by yourself, but part of you is yearning to go for it.

- People who have never sung in public before and who don't know if it is even possible for them to "sound good." You sing in the shower or along with the radio when you're alone in your car. You don't think you sing well enough to do it front of someone else, and you tend to move to the corner of the room when everyone is singing "Happy Birthday to You." All your life you've believed that you really can't sing, and you've always wished you'd been born with a voice. A little part of you thinks that maybe you could actually learn to sing with confidence and express your power and your passion, but you're afraid to trust that notion.

In this book I use the term "performance" to mean singing in front of one or more people. I use the term "audience" to refer to one or more listeners. And this is what I mean by the term "singer":

A singer is anyone who sings anywhere, to anyone or to no one at all. It doesn't matter whether you sing in the shower, in the car, to your child, in a choir, at a karaoke bar, at church, or on a stage in front of thousands of people. If you have started to explore your voice, you are a singer. Please think of yourself as one.

Singing with power, passion, and confidence enables you to reveal yourself through your voice. Sounds simple enough, right? Why, then, do most singers find it so hard to do? There are many reasons, but at the top of the list is fear. When we were children, most of us vocalized without worrying about how we sounded. We sang; we made funny noises; we used our voices as an extension of what we were feeling at that moment. If you ask a very young child if he or she likes to sing, dance, or draw, that child will usually answer with an emphatic "yes!" It isn't until we grow older that inhibitions begin to appear.

Many people have told me that they must have been in the wrong line when voices were being handed out—that you either "got a voice" when you were born or you didn't. Often this belief is formed by casual and careless comments by teachers, relatives, or others in authority: "Sweetie, why don't you just mouth the words while everyone else sings?" "Class, please don't imitate Johnny—his voice sounds terrible." Or the ever-popular "Suzie takes after my side of the family—the one that can't sing."

About Step 1:
Power—Make Friends with Your Belly

For many people, learning to sing is learning to undo bad habits. This is where Step 1: Power—Make Friends with Your Belly comes in. You'll learn to breathe and make sound the way Nature intends you to make it—and you'll learn how to *stop* trying to make sound inefficiently by identifying and overcoming the bad habits most of us have picked up during our lives. When you understand how your instrument, the body, is supposed to work, you can return your voice to its natural state. When you become aware of how energy flows through the body, you will be able to control your voice with much more confidence and you'll be able to make adjustments when the energy flow is blocked and the voice is working less than perfectly.

This is one of the major advantages of learning about the mechanics of singing: you will be able to make adjustments and repairs—often while in the middle of a performance. As singers, we need to get comfortable with this idea. We are the only musicians who regularly have to make technical adjustments to our instruments while we're "playing" them. A piano player never has to stop in the middle of a performance, pull out a tuning hammer, and tune a string (actually, I did do that once when I was playing in a recording studio, but that's another story). Once you learn how to make adjustments, you will find that you can make many of them as you are singing. Some will be done consciously by you; others will be done automatically by your trained "instrument"—your brain and your body.

About Step 2:
Passion—Make It Your Own

In this section, you'll learn how to make conscious decisions that allow you to move from simply employing good technique to creating art by revealing what you feel and what you have to say to the world. You'll learn how to use dynamics and emotion in your singing and you'll learn how to create your own style. The tools you'll discover in this step will help you to put your unique stamp on everything you sing.

The mechanics you'll learn in step 1 will open your eyes to the technique and style options that are available to you and will enable you to adjust various elements of your voice and your delivery when you sing. This ability gives you a huge advantage over a lot of other singers, who have to settle for living with the only sound they know how to make. In fact, most singers don't truly believe that it is possible to have options. I've heard many first-time students say, "That's the way my voice sounds—I can't change that." Yes, you can, and this book will show you how to do it.

About Step 3:
Confidence—Make a Move, Make a Connection

In this section, you'll learn the nuts and bolts of getting your audience to root for you and to want to hear what you have to share. You will discover how to look and feel comfortable when you sing by learning what to do with your hands, face, and body. You will also learn what to focus on while you're singing and what to focus on only while practicing.

These are the 3 Steps to Power, Passion and Confidence. If you follow this system, do the work, and are willing to explore new territory, you will see, feel, and hear the results.

Performing with confidence is really quite simple. When you open your mouth to sing and you know that, more often than not, what will come out is what you intended to have come out, you will sing with confidence. You can then begin to reveal your power, your passion, and your authentic self to the world and experience the joy of singing. This book is your guide on that journey.

Note from the Author

Singing has always been a part of my life. From the earliest time I can remember, I've always performed. Whether it was at family get-togethers, in church, or in school, I found myself an audience—whether they liked it or not. Pouring my feelings into song has allowed me to deal with the turbulent times of my life when I had no other outlet. The desire to sing has pushed me outside of my comfort zone and helped me build self-esteem. It has enhanced other aspects of my life, as well. My stage experience makes me a better presenter in all areas of my life. I am more comfortable with meeting new people and with speaking in public. In fact, I'm more comfortable in my skin, period. And it started with singing.

I wrote *Sing Free Now!* to share with you my experience as a singer, choir director, and voice teacher so that you, too, can find your power, express your passion, and feel confident when you sing. The principles, techniques, and exercises in this book will help you achieve your goals wherever you sing.

If you love to perform in the shower but wouldn't dare sing in front of anyone, you can have, in a very short time, the confidence you need to have the incredibly connecting experience of singing a song to someone else. If you've been told that you can't sing, can't carry a tune, or are tone deaf, you can let go of those beliefs. You *can* sing, and I will show you how!

If you sing in a choir, your skill level and confidence can grow in ways that make those around you ask, "What have you been doing, and how can I do it, too?" You may find others in the choir asking for your help. You may also decide you want to sing solos if you haven't before.

If you sing solo—at karaoke events, in a band, or in any other capacity—you can improve your skills and confidence and take your singing to "the next level." You will have more control of your voice, sing with more style, and connect more with the audience.

Wherever you are in your relationship with your voice, you can move forward to the place where you experience confidence and joy when you sing. We were *all* born with a unique singing voice and we *all* have our own story to tell through singing.

How to Use This Book

This manual can be used in a number of ways. Use it in whichever way works best for you in terms of your particular learning style.

- If you like step-by-step instructions and learning in small chunks that are eventually pieced together in a logical progression, work through the book from beginning to end.

- If you like to see the big picture, know the overall strategy, and experiment with different steps of a process, sometimes doing them out of order, look for the parts that interest you first. Then go back and check out what you skipped over. (For more information on learning styles, see chapter 11, page 246.)

- Throughout the book you will find exercises, techniques, and tips. I suggest you take on each exercise and technique as you come to it. After reading the instructions given for a particular exercise or technique, put the book down and experience it. This will allow you to devote your full attention to what you are experiencing.

- If you come to a section in the book that you don't connect with at the moment, move on and read it later. Other information in the book may help you to "connect the dots" when you return to that section.

Important Information About This Book and My Website

The instruction and advice I provide in this book go a long way toward helping you to learn to sing with confidence—but, when it comes to using your voice, sometimes you have to *hear* what you're being instructed to do in order to truly "get it." On my website you'll find exercises and audio samples created especially for you. These are designed to give you the auditory information you need to perform the exercises described in this book.

These exercises and audio samples are available at no cost to you. You do not need to register or provide any information in order to access them and you may listen to them as often as you'd like.

To access both the Vocal Power Workout exercise tracks and the Listen and Learn audio tracks, please go to: www.SingFreeNow.com. In the "Log In" box, type in the following:

User name: singfree

Password: 123confidence

Once you log in, you will have immediate access to all of the exercise and audio tracks for the book. These play very important roles in helping you to get the most out of this book, and I encourage you to take full advantage of them!

This book is divided into three sections—one for each of the 3 Steps. Make sure to explore each step; once you have, you will soon find that you are singing with more power, passion, and confidence and experiencing more joy when you sing!

Step 1

Power
Make Friends with Your Belly

1

If *I* Can Do It, *You* Can Do It

As I finish setting up the sound system and adjusting the microphones, I imagine what all of the singers who will appear on this stage tonight are feeling right now: excitement; fear; joy. A few may be asking themselves, "What have I gotten myself into?"

Twice a year I present Bosnian Vocal Studios Sing Free Now! Performance Night, an event that gives everyone who studies with me the chance to practice, in front of a live audience, what they're learning in their voice lessons. As is always the case, the volume of background noise and the level of excitement grows as it gets closer and closer to show time. As each singer enters the room, I hand him or her a program and offer a reminder: "Breathe—and be sure to have fun!"

Twenty-two people have signed up to sing in front of a packed house. Twenty-two souls with varying degrees of experience, from working musicians to folks who have never before sung a solo in front of anyone; from six-year-old children to folks who are well into their seventies. Each person is unique, but they all have one thing in common: these singers have said yes to sharing the story of their song to friends and family.

One by one, each singer takes the stage. Some are obviously nervous. Some hide their anxiety well. They all do a fantastic job. Does this mean that everyone is perfectly in tune, sings all notes exactly the way they'd intended to, remembers every word of the lyric, and is ready to start a national tour? Not at all. What I mean is that, during at least part of his or her performance, each singer tells the story of the song. All of them turn themselves inside out, allowing what they feel—who they *are*—to come out and connect with the world. Do these singers possess something that you don't? Some special talent or gift? The answer is an emphatic **no**!

Every one of us is born with a song that our soul wants to sing. I am blessed to have the privilege of helping others to claim their own "soul songs" and to find the confidence to share them with others.

My First Gigs

My own journey to finding my "soul song" began when I was four years old. Somehow I'd talked my mom into taking me to a taping of *Sheriff John's Lunch Brigade*, a local TV show that aired in Los Angeles in the early 1950s. My friends and I all considered this show the most fun thing on TV.

I sat there, basking in the thrill of watching my favorite show filmed before my eyes. This was, by far, the most exciting thing I'd experienced in all of my four years on the planet—and that excitement exploded when Sheriff John asked the studio audience whether anyone present would be willing to sing a song to win a prize. One horrified mother sat frozen in disbelief as her son bolted out of his seat and bounded onto the stage. Sheriff John thrust his microphone into the little boy's face. "What's your name, and what are you going to sing for us, young fella?" he boomed. Practically giddy with adrenaline, I shouted back, "My name is Mark, and I'm going to sing 'Davy Crockett.'"

As loud as I could, I belted out "The Ballad of Davy Crockett," jumping around wildly as I sang. Sheriff John and the audience cheered as my mom tried to figure out how to make it to the door without being seen. I said to myself, "Hey, this 'singing in front of people' business is *cool!*" Thus, my career as a professional singer and voice teacher was launched.

During the next few years I attempted to sing, tell jokes, and make weird noises in front of anyone I could. I thought it was great fun, but it came with a price. For some reason, my father became uncomfortable whenever I received accolades for singing, performing, or commanding attention at family gatherings. My guess is that he was frustrated that he wasn't playing music professionally (he could pick out melodies on a couple of instruments, but he'd never really pursued his own dream of making music). I began to associate singing with making myself the center of attention, which was dangerous—I would be punished for it. I did a lot of work over the years to come to the realization that I was, and am, no different from anyone else on this planet—we all want to "sing our song," whether it feels safe or not and whether we believe we *can* or not.

When the Beatles first appeared on *The Ed Sullivan Show*, I was one of thousands of kids who said, "I want to do *that*!" I was hooked on the idea of being in a band, and my brother and I, along with two of our friends, would pretend we were the Beatles by singing into vacuum cleaner hoses and strumming tennis rackets. The urge to sing would not go away, even though I regularly got into trouble for "drawing attention to myself." My dad finally accepted my interest in music and bought me an acoustic guitar when I was thirteen. In junior high school I learned enough to play and lead songs for a group that met every week. I had a great time, and again I thought, "Hey, this 'singing in front of people' thing is *cool*!"

At Katella High School in Anaheim, California, I had my first real gig (musician talk for performance) at a concert in front of all my fellow students. Everyone in the Folk Rock Club got to sing three songs if they wanted to. My songs went over well, and I finally got it: "Hey, this 'singing in front of people' thing is *really* cool—and I'm doing it!" I wasn't great, but I had a lot of energy and I enjoyed the opportunity to share something with the audience. I decided to pursue singing when I went to college.

College had to wait for a little while because I spent the next few months doing volunteer work in the Congo. I went with a group of kids, and we each had a particular "job." Mine was playing guitar and singing as a way of communicating with the locals. I had no idea at the time how powerful this experience would be. The cliché "music is the international language" became a reality of my everyday life. I traded singing songs with one villager who was about my age and we became friends—a pretty amazing accomplishment, considering neither of us could speak the other's language. We sang our stories to each other and, through the power of singing, came to understand each other. I was awed by this power, and I became even more committed to doing something with it.

"You Can't—Unless You Already Can"

After spending a few months in the Congo I returned home, excited to start my college career and to study music. I enrolled at California State University, Fullerton, and spoke with a registrar about freshman classes. I excitedly blurted out to him, "I want to major in music!" but, after finding out that I hadn't taken four years of band in high school, he told me that was impossible. The university's policy at the time (I've heard it has since changed) was that, if you couldn't already sight-read music well and didn't play a band instrument proficiently, you couldn't be a music major. In other words, "If you don't already know how to do something, you can't learn how to do it!"

This type of misguided thinking plays into many people's fears about singing, and I want you to know that it just isn't true. So many people have told me over the years that "you can't 'learn' to sing—you either *can* sing or you *can't*." I love showing people how false this belief is. Regardless of whether you've been singing all your life or you think you can't sing at all, *Sing Free Now!* gives you all the tools you need to sing with power, passion, and confidence.

Anyway, back to my story. After a lot of arguing, begging, and pleading on my part, eventually I was allowed to *minor* in music at Cal State. I was told to choose a main instrument and I was assigned an advisor for that instrument. I'd just started playing piano and couldn't wait to learn more. When I met with my piano advisor, however, the first words out of her mouth were,

"Let me see your hands!" I didn't know what to expect as I reached across her desk, and my jaw dropped in disbelief when I heard her next command. "Pick another instrument—your hands are too small to play the piano!"

Again I found myself face-to-face with a belief that you have to have the "right" stuff (hands; voice; talent; looks; intelligence; connections—the list goes on and on) to make music. What I proved to myself—and what I've proved to thousands of voice students—is that all you need to sing and make music is the recognition that you have a desire to do so. Learning the 3 Steps to Power, Passion and Confidence makes the process easier and faster, but it all starts with saying yes to your voice.

I was determined to prove my advisor wrong, so I threw myself into practicing the piano. I decided to start working on my voice, too. I was fortunate (I thought) to work with a very prestigious voice coach, who was available to music students at my college. But I soon became frustrated because every time I asked him about what was physically happening when I sang, he ignored me. Finally, when he could stand my questions no longer, he warned me to "quit worrying about what's going on in your body and just make this sound." Years later, when I became a voice teacher, I would use those words as a reminder of how *not* to coach students (you *need* to know what's "going on in there") but, at the time, they served only to shut down my desire to take voice lessons. "I'll just figure it out on my own, like everyone else," I told myself.

My first paid performance was in a small club that had an old upright piano in one corner. I convinced the manager to give me a two-hour gig one Saturday night, and I begged everyone I knew to come. I was so nervous that, during my first song, I had to stop singing and turn it into an instrumental— I couldn't catch my breath. (It was only later in my career that I learned how to use mechanics to breathe correctly—that's something this book will teach you how to do.)

After I'd finished performing, I sat down at a table to savor the moment with a few of my friends. "How did my playing sound?" I asked them.

"Great!" everyone agreed. "And my singing?" I nervously mumbled. "We're not sure—we couldn't hear it over your pounding on the piano." This was my first exposure to dynamics (specifically, my lack of them during that performance), and it would become a recurring issue. (In this book, I'll show you how to avoid making the same mistakes I did early on, and I'll give you the tools to using dynamics to portray emotion and create style.)

During my second year of college I joined Evermore, a rock band with a lead singer but no keyboard player. It was a great chance for me to rehearse and play songs with a group, which is very different than performing solo. I learned about fitting voices and instruments together to tell the story of the song. It was another step in my musical education, but we only played two gigs in two years, and I decided it was time to leave my hometown. There were so many bands in Southern California at the time that I was convinced I wouldn't play often enough to learn the art and craft of singing and playing. I was hungry to learn more, and I moved to Portland, Oregon.

Portland offered a fertile arts and culture scene that was (and that continues to be) alive with many kinds of music. In my first few years I played in blues bands, rock bands, country bands, and folk groups, and I learned a lot about the music business. I also heard about a great piano player who gave lessons, and I decided to give her a try. At the beginning of my first lesson, I told her I was making my living as a musician. "Play me something so I can see where you're at," she said. I started to tinkle the ivories on her piano and, after a few moments, she interrupted me. "You make money playing like *that*?" she berated. On the surface, this example appears to be about a teacher putting down the student's technique (there probably was some of that in her comment). I believe, however, that this was an example of a belief that's rampant among music teachers, especially those who teach singing—that there is one, and only one, "right" way to do it, and that one way usually corresponds to whatever style that teacher teaches. She played jazz; I was playing rock—to her, a far less legitimate art form, and one she told me she had no desire to play or teach.

I don't adhere to this perspective at all when I teach people how to sing. The truth is that you really *can* sing any song, and in any style, that calls to you. In this book I'll show you how to sing what *you* want to sing. You are not limited to singing what someone else decides is suited to your voice. The mechanics of singing are the same in opera, bluegrass, heavy metal, gospel, reggae, pop, country, or any other style. Once you learn the mechanics, you can sing anything your heart desires.

By the way, I told that piano teacher that I could get one of my friends to make fun of my playing free of charge and that I wasn't about to pay *her* to do it. It was a great gift from the universe to see negative reinforcement at work during a lesson—it showed me that it serves no purpose, and it helped me to see that we all respond better to being shown what we *can* do than to what we *can't* do.

Singing for My Supper

Over the next few years I started writing more songs and playing more gigs. Not only did I perform in bars and nightclubs, but I also sang at church services, festivals, and concerts. I had gigs at which I sang in front of five people and gigs in which I sang in front of twenty thousand people. I sang in radio and TV commercials, in studio sessions, and at the inauguration of the governor of Oregon. I sang the national anthem at NBA games and I won a songwriting contest that led to me singing my winning song live on the *Today* show and on *The Pat Sajak Show*. I led a live network telethon the week after 9/11. I have been a choir director, an arranger and composer, and I have toured the United States singing my original songs. I have been so nervous singing in front of people that I didn't know if my voice would work at all, and I've had so much fun singing at performances that I didn't ever want to stop.

I know what it's like to sing in practically every kind of situation singers find themselves. During the first 11 years that I sang professionally, I got so hoarse after most performances that I'd spend the next day wondering whether or not my voice would work that night. It was stressful, and I was never able to count on what I would be able to coax from my voice. I chalked it up to "that's what singers have go through." Little did I know that I was experiencing what singers have to go through when they don't know how their bodies are designed to breathe and to make sound. (In this book, I'll explain "what's going on in there" so that you, too, can gain the control you need to sing with power, passion, and confidence.)

When I was singing in Nu Shooz, a band whose hit "I Can't Wait" is still played on radio stations all over the country and at many NBA basketball games, I started studying voice with Tom Blaylock, a teacher who actually knew what our bodies are intended to do during singing. This awareness radically changed my relationship with my voice. As I learned how I was supposed to breathe and make sound by working with my body, as Nature intended, instead of fighting it, I was able to develop more power, more consistency, and more confidence. I had more fun when I sang because I wasn't worried about my voice. I realized one day how confident I'd become as a singer.

I nearly fell out of my chair during one of my lessons with Tom when he suggested that I train with him to teach singing. "I can't do that—no way!" I replied. The seed had been planted, however, and, as it grew, I realized that I really wanted to share what I had learned about singing. I trained with Tom and started teaching in 1986. I continued to train with him through 1998, and I went on to work with many other great teachers, coaches, and voice physiologists, weaving together what I learned from them with my decades of experience as a singer.

Sing Free Now! is a culmination of all of these experiences and of the insights and feedback of the thousands of singers I've worked with. I've taught singing to recording artists such as Meredith Brooks, Dan Reed, and Linda Hornbuckle. I also coached Courtney Love when she performed with her band Hole at the Rose Garden arena. I've taught thousands of private lessons since 1986, and for the past few years I've conducted a popular class called Sing Free Now! I've taught workshops and seminars on singing with confidence in both the United States and Brazil. I have helped working musicians to sing and perform better, I've helped choir singers to have more confidence and fun, and I've helped countless people who thought they were tone deaf to sing in tune and enjoy using their voice.

What's Different About *Sing Free Now!*?

From my experience as a singer, voice teacher, and choir director I've come up with a unique approach to helping you sing with confidence. In *Sing Free Now!* you will learn about:

- **The 3 Steps to Power, Passion and Confidence**: learning to breathe efficiently and to master other physical aspects of singing; "feeling" your way to the artistry of singing by using dynamics, emotion, and style; and making a connection with your listeners by mastering the elements of stage presence in order to sing *to* them, not *at* them.

- **Bosnian Belly Breathing**: a technique used to jump-start your return to the natural belly breathing you were born doing but have forgotten how to do over the years.

- **Using Interim Sounds**: the art of using temporary sounds that you *can* make right now to more quickly progress to making the actual sounds you want in your performances, but can't yet control.

- **Outsmarting Your Vocal Defense Mechanism**: how to override your body's involuntary responses when they're sabotaging your singing.

- **The Big Three Vocal Principles**: support (the resistance that is the foundation of your voice); resonation (the "treble and bass knobs" of your voice); and registration (the "automatic and manual transmissions" of your voice).

- **The Scale of 1 to 10**: how to clearly communicate to your body what you want it to do when you sing.

- **Incorporating Variety**: developing the ability to sing a line of a song in a number of different ways by changing vocal elements. This not only creates dynamics in your singing, but also the choices you make with these elements help to create and refine your style.

These are just a few of the tips, secrets, and techniques you will learn in this book that will help you to sing with more confidence and joy in just a few short weeks.

Imagine your own "Performance Night": During the day you calmly look forward to singing, knowing that your voice will do what you intend it to do. That night, as you take the stage, you feel excitement, and your excitement turns to exhilaration as you open your mouth and tell the story of your song. You balance the techniques employed in the 3 Steps to Power, Passion and Confidence, using the mechanics of your voice in a way that gives you control over your dynamics. You "own" the stage, causing your audience to root for you and leaving them wanting more. You look back and wonder, "Why did I ever think I couldn't sing like this?" Welcome to the beginning of your new vocal experience.

In this first step to singing with confidence, we will explore the nuts and bolts of using your voice, identifying the parts of the body that work together when you breathe and when you vocalize. We will look at how Nature intends us to use these parts—and at how almost everyone sings instead. My intention is to help you develop a solid understanding of the "big picture" of how your instrument, the body, actually works. This awareness will help you to use your body efficiently, have more power and control, and have access to a range of choices when you sing.

Until you know how your instrument works, you are in the dark as to what's happening when your voice works well and what's happening (or not happening) when your voice is not doing what you want it to. While mastery of the mechanics of singing alone is not a guarantee that you will be a good singer, it definitely serves as the foundation you need in order to sing with confidence. And it all begins by learning to use your instrument—your body—in the way that Nature intended it to be used.

Your Body, Your Instrument

Most of us never think about what happens when we vocalize. We open our mouths and sing a melody and some words, but we don't know what's happening inside us that actually makes the sounds. When you sing, your body—just like any other musical instrument—uses three main parts to make sound:

1. An energy source—something that *causes* a vibration.

2. A vibrator—the thing that actually *vibrates*, resulting in the sound.

3. A resonator—an object or space that *shapes* the vibration and makes it sound the way it does.

When you play a trumpet, the energy source is the force of the air you blow into the mouthpiece, the vibrator is your lips, and the resonator is composed of the metal tubing and bell of the horn, which make the sound louder and fuller. Your body works in the same basic way when you sing. The energy source is the force of the *air* that is moving from your lungs through your throat, the vibrator is your *vocal cords*, and the resonator is composed of your *mouth and other spaces in your head and throat*. It's important to learn how these three parts work together to make the sound of your voice. Let's start by exploring your torso, where you create the energy (the force of the air) that is used to sing. It all starts in your belly.

2

The Syringe—Your Torso

The great golfer Arnold Palmer once gave a lesson to a group of men who wanted to improve their game. He started by having each student tee up his ball, lay his club next to it on the ground, and stand back about 10 feet. Palmer then proceeded to pick up each club and drive each student's ball 200 yards straight down the fairway—one right after the other. When he got all the way through the line, he turned to the students and said, "Gentlemen, playing golf is not about your equipment!"

His point was that, if you know what you're doing, you can make a good golf shot with any club. The same idea is true in singing. It is not that some people were born with a good voice and others weren't. It's all about learning what is inside your body and knowing what to do with those parts in order to sing.

One of the most important parts is your torso. That's the trunk of your body—the part to which your neck, arms, and legs are attached. Your chest, abdomen, and pelvic area are all part of your torso, and many of your organs, including your lungs, are housed in it. Your torso allows you to control the air you need to fuel your voice, and it's used to help you create power in your singing.

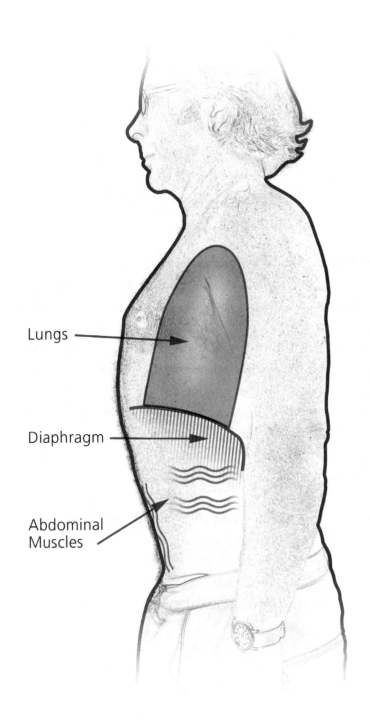

Lungs

Diaphragm

Abdominal
Muscles

Perhaps the easiest way to understand how the torso works to move air in and out is to think of it as a syringe. A syringe is composed of a tube, or *barrel*, a plunger, and a plunger handle. When the plunger is pulled down through the barrel, it causes air or liquid to be sucked into that barrel. When the plunger is pushed up through the barrel, air or liquid that is in the barrel is forced out. We are going to focus on the three parts of the body, each

A Syringe — Your Torso

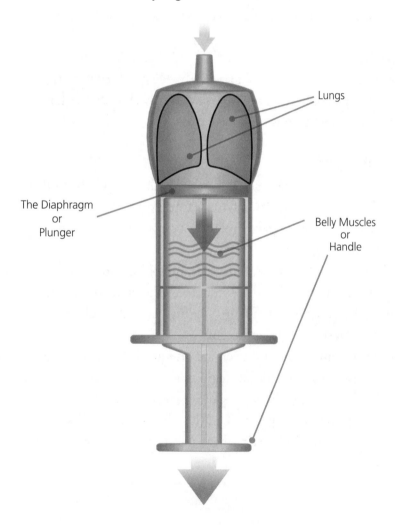

Lungs

The Diaphragm
or
Plunger

Belly Muscles
or
Handle

of which is found in the torso, that are primarily responsible for this action. These three parts work together to control the air we use when we talk or sing.

1. The diaphragm (the plunger).

2. The rib cage and the lungs (the barrel).

3. The belly muscles (the plunger handle).

Nature designed us to use each of these parts in a specific way in order to breathe or to make sound. Particularly when it comes to the diaphragm, however, many people have no idea what that way is. Some have never been told what the diaphragm is or what it does.

The Diaphragm

After I'd given my first performance in the Folk Rock Club at my high school (my first big gig), my faculty adviser came up to me and said, "Mark, you could be a pretty good singer if you'd just sing from your diaphragm instead of your throat."

When I asked him how to do that, he told me to "just focus here," and he pointed vaguely to my belly. I "focused" like crazy on my belly (whatever *that* meant) but nothing about my singing seemed to change. What was I doing wrong? What was the problem?

The problem was that I'd been tossed into the same boat that most people find themselves in when they begin to sing: most of us have heard that we should sing from the diaphragm—but no one has ever shown us how to do it. I feel confident that, once you've read this chapter, you will know what "singing from the diaphragm" really means and, most important, that you will know how to accomplish it.

Albert Einstein once said, "You don't really understand something until you can explain it to your grandmother." It's time to tell your grandmother about her diaphragm.

When I ask new students to show me where they think the diaphragm is, the answer I most often get is that it's somewhere in the front of the belly. When I ask people what it is, I hear, "It's an organ, like a lung" or, "It's a big blob of tissue" or, "I have absolutely no idea." When I ask whether or not the diaphragm moves, many people say, "Yes; in and out" or, "It inflates and deflates."

I ask my students these questions for one reason: most singers have been told, at one time or another, to "sing from the diaphragm." While this advice is meant to help, it is nearly impossible to follow if you don't know what your diaphragm is or where it's actually located.

The diaphragm is a muscle. In fact, aside from the heart, the diaphragm is the most important muscle of the body. Without the movement of the diaphragm, breathing stops. It lies horizontally at the base of the rib cage and it serves as both the floor of the chest cavity and the ceiling of the abdominal cavity (belly).

Exercise: Find Your Diaphragm

Here's an exercise that will help you to get a good feel (pun intended) for where the diaphragm is. Walk your finger down your breastbone until you first find soft tissue. Push in lightly and cough. You will feel the diaphragm pushing against the abdominal wall.

The diaphragm is located much higher in the belly than most people think. It looks like a section of a dome (see the illustration on page 42), and the top of the diaphragm is attached to the base of the lungs. When we inhale, the diaphragm pulls downward so that air is drawn in and it begins to flatten, making room for the air that is taken in. When we're breathing quietly, the extent of this movement is less than an inch. During exercise or singing, when the breathing becomes more active, the diaphragm can move much farther.

This is the job of the diaphragm—to move up and down in order to draw air into and push air out of the lungs. The diaphragm acts like the plunger in the barrel of a syringe. Pull the plunger down—air is sucked in. Push the plunger up—air is forced out. How much the diaphragm moves and how efficiently we breathe depends on *how* we breathe.

Breathing

The diaphragm, rib cage, lungs, and abdominal muscles all play important roles in breathing, so let's look at how they work together. Almost everyone who has ever sung has been told that breathing correctly is the key to good singing—yet hardly anyone can define "correct" breathing and even fewer people do it automatically. Many of my students have told me that they can breathe correctly (I prefer "efficiently") only when they concentrate on doing so.

Efficient breathing, like any other desirable action that's performed when singing, is of greatest value when it's done automatically. Of course, while you're in the process of learning how to breathe efficiently on a consistent basis, you'll be required to think about all the details that go into it as you practice. But rest assured that, by diligently practicing repetitions of the exercises found in the Vocal Power Workout, you'll create the "muscle memory" that allows you to automatically breathe efficiently when you sing.

Before you learn to breathe efficiently, it's a good idea to understand how most of us are breathing inefficiently.

Exercise: Test Your Breathing Efficiency

Sit comfortably in a chair. Imagine that you are standing across the room from your chair and that you are watching yourself. At a fairly loud volume, sing "Happy Birthday to You." Notice how many breaths you take while singing the song.

Most people take three to five breaths, but the exact number is not important. What *is* important is that most of us can literally see and hear ourselves take each breath. Ask yourself these questions: What cues did you rely on in order to count the number of breaths you took? Did you notice your shoulders lifting up? Did you hear each breath as you gulped in air? If you're like most people, you probably did both of these things—you lifted your shoulders and rib cage and you audibly sucked air into your lungs. Obviously, this method works—you're alive and you're able to make sound—but it's not the most efficient way to move air.

Let's look at the three ways that you can breathe:

1. **Shoulder breathing.** This is the least efficient method that we can use, yet more than 90 percent of us do it. Breaths that are taken by lifting the shoulders are shallow and tend to fill only the upper parts of the lungs with air. The diaphragm doesn't pull down as much as it could when you inhale, and when you breathe this way you may find yourself running out of air. It's pretty difficult to sing with power, passion, and confidence when you don't have enough breath.

2. **Rib cage breathing.** This involves breathing by expanding the rib cage like a set of bellows or an accordion while

keeping the shoulders fairly stationary. A person who has had experience singing or who has had some vocal training may be breathing this way. This method often kicks in during athletic activity or exercise. It allows a person to draw air deeper into the lungs, but it doesn't fill the lowest part of lungs with air. It is better than shoulder breathing but it's still inefficient.

3. **Bosnian Belly Breathing.** This is the most effective way to breathe. It involves expanding and contracting the abdomen to both *allow* and *cause* the diaphragm to move up and down. Your goal is to switch back from whatever inefficient method you're using to breathe currently to using this method, as it will have a huge impact on your singing. I say "switch back" because we were all born breathing from the belly—you can watch any baby's belly rise and fall as he or she breathes or cries. Somewhere along the way as we grew up (some scientists say this occurs at around age three), however, we make the unfortunate switch from belly breathing to one of the less efficient ways.

Why the Switch?

There are many theories as to why this switch occurs. I believe it happens because of the state of our bellies.

The belly is full of organs, connective tissue, muscle, and fat, which, taken together, is called the abdominal bulk (wonderful name, don't you think?). If you check in with your belly as you're reading this, you'll probably notice that you are tightening it or holding it in to some degree. In fact, it is difficult for most people to completely let go of tensing the abdominal wall. I believe this happens for three reasons.

Reason 1: We do not want our bellies to show. No matter what our gender, age, size, or shape may be, most of us (especially those who are heavily influenced by Western culture) want to make ourselves look skinnier. We've all been consciously or subconsciously trained to "hold it in" in order to appear to have a flat belly. I remember being told, as a boy, by gym teachers and even my dad, "Chest out, gut in!"

Reason 2: We want to have a stronger "core." The term "core" entered our vocabulary and our consciousness within the last few years. You may or may not know what your core is, exactly, but you probably have heard that it should be strong and solid. This is a popular concept in yoga, Pilates, martial arts, and other forms of exercise. In reality, participants in these activities are never encouraged to create too much tension in the belly—just the opposite! Nevertheless, adhering to the idea that we need to strengthen our core can consciously or subconsciously lead to overly tensing the belly.

Reason 3: We're stressed out. Way too many of us go through our daily lives in a low-grade state of fight-or-flight response, which is the body's method of reacting to perceived danger: "I'm going to be late!" "Did I leave the iron on?" "How will I pay that bill?" Stress can cause the release of adrenaline, increased heart rate, dilation of the pupils, constriction of blood vessels, tightening of the abdominal muscles, and rapid, shallow shoulder breathing. This can result in a vicious cycle: you become stressed; the stress causes you to tense your belly; the tension in your belly causes you to take in less oxygen; and a lack of sufficient oxygen causes you to become even more stressed.

The part of the body that reacts first to lack of oxygen is the brain. When we're stressed, it's critical that we breathe more deeply in order to reenergize our brain's ability to think clearly (or to remember the lyrics), to lower our blood pressure (so we don't "choke" under pressure), and to be able to make the sounds we want to make as singers. By practicing the breathing methods described below, you will not only become a better singer, but you'll also have more energy and be able to think more clearly. Belly breathing can actually help you in many ways that have nothing to do with singing.

I believe that our tendency to tighten and hold in the belly is the reason that you probably shifted, at an early age, from the natural, efficient way of breathing to the less efficient method that you use to breathe now. When the belly is tightened, all of its organs and other tissue are compressed and the diaphragm has almost no room to move downward. The only way to move air in and out is to take shallow "gulps" of air, which is usually done via shoulder breathing.

You may be wondering if it is worth the effort to change the way you breathe. Sure, belly breathing may be the most efficient method. But the way you're breathing now has allowed you to make sound in a way that's seemed OK—at least sometimes—right?

Let's look at the four main reasons that switching back to belly breathing will help you to sing with more power and confidence.

Reason 1: Shoulder breathing doesn't move the diaphragm as far as it can be moved. Think about the syringe and imagine pulling the plunger only about a third of the way out of the barrel instead of all the way out. There's less space for air or liquid to enter the barrel, right? The same holds true for our bodies. Less movement of the diaphragm means less air drawn in and squeezed out of your body. You may have noticed that you tend to run out of air when you sing. Shoulder breathing is one of the main reasons we experience this problem.

Reason 2: When you lift the shoulders to breathe while you're singing, your audience can "see" every breath you take. Not only do such actions tend to interrupt the flow of the music, but they also distract the listener. It's difficult to convey emotion and create a flow of energy from singer to listener when it appears that you are working hard to breathe.

Reason 3: Shoulder breathing causes us to gulp down air, resulting in a sound that is even more distracting than the sight of lifting shoulders or heaving chests. Amplify this distraction by singing into a microphone and you make it even more difficult to create a connection with your audience. If you listen to the radio with this in mind, you'll find singers, newscasters, and actors doing voice work in commercials whose breathing is loud and obvious. Notice how annoying this is.

Reason 4: Shoulder breathing causes you to dry out your instrument. The sound you make as you gulp each breath of air is the result of that air being sucked down your throat and past the vocal cords. This gulped air dries out the cords, which can lead to problems with tone, pitch, endurance, registration, range, and every other aspect of singing (don't be concerned if you don't know what these terms mean—you'll learn about them in this guide). This is the most serious of all the problems related to shoulder breathing.

Exercise: Dry Out

To better understand the effect that dry air has on your vocal cords, pant like a big dog a few times. Pay attention to what happens in the back of your throat. Notice the dryness? Singers who employ shoulder breathing can experience this irritation and dryness very quickly—often during the course of singing just one or two songs.

Bosnian Belly Breathing

I hope that, by now, I've convinced you to take the way you've been breathing, toss it out the window (you can always retrieve it later, if you really want to), and remind your body how to breathe the way Nature intended. To jumpstart this process, let's go back to the concept of making friends with your belly.

Making friends with your belly involves making room in your abdominal cavity so that the diaphragm is able to pull down as far as it can go. The way to do this is to use the abdominal muscles to expand the abdomen. I call this technique Bosnian Belly Breathing. Here's how it works:

Exercise: Get Acquainted with Bosnian Belly Breathing

Place one hand low on your belly. Using the muscles in your abdominal wall, push the hand out and away from the body. The organs in your abdomen will move out of the way, creating more room in the abdominal cavity. Your diaphragm will automatically pull down, causing you to take a breath (provided you don't fight your body's attempt to take in air)—you don't have to do anything but expand your abdomen.

Once you're used to it, it is actually easier to breathe this way. Because the diaphragm and the lungs are connected, when the diaphragm pulls down, the lungs are stretched open. This lowers the air pressure in the lungs. Unless you are holding your breath, the air around you will rush in and fill your lungs (the old "Nature hates a vacuum" principle that is demonstrated so clearly when a plunger is pulled down through the barrel of a syringe). You have just inhaled the way Nature intended! No need to suck air—just expand the belly!

When you breathe this way, the air is *drawn* into your lungs in an efficient stream instead of being sucked in with a turbulent gulp. This greatly reduces the drying effect of the air on your vocal cords and allows your audience to focus on your performance instead of on watching and listening to you breathe. Don't worry if you can't feel air moving into your body when you first try this. As you practice expanding your belly, doing the best you can each time, your abdominal muscles will get stronger and more coordinated, and the amount of air that is drawn in will increase. We will get more into the nuts and bolts of Bosnian Belly Breathing throughout the rest of this chapter.

To Breathe or Not to Breathe

I invite you to use the word "expand" instead of "breathe" or "inhale" when you think about bringing air into the body. This helps you to let go of shoulder breathing and to return to the belly—where Nature intends you to begin the action of moving air into and out of your lungs.

When you begin to relearn the process of belly breathing, it is easier to focus on expanding the front of the belly, but I want you to be aware that you can expand not only the front, but also the sides and the back of the abdomen.

Exercise: Feel Your Entire Belly Expand

Place your thumbs into the soft tissue of the sides of your waistline, just above your hips. As you expand your belly, feel your thumbs moving out slightly. Now place your fingertips on each side of your spine at your lower back. As you expand your belly, feel your fingertips moving out slightly.

The idea is this: the more you can expand every part your abdomen, the more room you can make for the diaphragm to pull down. The farther the diaphragm travels, the more air you can move into and out of your body. So, from now on, as you expand the belly, occasionally put your focus on your sides and back and work to expand these areas, too.

Obviously, when you sing, you also have to exhale—to move air out of the lungs. To do this naturally, you will do the opposite of expanding the belly: you will lift it in and up. I invite you to use the word "lift" instead of "breathe out" or "exhale." This lift causes air to be pushed out of your body in the same way that pushing a plunger through the barrel of a syringe causes the air or liquid in that barrel to be pushed out, and it's another important part of the Bosnian Belly Breathing technique.

Another way to think of this process is to imagine trying to squeeze all of the toothpaste out of a tube. If you squeeze at the tube's neck some toothpaste will come out, but much of it will be left, unused, in the tube. However, if you roll up the tube from the bottom, you'll be much more efficient at getting virtually all of the toothpaste out of the tube. Singing works in the same way. Most singers "sing from the throat," squeezing their neck muscles to produce sound and volume. A much more efficient way to get the desired results is to "sing from the diaphragm"—which, in the case of making sound, means lifting your belly in and up, which causes your diaphragm to pull up and to squeeze out much more of the air that's inside through your throat and mouth.

As you lift your belly in and up, even slightly, you begin to move the organs and tissue that are in your abdominal cavity up against your diaphragm, which is connected to your lungs. This squeezes your lungs, creating air pressure. This air pressure is the energy source that causes sound to be made when you sing. It is very much like squeezing a tube of toothpaste, playing the accordion, or squirting a squirt gun. If you squeeze something, whatever is inside of it will come out. By lifting your belly in and up, you are doing a controlled squeeze of your lungs to move air out while singing. In other words, you're "rolling up the toothpaste tube" from the bottom to get a steady flow of air to come out.

The idea of "rolling up your toothpaste tube" is one of the most important concepts when it comes to singing: whenever you sing a note, your belly's in-and-up lift must be constant.

This steady lift creates the air pressure needed to fuel your vocal engine. Without it, the throat tries to do the work of creating the air pressure to make sound. This results in what some people call straining or "singing from the throat." Actually, all of the sound produced when you sing originates in your vocal cords—it's the quality or volume of that sound that seems strained. This is what's usually meant by "singing from the throat"—producing a sound that is thin, strained, or forced. When you use Bosnian Belly Breathing, however, you transfer a large part of the workload of singing from the small muscles of your throat to the much larger muscles of your belly. This is what Nature wants you to do when you sing—your body has just forgotten to do it.

Remember the techniques used in Bosnian Belly Breathing by memorizing these two simple phrases:
To get air in, the belly goes out.
To get air out, the belly goes in.

As you experiment with expanding and lifting your abdomen, watch out for a couple of potential issues regarding your body alignment. While executing either of these techniques, some people inadvertently move their spines forward and back or rock their pelvises back and forth. This tends to be caused by your body wanting to "work smarter, not harder" (rocking the spine or pelvis often feels easier to your body than working the abs)—but, in reality, these rocking movements aren't very "smart" at all because they sabotage the actual expanding and lifting of your belly. See if this is happening with your body by performing the following exercise.

Exercise: Keep Your Body in Alignment

Stand against a door or a wall, making sure that your bottom and your shoulder blades are touching the surface behind you. Expand your belly to move air into your body. Now lift your belly in and up to move air out of your belly. If either of these actions causes your bottom or your shoulder blades to pull away from the wall or door, you know that your body is trying to "help" you perform the action. Unfortunately, this "help" will actually hurt your ability to sing. Practice keeping your bottom and your shoulder blades from moving when you expand and lift your abdomen so that your body becomes used to moving your belly independently from your pelvis.

So far, we've talked about the Bosnian Belly Breathing concepts of actively expanding and lifting the abdomen. But there is one more element that makes Bosnian Belly Breathing unique: the concept of keeping the rib cage and shoulders in the proper position. By that I mean not allowing your rib cage and shoulders to lift up and drop during breathing. This is what you are used to doing as you breathe, so you will probably find your body attempting to continue down this path even as you practice expanding and lifting your belly. The problem with your rib cage and shoulders wanting to "help" is that this motion causes your belly to work less and you will fall back to breathing inefficiently, moving less air in and out of your body. When you lift your belly in as far as you can, your shoulders and rib cage will be in the proper position for Bosnian Belly Breathing.

Here's an exercise to help you learn to keep your rib cage and shoulders positioned correctly:

Exercise: Expand Your Rib Cage

Imagine putting on a pair of pants that are two sizes too big and way too long. Visualize pulling them up until they are just below your armpits. Your job is to hold them in this position. The only way you can do this without the aid of a belt or suspenders is to expand your rib cage against the pants. As long as you keep the rib cage expanded, the pants will stay up. Be sure not to hold your breath or tense up your shoulders or the muscles between your ribs; instead, focus on letting your *awareness* of your rib cage keep it in the proper position. Now expand your belly without letting the pants drop. Next, lift your belly up and in without letting the pants drop. With just a little practice, you will be able to develop the awareness needed to keep your rib cage and shoulders in the proper position when you sing.

When you are able to correctly expand your belly, lift it in and up, and maintain the proper rib cage position, you will be effectively using all the components of Bosnian Belly Breathing.

It's important to note that the techniques used in Bosnian Belly Breathing may go against the instructions on "correct breathing" that some singers have been given in the past. This is particularly true when it comes to expanding the belly. I have often come across—in books, workshops, and lessons—advice that encourages singers *not* to actively expand the abdomen when inhaling. Many singers have been taught to simply allow the expansion to happen. Some teachers point out that, during inhalation, the diaphragm moves downward and the abdomen moves outward on its own. While this is true, it overlooks the real question: Is the diaphragm moving downward and is the abdomen moving outward to the fullest extent possible in order to give your voice the maximum amount of support your body can give it? Unless a singer is using the techniques that make up Bosnian Belly Breathing, the answer is almost always no. Mere awareness that this is supposed to happen doesn't *cause* it to happen; you have to actively move your belly in order to teach your body how to automatically breathe efficiently when singing.

I think I understand why some teachers don't coach singers to actively expand the belly. The act of simply moving your abdomen in and out, with no understanding of why you're doing it or of what it can help you achieve, will not bring you to natural breathing or help you to sing with power, passion, or confidence. And without the proper support (which we'll discuss in the next section), belly breathing will not be of much help when it comes to singing the way you want to. The problem with the "just let it happen" approach is that it has been so long since most people breathed efficiently that just "telling their bodies" how breathing is supposed to work won't automatically result in the desired change. Your body needs a jump start, and this is what actively expanding, lifting, and keeping the rib cage in the proper position is designed to do. This active movement is how Bosnian Belly Breathing returns you to breathing naturally—and, with practice, automatically—while you sing.

Remember that you have to practice with conscious effort when you're breaking an old habit and creating a new one. As your body becomes accustomed to breathing this way, it will require less and less extreme expanding and lifting in order to move air efficiently. However, in the beginning, it is very important to expand and lift to the maximum extent that you can.

Let's revisit our toothpaste tube analogy for a minute: As we discussed, most people sing by "pinching the tube"—tightening the muscles surrounding the airway—just below the neck, causing a small amount of "toothpaste"—air—to escape. They are, figuratively speaking, "singing at the top of their lungs" because they allow their bodies to access only a small portion of the air that's contained, or that could be contained, in those lungs. When you use Bosnian Belly Breathing, you "roll the tube" from the bottom up (or, to continue the analogy, "sing from the bottom of your lungs"). By expanding, lifting, and keeping your rib cage in the proper position when you practice the exercises in this book and when you sing, you will build the strength and coordination in your abdomen that will help you control your voice. And control is a major factor when it comes to singing. Once you make friends with your belly, you'll be well on your way to making friends with your voice.

Filling the Bucket

We know that air enters the body through the nose and the mouth, that it passes down the throat, and that it can travel only as far as the bottom of the lungs. The question is this: can you take in more air than you've been taking in—and can you direct it to go where you want it to go? The answer is yes. If you think of the body as a bucket that fills up from the bottom first as you "pour" in air, you will tend to have more control of the airflow and you'll increase the amount of air you can use when you sing.

Lying horizontally at the base of the pelvis is a system of muscles called the pelvic floor. Your pelvic floor can act like a "second diaphragm" to help you draw more air into your lungs.

As you expand the belly and the diaphragm draws downward, you can also energetically lower the pelvic floor. Visualize the air being drawn clear down to the base of your spine. It's as if you are pouring liquid into a bucket, and that bucket's bottom is located where yours is.

Obviously, the air doesn't reach your pelvic floor, but when you visualize the energy of the air filling and emptying the "bucket" that is your torso, your pelvic floor muscles can engage along with your diaphragm. You will notice how much more air you have to sing with and how much easier it is to control the airflow.

Through the Nose or the Mouth?

Here's a question I hear frequently: "Should I breathe through my nose or mouth when I sing?" Ideally, you would always breathe through your nose—the little hairs in the nasal passages, called nasal cilia, help clean out dust particles and other harmful alien invaders. The mucus membranes in your nose also help fight infection and moisten the air that flows through.

However, there are two main problems with trying to breathe only through the nose.

1. It is very difficult to train yourself to do this. You cannot keep your attention on it constantly, and even practicing it will not cause it to be automatic.

2. Research shows that your nasal passages constantly alternate between being open and being partially or completely blocked. Air moves into your body more quickly if it moves through the mouth as well as the nose.

The easiest way to breathe is to simply allow the air to enter your body however it easily and naturally can. This usually is through a combination of both your nose and mouth.

Training Your Body to Breathe Efficiently

Breathing is one of the few processes performed by our bodies that can be both consciously and unconsciously controlled. You are conscious of the mechanics as you practice Bosnian Belly Breathing. When your focus shifts away from your breathing, your body subconsciously takes over, reverting to its "default" breathing patterns. As you begin to reprogram your body to breathe naturally, you will probably notice that the inefficient way of breathing creeps back into your routine at times.

You may also notice that, despite your best efforts, your shoulders sometimes still lift up when you expand to bring in air—an indication that your body has reverted to its old habit of trying too hard to inhale. Usually this occurs because your subconscious (and possibly your conscious) mind is not convinced that expanding your belly will bring in all the air you need. From the time you stopped breathing naturally as a child to the moment you began to practice Bosnian Belly Breathing, your body's only way of "knowing" that you'd taken a breath was to feel and hear the air as it entered your body. And let's face it: if you didn't take in enough oxygen, you would die in a matter of minutes. So your body is very protective of the breathing process and it may not want to let go of the way you've been doing it for years. Your body may be telling itself, "Just because this Mark guy says that expanding and contracting the belly makes us breathe doesn't mean we buy into it."

This is completely normal. One of the best ways to help your body switch back to natural breathing is to notice every time your body makes its own effort to inhale (lifting the shoulders; actively gulping in air) on top of your conscious action of expanding your belly. The simple act of self-monitoring can help your body to realize that you don't want it to "inhale"—

and that you don't need it to. You can use your ears to help, too. If you hear air during or after your expansion, you are probably inhaling the inefficient way. Remember: this can dry out your vocal cords and tire you out. If, after a week or two of practicing Bosnian Belly Breathing, you still catch yourself lifting your shoulders or audibly inhaling, try this exercise to help things along.

Exercise: Monitor Your Breathing

If you find that your body too easily reverts to old, inefficient breathing habits, use a length of rope, a belt, or a rolled-up towel as an inhalation monitor. Wrap it high around your rib cage under your armpits and hold it snug against your chest as you practice singing or breathing. If you lift your shoulders or gulp in air when you expand, you will feel the tightening movement of the inhalation monitor against your skin. Correct your breathing and, when you can feel that you are no longer "inhaling," let the inhalation monitor drop and check your breathing as you face a mirror. Use the inhalation monitor whenever you need to remind your body of how it naturally breathes.

The more aware you are of each inefficient breath you take, the easier it is to retrain your body to breathe the way Nature intended it to.

Important Points to Remember

- The diaphragm is a muscle that lies horizontally on top of the belly.

- The diaphragm moves up and down, acting like the plunger of a syringe, to draw air into and push air out of your body.

- "Singing from the diaphragm" means using the diaphragm in the way that Nature intended in order to breathe efficiently; it doesn't mean that sound is actually made by the diaphragm.

- Belly (natural) breathing is the way that Nature intended us to breathe, and we all breathed this way when we were young.

- Breathing naturally greatly reduces the drying effect of air and gives you a greater air supply when you sing.

- Bosnian Belly Breathing involves active expansion and contraction of the belly, which both *cause* and *allow for* natural breathing.

- Think of the body as a "bucket" that you can "pour" more air into, filling it from the bottom up.

- It is more efficient to let the air enter the body through both the nose and the mouth than to try to direct it through the nose only.

- Become aware of every time your body tries to "inhale" on top of Bosnian Belly Breathing—this awareness will help your body to let go of this unnecessary action.

3

The Megaphone—Your Vocal Tract

I got a call one day from a friend of mine who was a student at Oregon Health Sciences University, one of the leading education and research hospitals in the country. He was aware of my fascination with the anatomy and physiology of singing, and he had a question for me: "Mark, we have the victim of a fatal car crash here in the morgue. After the autopsy, would you like to dissect her larynx?"

I was stunned at the thought, but I managed to mumble that I would be there as soon as I could. Forty-five minutes later I was in a gown and gloves, nervously waiting to see something I'd only ever been able to view in a book. Unfortunately, the autopsy took longer than expected and, disappointed, I told my friend that I wouldn't be able to stick around much longer. "Hang on a second," he said. "Let me see if you can work on the neck we have in the storage refrigerator instead." (And I thought I had some strange things in my fridge!)

As I cut open the part of the body that actually makes the sound when we sing, I was in awe of the mechanism. It's small, delicate, and elegantly designed. Excited, I began to pepper the two doctors who were in the morgue with questions. "Do the cricoarytenoid muscles always . . ." The doctors stared at me. "Whoa, slow down there, Mark," said one of them. "We have no idea what you're talking about." I couldn't believe it!

My friend proceeded to explain to me that, in med school, students spend only about four hours studying the larynx; usually, only those who specialize in otolaryngology (ear, nose, and throat medicine) go on to learn more. I thought to myself, "If most doctors don't really know how the human vocal mechanism works, imagine how in the dark most singers must be on the subject."

Open up and say "ah"—it's time to shine some light on your vocal tract.

In the last chapter we examined the parts of the body that create the energy (the force of the air) during singing, but what actually makes the sound? If you sing a note and think about what happens, you will find that making sound involves three main factors.

1. Air must be taken into the body.

2. Air must be moved out of the body.

3. The moving air somehow causes something in the throat to make a sound.

There is a fourth factor, as well—but, before we look at that, let's begin our journey through the vocal tract.

The Vocal Folds

The vocal folds, which are commonly called the vocal cords, are housed in the larynx, which is commonly called the voice box. The larynx, an organ in the throat, has the most complex movement of any muscle-based system in the human body, and it works in an almost mystical way to create what we call the human voice.

Although most people refer to the vocal folds as vocal cords, that term is a little misleading. Many people picture the vocal cords as guitar string–like tendons that run vertically somewhere in the neck. In reality, the vocal cords—or vocal folds—don't look like strings at all; they are actually folds of muscle tissue (hence the more appropriate name "vocal folds"). There are two of them, shaped in a V, and they lie horizontally in your windpipe, with the point of the V just behind your Adam's apple.

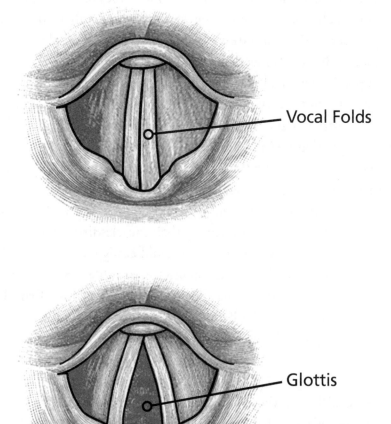

The Vocal Folds

This illustration shows the vocal folds from the viewpoint of looking straight down the windpipe from the top of the head. The two bands shown in the illustration are the vocal folds, and the space between them is called the glottis.

Your vocal folds are very small: in most women, they are one-half to three-quarters of an inch long; in most men, they're three-quarters of an inch to one inch long. The most important thing to realize about your vocal folds, however, is that they are muscles—and, like all muscles, they need to be warmed up in order to work at their best.

Singing is very much like an athletic event in that it requires you to use lots of energy and to work muscles vigorously. A good coach, dance teacher, or exercise instructor starts every practice, lesson, or workout with stretches and warm-ups. Warmed-up, limber muscles aren't injured as easily and they can stretch farther. In addition, people who warm up their muscles before using them have much more endurance than those who try to perform with cold, stiff muscles. Most runners don't hop out of bed and start sprinting down the street; if they didn't warm up their muscles first, they wouldn't have the endurance to run very far and they could easily pull a muscle. Unfortunately, most singers don't think of themselves as athletes who need to warm up their instruments and, as a result, they sing with cold, stiff vocal folds. If you warm up your vocal folds before you use them to sing, the results will be more satisfying, you will have more confidence, and you will experience more joy. In addition, the stronger and more prepared your muscles are, the more "effortlessly" you can appear to sing.

The Vocal Power Workout exercises found on my website (see page 25) are a great set of tools that are specifically designed to warm up your vocal folds and properly prepare your voice to make sound.

How the Vocal Folds Work

What do the vocal folds actually do? For one thing, they open and close, acting as a valve that controls the air going into and out of your body. During breathing, this space is relatively large. But you must close the folds and make the glottis smaller in order to sing a pitch.

Note, Pitch, and Tone—What's the Difference?

The words "note," "pitch," and "tone" are often used interchangeably to refer to a musical sound of a specific frequency. Technically speaking, however, these terms do have different meanings. The term "note" refers to musical steps on a scale and the letter names assigned to those steps—A, B flat, C sharp, and so on. (In one system, called the Solfége system, these steps are named do, re, mi, and so forth.) "Pitch" refers to how accurately an instrument or voice matches a desired frequency—in other words, it refers to whether or not it is in tune. The colloquial term "pitchy," as in "her singing sounds a little pitchy," means "not exactly in tune." Last, "tone" describes the character or timbre of a sound. It is what allows you tell a piano from a flute when they are both playing the same note.

Here's an example of all three terms used correctly: "When Bob sang the aria, his high note was in pitch and it had a bell-like tone."

The way your vocal folds work to make sound is similar to the way your mouth works when you whistle: You can make a sound if you tighten the lips and make the space between them small enough. If you blow air through loose lips, the space involved is bigger and it's more difficult to make a sound. The same is true with the vocal folds—make the space (the glottis) between them small enough, and moving air will cause the folds to make a sound, like singing.

Want another example? Visualize a pop bottle and a mayonnaise jar. If you blow over the top of a pop bottle you will hear a note, but blowing over the top of a mayonnaise jar won't make a sound at all—there's just too much space. So this is the fourth step in singing a note—you must close the folds and make the glottis smaller.

In order to sing a note, you must close the vocal folds and make the glottis smaller.

There are two ways to accomplish this. Nature intends us to tighten the folds and close the glottis in the same way that we move any muscle—through a nerve impulse. Most people, however, close the glottis in an inefficient way, using what are called the "swallowing muscles."

The swallowing muscles are attached to the base of the tongue and, you guessed it, are used to swallow. During singing, most people unknowingly use these muscles to squeeze their vocal folds closed, interfering with the way that Nature intends us to close the glottis. Your swallowing muscles can also pull your larynx higher in your throat, which can make it harder to sing. You need to train your swallowing muscles to stay out of the process. Here's an easy way to do that.

Exercise: Suppress Your Swallowing Muscles

Swallow normally and feel the action of these muscles. Now open your mouth as far as you comfortably can. With one hand placed under the jaw, hold your jaw open and don't let it close. (See the illustration on page 71.) With your jaw open, try to swallow again. You'll find that it is virtually impossible.

When you perform the exercises in the Vocal Power Workout section of my website (see page 25), be sure to hold your jaw open. Each time you physically interfere with the action of the swallowing muscles, you train your body not to rely on them for assistance in closing your glottis when you are singing songs. By singing exercises while holding your jaw open, you encourage your body to close your glottis efficiently and naturally. Yes, holding your jaw open during the exercises will look and feel pretty silly at first, but you will quickly get used to it. Remember that this technique—along with every other technique you initially use in order to train or retrain yourself—is designed to help you both develop the right habits and strengthen needed muscles. This is *not* the way you'll eventually sing when you perform, but it is a critically important part of practicing correctly.

It is important that you hold your jaw open by placing your hand *under* your jaw. If you hold your jaw with your hand in front of your face, you will block your mouth, making your voice sound more muffled than it actually is. This could cause you to make vocal adjustments that are counterproductive.

Correct

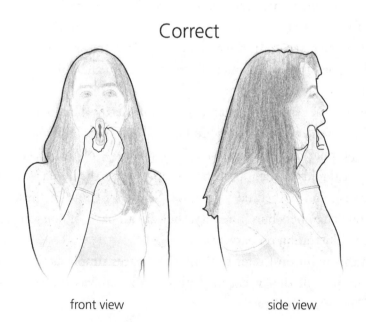

front view   side view

Incorrect

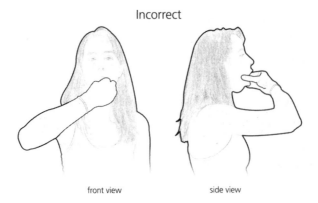

front view   side view

The Resonation Chambers

Once the glottis is closed, air that moves through your vocal folds causes the folds to vibrate and create a sound. This sound is then shaped, amplified, and defined by the spaces in your head. (I knew the spaces in my head were good for something!) This is called "resonation." The space in which sound resonates is called a resonation chamber. A good example of a resonation chamber is the wooden body of an acoustic guitar. Without this chamber, you would hardly be able to hear the sound created by the vibration of the strings. The main functions of a resonation chamber are to make the sound louder and to add character to it. In the case of the guitar, the size and shape of the box and the type of wood it's made from affect both the guitar's volume and tone qualities.

There are four resonation chambers in your head. The mouth is the largest one. The other three chambers are located in the back of your throat and are called the pharyngeal resonators. They are parts of the space that goes from your vocal folds at the top of the windpipe, past the uvula (the dangling piece of tissue), and up behind your nose. Scientists think of these as being three separate chambers but, in reality, they are all parts of one long space, or tube (see the illustration on page 73).

From this point on I refer to these four spaces simply as the resonators. They are the part of the "vocal megaphone" that makes the sound of your voice loud enough to be heard.

In most developing singers, almost all of the sound created by the vocal folds is dumped into the mouth to resonate. This presents a challenge because, unlike the hollow body of an acoustic guitar, your mouth is not an empty chamber. It contains your tongue, teeth, the hard and soft palates, and pooling saliva, each of which is of a different density. This causes a damping effect on any sound that resonates in your mouth, and it can make that sound seem dull and muddy. Imagine the dull, muddy sound you'd get by playing a guitar after putting a tennis ball, a banana, and a can of soup in the instrument's body. Not a great idea!

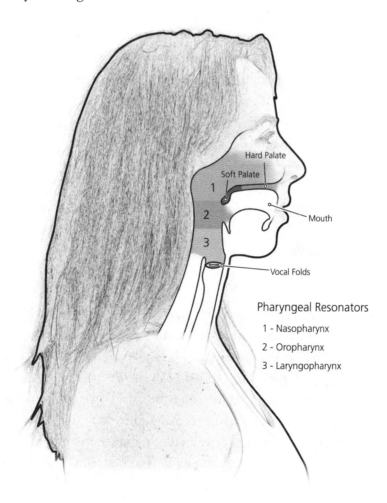

Hard Palate

Soft Palate

1

2

3

Mouth

Vocal Folds

Pharyngeal Resonators

1 - Nasopharynx

2 - Oropharynx

3 - Laryngopharynx

One way to lessen this damping effect is to reduce the amount of sound that resonates in your mouth. We want at least some of the resonation to take place in the other resonators. How can we train your body to do this? It's simple.

Exercise: Use Your Other Resonators

As you hold your jaw while you vocalize (sing exercises), squeeze together the part of your cheeks between your upper and lower teeth. Don't squeeze hard enough to cause discomfort—just enough so that the width of the opening of your mouth is narrowed by half. This action creates back pressure that diverts some of the sound from your mouth into your other resonators. If you practice this exercise regularly, your body will eventually "learn" to divert sound into your other resonators automatically while you are singing.

The advantage to having sound resonate in these other chambers is that these spaces are open and empty. Because there is no tongue or anything else in them to dampen the sound, that sound has a richer, more pleasing tone.

The Tongue

Another important part of the vocal tract is the tongue. It is instrumental (don't you just love musical puns?) in creating the different vowels and consonants that we sing. It is a muscle, and it can be strengthened through exercise. A strong tongue allows you to hold the correct position for each vowel. In fact, the position of the tongue—and the effect that position has on the size of the space in the back of your throat—are what largely determine the sound of each vowel you sing. For example, some vowels require the tongue to be arched; others require a flatter tongue. The exercises in the Vocal Power

Workout (which are found on my website; see page 25 for instructions on accessing the site) will help you to gain control of and strengthen your tongue.

In addition to being strong, your tongue must also be coordinated and flexible so that it can move independently of your jaw. This independent movement allows your tongue to create vowels and consonants and helps to stop your jaw from closing during singing—and an open jaw serves not only to keep the back of your throat open, but also to keep those pesky swallowing muscles out of the picture.

The Palate

The other major part of your vocal tract is the roof of your mouth, which is called the palate. It consists of two parts: the hard palate, which is made of bone, and the soft palate, which is made of muscle fibers that are sheathed in a mucus membrane. If you run your finger along the roof of your mouth, starting just behind the front teeth and moving back toward your throat, you will feel the hard palate. The soft palate begins were this bone ends. The soft palate is moveable, and the way in which it is moved can change the sound of your voice.

We can compare it to a railroad switch that directs a train onto one set of tracks or another. The soft palate opens and closes in the same way, directing the sound through the nasopharynx resonator (behind your nose) or the oropharynx resonator (behind and into your mouth).

Ideally, we want the palate to allow a certain amount of sound to resonate in both spaces. Occasionally, the soft palate will be in the wrong position and the balance of sound between the resonators will be off. We will look at this in more detail in chapter 5. For now, just study the illustration on page 73 to familiarize yourself with the location of your resonators and your palate.

Important Points to Remember

- Your vocal tract—the path from your vocal folds (commonly called the vocal cords) to your mouth—acts like a megaphone. The sound is made at the small end (by the vocal folds) and is amplified by the bigger end (the throat and mouth).

- The vocal folds are a pair of small muscles that lie horizontally in the windpipe. Like all muscles, they must be warmed up in order to work efficiently.

- When you sing a note, the space between your vocal folds, called the glottis, must be almost completely closed.

- By holding your jaw open while vocalizing, you help your body to close the glottis the way Nature intended, allowing you to make the sounds you're aiming for.

4

Support—The Foundation

Right around the corner from my house there used to be a pretty busy construction site. I'd seen big trucks driving by and heard the sounds of something major going on for days before my curiosity finally got me to ride my bike over there. I found a crew of workers bustling around a good-sized two-story house that was jacked up on blocks. Underneath the house was a giant hole in the ground. On the side of one of the trucks was the name of a company that repairs home foundations. I talked to one of the workmen, who told me that the foundation of the house was basically rotten and that they were in the process of replacing it. "That sounds like a lot of work!" I said. He replied, "Yeah, but if we don't do it, the whole thing could come crashing down."

In terms of singing, this is exactly what support is—the foundation for your voice. In this chapter you'll learn how to build your voice correctly from the foundation up. Once you know what support is and are able to use it throughout your vocal range, you won't ever have to have your voice "jacked up on blocks" while you try to repair it.

Singing involves the application of what I call the Big Three Vocal Principles: support, resonation, and registration. In this chapter we will explore the most important of these: support. In order to properly develop your voice, you must know how to create the support that is required to serve it. If you don't have that support, all of your other efforts to learn to sing with power, passion, and confidence will be like repainting a used car and calling it new: the major problems will still be there; they'll just be covered up. You may often run out of gas, your engine might idle roughly, and you won't have the power you want when you "put the pedal to the metal." It is almost impossible to sing with power or confidence unless you know how to create support.

What Is Support?

I sang professionally for 11 years with absolutely no concept of support, and it was very difficult for me to maintain my voice during that time. I got hoarse often, I had serious trouble with singing high notes, and, if I sang a song loudly and aggressively, I couldn't come right back and sing another song "cleanly" (without noise) and gently. I often spent each day worrying about whether or not my voice would work that night. It wasn't a lot of fun to have so little control over my voice, but I believed that was what singers had to put up with. Looking back, I know now that much of my trouble had to do with the fact that I was "singing from the throat" instead of using my support system.

So what is support? I ask this question of each singer who comes to my studio for his or her first lesson. Some people have never heard the term; some have heard it but, much as they don't understand the concept of "singing from the diaphragm," they have no idea what it means. Still others have a vague idea that support has to do with singing from the diaphragm, that it's related to rib cage alignment, or that it involves air supply or "correct" breathing, standing up straight, projecting, and so forth. The concept of support is fuzzy to most singers, even though they know they're "supposed" to be doing something with their abdominal area.

A teacher once told me that support could be defined as "the result of the opposition of the inhalation muscle movements versus the exhalation muscle movements." Huh?! What does *that* mean? Well, that's just a confusing way of saying that support is all about resistance. In the television show

Star Trek: The Next Generation, the Borgs often said, "Resistance is futile." The opposite is true in singing. You're going to see that resistance is absolutely necessary to create support.

Here's how I define support:

Support is the control of the airflow during singing. This is accomplished by resisting the lift of the belly.

Each time you use Bosnian Belly Breathing to expand your belly, filling your lungs with air as you prepare to sing a note or a line, you are performing the "inhalation muscle movement." As you sing, you lift your belly in and up to move air out of your body. This is the "exhalation muscle movement." However, if there was no resistance to the in-and-up lift of your belly, your abdominal wall would move in instantly, all of your air would gush out in a fraction of a second, and you would have no way to sustain a note. You would also make a breathy sound that wouldn't project well. So somehow, in addition to lifting the belly in and up as we sing, we also have to *resist* that in-and-up lift to control the speed and intensity of the air as it flows out of the body.

Before we discuss how this is done, try this exercise—it can help you to better understand the concept.

Exercise: Understand the Concept of Support

Put the palm of one hand on top of the other. Lift with the lower hand and resist the force of that lift with the upper hand. (See the illustration on page 80.) You have just imitated the support you're going to create in your torso. It's as simple as that.

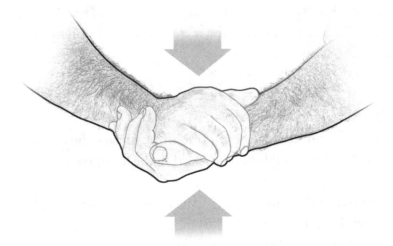

In other words, when you sing, you can change how fast and how hard the air flows out of your body by changing the intensity of the lift and resistance of your belly muscles. These actions have a big impact on many aspects of your singing, including your ability to:

- project
- use both halves of your voice (registration)
- create the tone you want (resonation)
- sing in tune
- control vibrato
- reduce breathiness
- increase endurance
- and more

Support is the engine of your vocal vehicle—it's what drives the voice and gives you command of the mechanics of singing.

This is the critical piece of the puzzle that is missing in most singers. I often watch vocalists struggle to sing while tightening, squeezing, tensing, or overworking the muscles of the upper torso, neck, and throat. In contrast, when the support system is hooked up and working automatically while you sing, you are harnessing the larger, stronger belly muscles to do most of the work. This is what Nature intended. It is more efficient and easier on the body than straining the neck and throat to make sound.

This support action can be felt whenever you try to lift an immovable object. To experience this for yourself, try this exercise—it's great way to get in touch with how you engage the muscles that control lift and resistance:

Exercise: Lift and Resist

Place your hands under a kitchen counter or some object that is too heavy for you to move. Being careful to protect your back, slowly and safely try to lift the immovable object (while singing the line "to dream the impossible dream"—just kidding). Can you feel your abdominals tightening?

This is very similar to what your abdominals do when you engage support to sing a high note at a loud volume. Now try this:

Exercise: Sing While You Support

Try as hard as you safely can to lift that immovable object again—but this time, sing a high note loudly as you do it. Then stop lifting, wait a minute or two, and sing the same note one more time. Many singers notice that the note they sang while lifting sounded fuller and louder. This is due to the fact that, during heavy lifting, your body uses the same type of muscle action it uses when you sing with support. That's why the second note, which you sang without support, sounded thinner and quieter. If you heard no difference, you may be one of the few singers whose bodies automatically incorporate the movements of heavy lifting into the action of vocal support.

The exercise above demonstrates what support can feel like when you sing a high note at a loud volume. But when you sing at a lower pitch or at a lower volume, less intense lift and resistance are needed. The amount of support you need at any given moment is determined by the sound you choose to sing at that moment, and you can change that amount of support on command. It's important to understand this so that you don't become overwhelmed by the idea that you have to work hard whenever you sing. I've had singers tell me, after completing the "immovable object" exercise, that they don't want to have to work that hard to sing. "That feels wrong," one singer said. "I thought correct singing should feel relaxed and easy," said another.

When you're singing quietly, as you might when you perform a ballad, you *will* feel like you're working less. But if you want to sing in the way that's commonly called "belting" (I don't like that term—I prefer "singing powerfully"), you need to understand that you can't do so correctly without incorporating a lot of abdominal lift and resistance. Remember that when you create support correctly, the majority of the work will be done by your abs rather than by your throat—and that, because the abdominals are larger, stronger, and intended by Nature to do this job, your voice will work better and last longer when you do use your abs instead of your throat.

A different way to look at support is via the following equation: power = lift + resistance (I know, you thought there'd be no math involved). This means the more intensely you lift and resist, the more power you create.

The good news is this: the stronger your muscles get, the less you'll have to work to create support. The more you practice creating support, the easier it will get.

How Do You Create Support?

How do we create the lift and resistance that make up support? There are two main ways: by putting our abdominal muscles to work and by keeping the bones of the upper torso stationary. First let's look at the abs.

When you use your abs to create support, you can call on parts of all four sets of the abdominal muscles to help create both the in-and-up lifting motion and the resistance action.

These actions are performed by your abdominal muscles in much the same way that your hands performed them in the opposing hands exercise. There is one big difference, however: you don't have to consciously direct your abdominal muscles to perform these activities as long as you train them to create support automatically.

When you practice singing a powerful, supported sound—say, at least a 6 or a 7 on a volume scale of 1 to 10—you call on the abdominal muscles to lift and resist each other with a lot of intensity. This creates the appropriate amount of power to sing loudly when that's what you intend. It also teaches the muscles what they need to do to create support. And, because those muscles do have to work hard to create that kind of support, they tend to learn how to do it fairly quickly. When you sing at, say, a 3 volume, the abs don't have to work very hard, so it takes longer for the muscles to figure out that it's their job to provide support. This is why initially you'll want to practice creating support by singing high notes at a loud volume. The more support you need, the harder the abs have to work—and the faster they will strengthen. I call this "vocal weight lifting."

Eventually, the belly muscles will automatically lift and resist to the right degree no matter how loudly or softly you want to sing. (It's just like learning to ride a bike—after you've "gotten it," you rarely have to think about your balance no matter how slowly or quickly you're pedaling.) Some singers find that it takes only a few days for their abdominal muscles to "get it"; for most singers, however, it takes a few weeks.

It's important to note that creating support doesn't mean always lifting and resisting with great energy. Support must be constant, but the level of *intensity* of that support can vary with each note you sing. The more powerful the sound you intend to sing, the more intense the lift and resistance has to be. The less powerful the sound, the less energetic the support needs to be. (Unfortunately, the majority of people I've heard sing don't use *any* lift and resistance. As a result, their sound is much thinner, breathier, and less projected than it could be.)

You can also stabilize the bones of your upper torso to create support. When you keep the upper ribs, collarbones, and shoulder blades from moving up and down during singing, they will act like a wall of bone that resists the in-and-up lift of your belly. Think about your upper torso in terms of that "opposing hands" exercise we did earlier. Allowing your upper torso to lift up is similar to not using the force of your upper hand to push against, or resist, the force of your lower hand as it lifts up. If the lower hand faces little opposition, little pressure is created. It's the same with the bones of your upper torso and your abdominal muscles.

Here is an illustration that shows both the correct position of the shoulders and upper torso for creating support and the incorrect position that you should avoid.

Shoulders and upper body

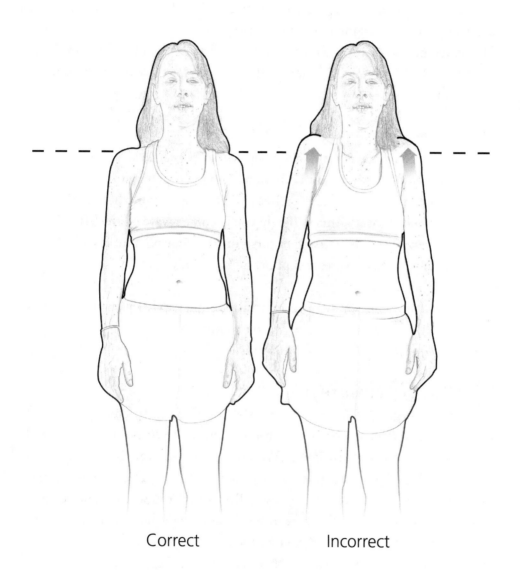

Correct   Incorrect

It is critical that you correctly create the air pressure that's needed to sing. Unfortunately, many singers try to do this in the throat instead of using the support system. By keeping your shoulders from lifting up, you can more efficiently create the right amount of pressure *in the torso* to sing with power. This is yet another reason to break the bad habit of "shoulder breathing" and to use the techniques of Bosnian Belly Breathing to relearn to breathe as Nature intended.

I have a mirror in my studio that helps my voice students see what their bodies are doing while they sing, and I encourage you to do exercises in front of a mirror whenever possible, as well. This will help you become aware of any lifting or falling of your upper torso during singing, and it will help you learn to create support more quickly.

Does this mean you have to remain motionless when you sing? Not at all. You can move in whatever ways you want to when you sing—*as long as you keep your shoulders from rising and falling.*

The "Yoh-Oh" Exercise

To help you begin to change the way you breathe and to create support, I invite you to start practicing the "yoh-oh" exercise (track 1 of the Listen and Learn section of the Vocal Power Workout, which is available on my website; see page 25 for instructions on accessing the site). This exercise brings into play all the aspects of Bosnian Belly Breathing. You will lift and resist—and, in doing so, you will begin to teach your body how to make a supported sound. This will prepare you for the other exercises in the Vocal Power Workout (see chapter 8). Listen to the exercise first, then continue reading as I walk you through it.

Let's break this exercise into two parts: the movements you perform and the sounds you make while doing it. First we'll work on the movements.

1. Start by sitting in a comfortable position. Check your body alignment, making sure that your shoulders are directly over your hips and that you are not leaning forward or slumping back. Correct body alignment makes it easier to expand and lift your belly.

2. Now, without making a sound, rest a hand low on your abdomen, expand your belly, and see how far out you can push your hand. Next, lift your belly up and in, and see how closely you can pull it in toward your backbone. Keep your hand resting lightly on your belly but make sure it's not doing any work. It's only there to help make you aware of what your lower abdomen is doing.

3. Notice the distance between "all the way out" and "all the way in" and note the halfway point between the two.

4. Now lift your belly until it reaches that halfway point. Next, vocalize the syllable "oh" while lifting. Then lift your belly all the way in. Be sure to make these two distinct, separate lifts and to make them as equal in distance as you can. It may feel like you are performing a Heimlich maneuver (a technique used to dislodge material from the throat of a choking person by applying sudden upward pressure to the abdomen) on yourself.

5. Make sure you're not holding your breath as you do three repetitions of this "lift-lift" motion—this is the movement you'll do for the yoh-oh exercise.

Now let's move to the sounds. You will be vocalizing a "yoh" followed by an "oh." The challenge is to make the "y" sound while keeping your jaw open.

1. Place one hand below your jaw to feel that your jaw stays open (see the illustration on page 71). If your jaw closes at all, the swallowing muscles will attempt to help, and you don't want that to happen. Keep your lips from closing or moving, as they are connected by muscles to the soft palate and the back of the throat. If your lips pucker at all, the back of the throat will begin to close.

2. Squeeze your cheeks, narrowing the width of your mouth's opening by half (see the illustration on page 71). Remember: this is to help divert some of the sound into the pharyngeal resonators (see Exercise: Use Your Other Resonators on page 74).

3. Make a "y" sound without moving your lips. How do you do this? *You have to let your tongue be in charge.* Check yourself in the mirror to make sure that you are keeping the jaw and lips as open as you comfortably can, and then say "yoh." If you let your tongue move freely, it will make an approximation of the "y" sound.

4. Be sure you're not doing your impression of a pirate by vocalizing "yoh-*hoh*" instead of the desired "yoh-oh." Pronouncing a hard "h" results in an extra blast of air against the vocal folds and the back of your throat that can act like a sandblaster, wearing you out sooner and potentially causing your voice to get hoarse.

5. Now comes the fun part. Rest one hand low on your belly, hold your jaw open with the other hand, and vocalize "yoh-oh," lifting the belly in to the halfway point on the "yoh" and all the way in on the "oh."

6. Perform three repetitions of this exercise. After each set of three repetitions, stop for a few seconds to give your body a chance to rest.

Most people feel pretty uncoordinated the first few times they perform this exercise, so don't worry if it's awkward. Even if you look and sound silly in the beginning, consider all that's taking place in this exercise. By expanding and lifting, you continue to train your body to breathe in a way that provides for a natural, efficient air exchange. If you vocalize a clean (not breathy) sound with the volume at about a 7, the belly muscles will be lifting and resisting intensely enough to create strong support. (Be sure to listen to track 1 of the Vocal Power Workout so that you can hear a model of the sound you want to make.)

If you keep the bones of the upper torso from lifting up and down, you will create more support. By holding the jaw open, you will help to keep the swallowing muscles out of the picture, causing the glottis to close the natural and efficient way. Keeping your lips open helps to keep the back of your throat open. And squeezing the cheeks helps to direct some of the resonation out of the mouth and into the other resonators, making for a much fuller sound.

And to think that you get all of this just by performing an unusual-looking (and unusual-sounding) exercise!

How to Practice "Yoh-Oh"-ing

It's important to do this exercise often, but in short bursts. I recommend practicing the exercise three or four times, then waiting at least a few minutes to give your body a rest before you do it again. It doesn't help to do more than a few exercises at one sitting. Lots of short practice sessions, sung each day, help your muscles to learn new actions more quickly than they will if you sing one or two longer sessions. Whenever you think of it and you are somewhere that you can comfortably practice, sing three or four exercises. Soon, you will begin to create the muscle memory you need in order to automatically sing with support using Bosnian Belly Breathing.

All of the other exercises in the Vocal Power Workout call for you to use the techniques you employ in the "yoh-oh" exercise, so the more you "yoh-oh," the faster the correct mechanics will become automatic. I suggest you stick to the "yoh-oh" exercise for a few days before moving to the next exercises in the Vocal Power Workout. This will allow your body the time it needs to get used to using Bosnian Belly Breathing, creating support, and holding your jaw.

Maintain Your Speed

Another important aspect of singing with power, passion, and confidence is the creation of a consistent amount of support. To achieve this, you must keep the speed of your lift consistent from the first to the last note—don't slow down or speed up.

It's very common for singers who are learning to expand and lift the belly (the essence of Bosnian Belly Breathing) to experience the lifting motion slowing down or speeding up. Practice lifting at the same speed from the first note to the last note of each line you sing.

One day in my studio I was working with Sam, a young rockabilly singer. As he went through his exercises, he would lift with a fairly even rate of speed on most of the notes, but he would consistently use about a third of his lift on the first note. As a result, that first note was louder than the rest of the notes, and Sam frequently ran out of air before he reached the end of the line.

It may feel as though more lift is needed just to "turn on" your voice at the beginning of each line. However, if you maintain the same rate of speed of your lift from the first note to the last note, you will smooth out the air-flow and have more control over your volume and air supply. It's not how far you lift on the first note, but the right amount of *resistance*, that helps you to "turn on" your voice in a smooth manner. Experiment with different amounts of lift and resistance, working toward the goal of maintaining a steady volume for each note you sing, as you practice "yoh-oh"-ing. This a great way to build vocal control.

If you were rowing a boat and your stroke was uneven or jerky, the boat would move in the same uneven, jerky way. Smooth out your rowing and you will smooth out the movement of your boat. Need another example? To maintain a car's speed, you apply a constant level of pressure to the gas pedal; you don't press your foot down and lift it off rapidly. The same applies to expanding and lifting.

Many voice teachers and singers use the word "attack" to describe the beginning of the sound when singing, but I think this term can lead you to lift too fast, too far, and too hard on the first note. I prefer to call the beginning of the sung note the "start-up." If you practice your start-ups while lifting the belly slowly and evenly, it will become second nature. With intention and practice, your belly will lift at the right rate of speed every line you sing.

You may be asking yourself, "But how *far* should I be lifting?" Here's the rule of thumb:

As you begin to sing each line, create and maintain a lift that allows your belly to travel about seven-eighths of the way in by the end of the line. This applies to both

lines sung in exercises and lines of songs. This way, you've always got a small reserve of air in case you decide to improvise something at the end of the line or decide to hold the last note longer—and, because you won't be trying to conserve *too much* air, you will make a fuller tone and have better projection.

If you practice lifting this seven-eighths distance as you perform the exercises (and I mean that approximately—don't worry too much about an exact measurement), your body will learn to automatically do it when you're actually singing in front of an audience.

As you "yoh-oh," notice whether your belly ends up almost all of the way in. If you find that, by the end of the "oh," your belly is only halfway in, it's probably because your body is smart. It may be saying to itself, "If we don't lift in so far, we won't have as far to go to expand fully for the next line." On the surface this makes sense—it's the "work smarter, not harder" concept. However, there are two problems with lifting less than seven-eighths of the way in:

1. You will use less air than you need to project and make a full sound.

2. You won't be working your belly muscles as much as you could be. As a result, it will take longer for your abs to build the strength they need to sing with power and control.

Think of expanding and lifting when you sing as building strength in your biceps by lifting a barbell. It's easier to lift the weight only a few inches in either direction than it is to flex and straighten your arm completely, but it will take a long time to build any strength if you don't move to the extremes.

How Do You Know When You're Singing with Support?

It's a challenge to sing with support until you can recognize what it sounds like. Tracks 1 and 2 of the Listen and Learn section of my website (see page 25) model both a supported and an unsupported sound for you.

You can learn not only to *hear* the difference, but also to *feel* it. It's helpful to establish a number, on a scale of 1 to 10, that corresponds with the power, workload, or intensity (any of these words can be used) needed to make a supported sound on a note. Having a number in mind when you practice support (or any other vocal element) will make it easier to hit your target consistently. In the beginning, you'll want to practice singing notes with lots of power to help you gain an awareness of support. (You'll also be singing these notes in what's called "pure heavy register," which is discussed in the next chapter.)

You also need to know about Bernoulli's principle. What's that, you say?

Bernoulli's Principle

I recently worked with a singer on managing power to keep her voice from sounding like it was falling apart. She had a tendency to underpower certain notes, especially higher ones, which caused them to crack, warble, and generally be unstable. This is where Bernoulli's principle comes in. In 1738 a mathematician named Daniel Bernoulli discovered that the faster air moves, the lower its pressure.

What does that mean? Let's look at a simple example of Bernoulli's principle in action. If you blow over the top of a sheet of paper, the paper will lift up (try this—it's fun!) because the stationary air on the underside of the paper has more air pressure than the moving air on top of it. This effect plays a very important role in singing.

During singing, when enough air is moved through the vocal folds to lower the pressure between them, the higher pressure outside the folds helps to hold them together. When singing at lower power, the pressure difference is not enough to help hold the folds together, and the folds themselves must take up the slack and flex more to prevent pulling apart. Oftentimes this causes a singer to produce a noisy, unstable sound. This is particularly true in the case of a developing singer, especially when he or she hits high notes, because the singer's vocal folds are not yet strong enough to hold themselves together.

That's why it's easier to hit higher notes when you sing "loud and proud"; you're moving more air, which causes there to be less pressure between the vocal folds than there is outside of the vocal folds—and that difference in pressure causes your vocal folds to be held together more easily. This is often the exact opposite of what feels safe to your body, but the more power you use, the more Bernoulli's principle works to your advantage. Learn to use your power—there's no question that it's challenging at first, but it's a huge part of singing with confidence.

As you're learning how much power to exert when you sing, you may sometimes find that your body uses less power than it needs, especially when it comes to singing high notes. On the other hand, some people may actually go overboard and use more power than they can control, causing them to lose stability. It can be challenging to know exactly how much power, on a scale of 1 to 10, you need in order to sing a note with the minimum amount of support that's required. To help find the minimum amount of power required to make a supported sound, first learn what your maximum amount of power feels and sounds like. This may put you right up against the wall of what feels "right" or comfortable, since it may, at first, feel as though you are straining.

Finding Your Power

Before we start on the concept of singing with power, I want to define the word *strain*. Many singers use this word to describe the sensation of working hard to sing a note. I define straining as going beyond working hard to a place where the voice gets noisy, the folds won't hold together, and you may notice discomfort. **Please give yourself permission to work hard to sing a note**—this is an important tool in learning about support. I know this goes against what you may have heard about correct singing ("it should always be relaxed"). We will examine this "relaxation" misconception in more detail later.

So, back to our exercise of finding the minimum and maximum amount of power to use when singing a note. As you sing a note, increase the volume until you're on the edge of straining or until you can hear noise creeping into your voice. Then reduce the power just enough to get rid of the noise and the feeling of strain. On a scale of 1 to 10, put a number on that workload—this is your current maximum power for that note.

Now begin repeating the note, turning down the power a notch each time until you get to the point where noise creeps in, your voice feels unstable, and you have a sense that "it's about to fall apart." Raise the power slightly until the stability returns and the noise lessens. Put a number, on a scale of 1 to 10, on that workload—this is your current minimum power for that note.

You now have concrete numbers for a range of power you can use to sing that particular note on that particular vowel. I mention the vowel because, with each note that's sung, the vowel that's vocalized has a slightly different minimum and maximum workload setting. This might seem overwhelming at first—you may think that it's an impossible amount of information to keep track of. What makes this manageable is the intelligence of our bodies.

For example, I have a friend whose contact lenses are designed for "monocular vision"—his right contact lens allows him to see clearly at distance, while his left lens enables him to read without needing special glasses. How does he not get confused? Why does he not just see everything as a blur? He told me that, although it did take a few days to get used to them, pretty soon his brain figured out what to do. Now he rarely has to make a conscious decision about "which eye to look out of"—yet he can still see at distances both near and far.

In the same way, as you practice keeping notes stable, your body will begin to memorize the support settings for each circumstance. Eventually, you won't have to think about numbers on a scale of 1 to 10. In the beginning, though, this is a great way to teach yourself how to stabilize your voice.

I refer to scales of 1 to 10 throughout this book because using them is a great way to become an intentional singer. When you can tell your body, by assigning a number to your desired outcome, what you want it to do, you'll be much more likely to get the results you want. You'll easily be able to control volume, tone, pitch, emotion, dynamics, and any other element of singing. Think of it like this: If the captain of a ship simply ordered his crew to "go forward," the crew would be scratching their heads and wondering "what heading?" and "what speed?" In the same way, your body responds much better to "sing with a 7 power" than it does to "I hope I hit this note!"

From now on, whenever I ask you to sing something at or with a certain number, know that I mean a certain number on a scale of 1 to 10.

Important Points to Remember

- Support is the most important of all the vocal principles. It is the engine of your vocal vehicle—it is what drives your voice and gives you command over the mechanics of singing.

- Support provides you the means to control air during singing by resisting the in-and-up lift of your belly.

- The four sets of abdominal muscles can be trained to create the lift as well as the resisting motion during support.

- By varying the intensity of support, different options (in terms of registration, volume, vibrato, and so forth) become available to you during singing.

- By keeping the bones (the ribs, shoulder blades, and collarbones) of your upper torso from moving up and down during singing, you increase your level of support.

5

Resonation—The Tone

As I began to sing professionally I started to hang around other singers, and I would sometimes hear them talk about things I didn't understand. "Placing the voice" was a phrase that was so mysterious to me. I heard someone else say "resonate the sound in the mask." Were these singers performing at a Halloween party? One day, as I thumbed through a how-to book on singing that I'd found, I saw a drawing that showed arrows pointing out the back of the head, with instructions to "direct the sound out of the crown of the head."

I was so thoroughly confused—were these other singers strange beings from another dimension that could make sound come out of places other than their mouths? Once I began to train as a voice teacher, it finally became clearer to me: the strange phrases I'd heard and read were some of the many ways that resonation is described. If you are as confused as I was, read on!

Resonation is the second of the Big Three Vocal Principles. Using this principle, you can change the tone of your voice by consciously and subconsciously manipulating the resonation chambers in your head—the mouth and the open spaces located in the back of the throat (see the illustration on page 73). By "manipulating," I mean changing the size, shape, and tension of the walls of a space. One of the main vocal elements affected by resonation is vowel color.

Vowel Color

This term describes the quality of vocal tone that is similar to treble and bass. Perhaps you have experienced the effects of adjusting the treble and bass controls on a stereo or radio. Turning up the treble causes the upper frequencies of the sound to become exaggerated. The vocal equivalent of this effect is called *bright vowel color*. Examples of artists whose voices have bright vowel color are a young Jerry Lewis, Ethel Merman, Pee-wee Herman, Cyndi Lauper, Fran Drescher, Alison Krauss, and Lucille Ball. In the extreme, this vocal quality can make a person sound as though he or she has inhaled helium. Listen to track 3 of the Listen and Learn section found on my website (see page 25) to hear an example of bright vowel color.

Bright vowel color is often equated with a nasal sound. The two are quite different, however. If you make a parody of the "on" sound in the French word *garçon* you can hear a nasal sound. The test for nasality is to pinch your nostrils together while you are singing. If the sound stops or is very restricted, you are probably making a nasal sound. If you're making a very bright sound, however, pinching your nostrils together will have little effect on what you're singing because most of the sound is coming through your mouth. Think of bright as a "mouthy" sound, in contrast to a "nosey" nasal sound.

Interestingly, some people interpret a note sung using bright vowel color as being higher than it actually is. Vowel color does not affect pitch, and bright vowel color may be used when singing either low or high notes.

Turning up the bass knob on a stereo amplifies the lower frequencies of the sound; the vocal equivalent is called *dark vowel color*. Examples of artists whose vowel color is naturally dark are James Earl Jones (*Star Wars*'s Darth Vader), Tiny Tim, Barry White, Julia Child, and virtually all opera singers, from Leontyne Price to the late Luciano Pavarotti. In the extreme, a singer who uses ultradark vowel color can sound like an exaggerated parody of an opera singer. Listen to track 4 of Listen and Learn to hear an example of dark vowel color.

Just as some people interpret notes sung using bright vowel color as being higher than they really are, some folks interpret notes sung using dark vowel color as being lower than they actually are. Again, vowel color doesn't change pitch, and dark vowel color may be used when singing any note.

To get an idea of what's involved in changing vowel color, try this exercise:

Exercise: Experiment with Vowel Color

Pick a note that's in the middle of your range and sing it with an ultrabright vowel color (feel free to refer back to track 3 of Listen and Learn). Next, sing the same note with an ultradark vowel color. What physical differences did you detect? Some people observe that, when they "sing bright," it feels as though the sound resonates more behind the nose and that, when they "sing dark," it resonate somewhere lower. Sing the note both ways again and pay attention to what happens to the back of your throat. Could you feel the throat opening more for the darker vowel color? (If you didn't, don't worry; just know that your throat *was* opening more—it has to in order to produce a dark vowel color.)

This is the main reason that I'm going to ask you to **temporarily** (and I really mean temporarily!) sing your exercises and a practice song or two using an ultradark vowel color. This may be the place where you say to yourself, "I knew it. Voice teachers try to turn everyone into opera singers." Nothing could be further from the truth. If you want to sing opera songs, great; I do too, occasionally. But I also sing rock, country, pop, bluegrass, zydeco, gospel, and a bunch of other styles of music. I have no desire to steer you toward *any* particular type of music, and I think you should sing any and all songs that call to you.

While it may be true that some voice teachers who come from an operatic or classical background have difficulty applying the mechanics and techniques that they teach to popular music, it's important to realize that even teachers who are skilled at teaching pop or other styles frequently use classical music as a way to instruct their students on the value of dark vowel color. When I first began taking voice lessons, my teacher started me out with an aria from an Italian opera. I could feel serious inner resistance to singing a style that was so *weird* to me—not to mention the resistance I felt to singing a song in a foreign language—and I assumed that the teacher had a secret agenda to turn me from being a rock and pop singer into a singer who embraced the "dark side" (meaning a singer who consistently uses ultradark vowel color). What I soon discovered was how helpful learning to sing a dark vowel color was to the rock and pop singing I was doing professionally.

Why Sing Dark?

The reason I want you to **temporarily** sing with an ultradark vowel color is that I want you to learn to open your throat when you sing—and you have to open your throat in order to create a dark vowel color. An open throat has four positive impacts on your singing:

> **It creates a bigger chamber for sound to pass through.** More space helps you to create a bigger sound. The bigger the garden hose, the more water that passes through it, provided your water pressure is good. The same principle applies to your voice. By "singing dark," you teach your throat to stay open much more so than it would otherwise—and, once your body has learned to do this, your throat will stay open no matter what vowel color you employ.

> **It helps your body learn how to clean up noise.** Most singers have some unwanted noise in their voices at least some of

the time. This is often referred to as a scratchy, crackly, raspy, or breathy sound. I call any unwanted noise in the voice *vocal interference*. This interference can be due to the walls of the resonators, which consist of soft tissue, flapping like sails on a sailboat. Singing a dark vowel color causes the throat to open, which stretches the walls of the throat more tightly and, as a result, helps your boat—your voice—to move more smoothly.

If we continue our sailboat analogy, this is like trimming the sheets (for you non-sailors, that means tightening the lines that are attached to the sails in order to prevent the sails from flapping). In the throat, "singing dark" helps to prevent the walls of the throat from creating vocal interference. Eventually, the body learns how to do this on its own and the walls adjust to make a clean sound whether you're singing dark, bright, or in between. If you want to deliberately add noise as an effect, you'll certainly be able to do so—but, for now, let's concentrate on boosting your level of voice control and your ability to clean up *unwanted* noise.

It helps you to create a more fully resonant tone. In most developing singers, the walls of the throat don't reflect all of the frequencies of the voice because those walls are made of soft tissue—and soft tissue doesn't make for the greatest surface when it comes to reflecting sound. Think of it as being similar to the sound an acoustic guitar made of Styrofoam would produce; much of the richness and presence found in the sound of a normal guitar would be lost. The throat's soft tissue acts as Styrofoam in many ways, causing only some of the frequencies of most voices to be amplified, and the result is a sound that's duller and muddier than it could be. To hear an example of this, listen to track 5 of the Listen and Learn section of my website (see page 25).

By singing a dark vowel color, which causes the throat to stretch open, you exercise the walls of the throat. As they get stronger, they are better able to amplify and reflect all of the frequencies of your voice—darker, brighter, and everything in between. This is what's called a fully resonant sound.

It helps you to create a consistent vowel color for all the vowels. Each vowel has its own natural vowel color, which is different from the color of every other vowel. Some vowels are naturally darker, some are brighter, and some are in the middle (see Figure 1, page 105). Most singers don't realize this and are unaware that, in any given song, the natural colors of the vowels that are sung may vary greatly. While this may not be something that your audience consciously identifies—"Gee, you sound pretty good, but your vowel colors are all over the map!"—it is likely they will subconsciously notice that something about the sound of your voice just "isn't right."

I have found that the easiest way to learn to make vowel color consistent in a song is to sing all vowels ultradark. Practice singing an entire song "dark" without letting any of the notes change in color. Once you can do this, you'll find it easier to keep an even vowel color line regardless of whether you're singing a song dark, bright, or anywhere in between. When the colors of all the vowels sung in a song are in the same general color line, it makes for a more effective delivery. You will no longer sound as though someone is spinning the treble and bass knobs while you are singing.

There's an exception to every rule, of course. Sometimes you do want to intentionally vary vowel color as a dynamic effect, and we'll explore that later in this book—but you need to learn to match your vowel colors first.

Figure 1
Vowel Color Line

Darker Vowel Color   Brighter Vowel Color

Too – Took – Toe – Tut – Turn – Taw – Tot – Tah – Tight – Tap – Tare – Taste – Test – Tin - Tee

As you can see, singing with an open throat is critical. Again, this is why it's important to temporarily practice the exercises and a song or two using an ultradark vowel color. Remember to always vocalize the exercises with the jaw and lips held open. This also reinforces an open throat position. By doing both, you tell your body that you want an open throat as the default position for singing.

If you have any trouble determining whether or not your throat is open, the following exercise can help.

Exercise: Feel Your Way to a More Open Throat

First, try a visualization technique to get a sense of what an open throat feels like. Visualize that you are beginning to yawn or that you are biting into an apple. As you do, you may be able to feel your throat open.

Next, place a finger across your windpipe, just below your Adam's apple, and gently move your Adam's apple downward by opening your throat. Feel the resistance against your finger as your throat opens. If you sing before and after doing this exercise, you will likely hear the vowel color become darker once you've opened your throat.

Adapting Vowel Color to Pitch

A big advantage to learning to sing with a dark vowel color is that it will make it easier to sing high notes in your heavy register, which is commonly called the "chest voice." (We will explore the concept of registration further in the next chapter.) As a note goes higher in pitch, it tends to get brighter. This can cause you to experience more tension in the walls of the throat and to sound and feel strained during singing. By making an exaggerated dark vowel color, your support system will carry more of the workload, the throat will open, and your vocal folds will feel as if they aren't having to work as hard to produce the sound. (See Appendix B.)

Once you have determined how much support and what vowel color you need to stably sing a high note, you can then keep the workload of the abs and the openness of the throat as close as possible to the same settings even when singing a different vowel color.

We've already recognized that as notes get higher they also tend to get brighter. The opposite applies to low notes. These tend to sound duller and muddier as you get closer to the bottom of your range. This is true for both men and women and for all voice classifications, from bass to soprano. As counterintuitive as it may be, it's important to learn to sing with a brighter vowel color as you go lower in pitch. By listening for this in others, you'll begin to notice that most singers unconsciously "turn up the bass" by singing darker as the pitch gets lower. Doing the opposite will give your lower notes more presence and will make words more understandable.

Remember—to establish an even vowel color line, you will need to sing high notes darker and low notes brighter. Otherwise, notes sung at both ends of your range will be of a different vowel color than those that are in the middle of your range.

Vowel Color and Diphthongs

Keeping an even vowel color line (all the notes the same color) throughout a song will also help when you sing diphthongs. A diphthong is a sound created by two different vowel sounds that glide from one to the other. Table 1, below, shows some common diphthongs in the English language and the two sounds that are combined to make them. If you say the diphthong slowly, you will probably be able to hear the two sounds.

Table 1

Diphthongs

1.	I, as in lied	ah + ee
2.	OY, as in toy	oh + ee
3.	OW, as in cow	ah + oo
4.	EW, as in pew	ee + oo
5.	A, as in play	eh + ee
6.	OH, as in low	oh + oo
7.	OU, as in loud	ah + oo
8.	EER, as in here	ee + er
9.	AIR, as in pair	eh + er
10.	URE, as in lure	oo + er

The challenge in singing diphthongs is that, if you move to the second sound too quickly, you tend to close your mouth to some extent, which makes it more difficult to keep the pitch and the vowel color stable.

Let's look at a few diphthongs: the long "i," as in lied, spied, and ride (if you pronounce the "i" slowly you will hear ("ah-ee"); the long "a," as in play, wait, and hate ("eh-ee"); and "oy," as in toy, joy, and boy ("oh-ee"). Because the second vowel sound of all of these diphthongs is "ee" (check out where "ee" is on the color line shown in Figure 1, page 105), it tends to brighten the vowel color of the note. Unfortunately, many singers make the mistake of gliding from the first vowel to the second somewhere during the "middle" of the note being sung, causing the vowel color of the note as a whole to be unstable. If you wait until just before the note ends to glide to the second vowel, however, you'll be able to keep the vowel color stable, and you'll also be able to sing the word more easily. You can hear examples of this on track 6 of the Listen and Learn section of my website (see page 25).

Notice that the second sound of the diphthongs numbered 8, 9, and 10 in Table 1 is an "r." This sound tends to affect color and pitch as well because most singers produce it by closing the jaw—and a closed jaw usually means a brighter vowel color. Again, the key is to wait until *just before* the note ends to glide to the second sound of a diphthong.

To become better at creating the vowel color you want when you sing, there are three different approaches that you can use.

1. **Change the size and shape of the back of the throat.** An open, elongated throat creates darker vowel color; a smaller, flatter throat opening creates brighter vowel color.

2. **Change where the sound resonates in the mouth.** Visualize moving sound to the back of the throat to make it darker and toward the front of the mouth to make it brighter. (If you can't actually feel this happening, don't worry. Some people can feel it, some can't.)

3. **Change the position of the lips.** By moving your lips, you change the tension in the back wall of the throat—which, in turn, changes the vowel color. Stretch your lips vertically into an "oh!" ("surprised mouth") for darker vowel color; stretch your lips horizontally into a smile ("happy mouth") for brighter vowel color.

Use whichever of these techniques works best for you and is easiest to remember. Many singers use a combination of these techniques.

Vowel Color and Style

An important aspect of vowel color is the degree to which it allows the singer to produce stylistically authentic sound, or sound that is accepted as being "right" for any given style. For example, I once heard an album of pop songs sung by a famous opera singer. Because he sang them using his typical exaggerated dark vowel color, every song sounded like an aria from an opera. I could only guess that the singer either had no awareness of what makes pop "sound like" pop or just didn't care to sing in the authentic pop style. Maybe he believed that having a great instrument was the only factor in singing well. The result was about as rewarding as hearing a pop singer sing arias with a very bright vowel color, as if they were pop tunes. It just didn't sound "authentic." In fact, using a stylistically inauthentic vowel color when singing almost never works, no matter how impressive the vocal instrument! See Figure 2, below, to get an idea of the vowel colors that are generally accepted as being "right" for various styles.

Figure 2
Vowel Color and Style

Darker Vowel Color   Brighter Vowel Color

Opera – Classical – Art Songs – Jazz – Blues – Rock – Reggae – Pop – Country – Folk – Bluegrass

If the opera singer had sung the pop songs more brightly, he probably would have sounded much closer to the mark in terms of his performances sounding authentic.

Obviously, there is wiggle room to "color outside the lines" (pun intended) no matter what style you sing, but it's helpful to know where on the color line the generally accepted style of your song "belongs." Think of this as a good starting point. Of course, if you don't like the results or if you want to make the song "your own," you can experiment with the vowel color. The key is knowing where you're departing from and where to return to if you don't like the results.

Resonation and Vowel Production

In addition to vowel color, a critical part of resonation is vowel production. The ways in which you pronounce, sustain, and change vowels can radically affect your pitch, tone, and style, as well as the audience's ability to understand the words you are singing. Vowels are defined as sounds made by the vibration of the folds that travel through the vocal tract without any friction or interference. As is illustrated in Figure 1 (page 105), there are many more vowel sounds than the "a, e, i, o, and u" that are traditionally taught in English class.

So what do you need to know about making vowels? Let's start with learning how to create vowels effectively.

Exercise: Create Vowels Effectively

Hold your jaw open, keep your lips from moving, and vocalize the following vowels: oo, oh, ah, ay, and ee. Can you feel your tongue moving? The back of your throat changing? The positions of the tongue and the back of the throat are the primary physical factors that determine the different sounds of vowels.

This exercise shows that vowels can be created without any lip involvement. You can make vowels by changing, at the same time, the tongue position and the size and shape of the space between the back of your tongue and the back wall of your throat. (This is a critical skill for ventriloquists to master.) The vowels won't sound like what you're used to hearing—they'll tend to sound darker and muddier; however, by training yourself to start the vowels in the back of the throat instead of with the lips, you will learn to create purer vowels, which leads to better pronunciation, better pitch, and better tone. Then, when you bring your lips into play, both your vowels and your pronunciation will be clear.

Most American English speakers enunciate vowels by using the lips as a starting point instead of using the back of the throat as the starting point— and, because we have lazy lips (a result of not using them in precise ways), we produce mushy, ill-formed vowels. Sadly, "Hey, wus gone on witch you? Nat mush!" has become an accepted style of speech. It can be quite a challenge for anyone who is just learning to speak English to understand most Americans' speech. It takes effort to make vowel sounds that are clear, precise, and easily understood—and it takes even more effort to do this when you're singing.

If you begin to make a vowel sound in the back of your throat instead of with your lips, you will make a better vowel sound. This is one of the bonuses of holding the jaw open while singing the exercises—you'll build this habit into muscle memory.

Obviously, when you let go of the jaw and you sing actual words, the position of the tongue and lips will determine not only the vowel you sing, but also the *integrity* of that vowel. Integrity refers to the purity of your pronunciation and tone. If you sing the word "fall" and the "a" vowel sounds more like an "uh" than an "ah," you're likely to sing the pitch flat (lower than you intend to) and have a duller tone. To hear an example of this, listen to track 7 of Listen and Learn, which is found on my website (www.SingFreeNow.com; see page 25 for instructions on accessing the audio tracks). Many singers are amazed that the way in which they pronounce a vowel can affect their tone and pitch. This is one of the keys to good singing that is often overlooked.

By using body awareness (i.e., noticing the way something feels) as well as auditory awareness (i.e., noticing the way something sounds), you can better key in on small differences in the pronunciation of vowels. This will help you to improve your vowels' integrity. When I coach singers that are having pitch problems, this is one of the first areas we look at.

Exaggeration is a great tool when it comes to learning, and it can be used to help you become more aware of vowel integrity. By keeping the jaw wide open and exaggerating vowels during the early stages of learning to sing, you can more quickly teach your body how to make pure vowel sounds.

Try improving your vowel integrity by completing the following exercise.

Exercise: Improve Your Vowel Integrity

As you sing this exercise, try exaggerating the "uh" and "oh" vowels; this may help you to more easily pick up on the changes that take place with your tongue and the back of your throat as you sing the vowels. Be sure to hold your jaw open as instructed in each step of this exercise.

1. Pick a comfortable note in the middle of your range. Alternate singing an "uh" and an "oh" while holding the note for a few seconds. Don't let your jaw close or your lips move at all. Focus on the small changes made by your tongue and the back of your throat as you alternate singing "uh" and "oh."

2. Next, while singing an "ah" vowel on a comfortable note, alternate between a fully lowered jaw and a half-closed mouth. Notice the difference in vowel purity. Your "ah" will probably begin to sound more like "uh" as the jaw closes.

3. Now sing the note again—but this time, try to keep the pronunciation of the vowel from changing as you move from a fully open to a half-open jaw. Be sure to use both your ears and your body awareness to help you keep the vowel sound consistent. Practice this until you can open and close your jaw with little or no change to the pronunciation of a vowel.

4. Last, sing a song that contains a challenging high note. As you sing that note, exaggerate the openness of the jaw and throat. The vowel color will probably be very dark. Don't worry about this for now. Remember, you'll be using these exaggerated movements only temporarily in order to get your voice from where it is now to where you want it to be; this won't be the way you'll sing during performances (unless you are singing opera, classical, or some choral pieces).

Over the course of teaching thousands of singers, I've learned that singing a "temporary sound" that builds a desired skill in your voice is often the fastest way to develop a good performance sound—*a lot* faster than continued attempts to create a performance sound that you can't yet make.

This idea of using exaggerated sounds and movements takes getting used to. You may feel awkward at first, and the voices in your head (not *those* again) may be shouting, "Why is he having me make that sound? That doesn't sound like good singing!" You have to learn to trust that, sometimes, making a strange sound is the fastest and best way to build strength, coordination, and confidence.

By exaggerating the openness of your jaw and throat, you teach your body how to adjust your resonators and tongue to create as pure a vowel as possible. As you become able to sing this high note with stability, you can begin to close your jaw in order to make the vowel color brighter and to sound stylistically authentic. In other words, you may start practicing a line of a song by singing a challenging note with a wide-open jaw and a 3 vowel color (1 being as dark and 10 being as bright as you can sing). Then, as your body learns how to sing the note in pitch, you can change the vowel color to, say, a 6 (or whatever number corresponds to your desired target color). This may not happen immediately, and it may take many repetitions before you get the results you want. However, by temporarily using a dark vowel color, you'll much more quickly be able to sing a high note brightly than you would if you went straight for the bright vowel color and, as a result, ended up singing the wrong pitch or having your voice crack, yodel, or otherwise be unsteady.

Modifying the Vowel

There is a physical place in the body where each note should begin resonating in order to be in tune. The lowest note you can sing starts resonating just above your vocal folds. The starting point of resonation of each successively higher note moves up slightly in the back of your throat. This is why some singers say they feel lower-pitched notes low in their heads and higher-pitched notes in or near the bridge of their noses. (Please don't worry if you can't feel this happening—for every great singer who does notice these physical sensations, there's a great singer who doesn't.)

The challenge you face is that, at a certain point in your range (and this point constantly changes), you will feel and sound like you are up against an "invisible ceiling." Notes begin to get harder and harder to sing. You might experience difficulty keeping them in tune or making them sound clean. This often has to do with the position of the soft palate. It can act like a gate, opening and closing across the back of the throat. If your soft palate is blocking the nasopharynx, or upper resonation chamber (see the illustration on page 73), and you want to sing a higher note, it will be harder for the note to physically rise to its correct starting point of resonation. You may feel like you're trying to walk through a closed gate. Even with lower notes, you may feel like you're pressed up against this invisible ceiling.

This is the point where singers often tell me, "I'm at the end of my range," or, "Sometimes I can hit that note, but not today." The truth is that they're not necessarily at the end of their range. In fact, there may be many more notes they could reach, and reach comfortably—if only they would "open the gate," or "remove the invisible ceiling."

You can teach your body to do this is by using a technique called vowel modification. Vowel modification involves changing the pronunciation of a vowel from its normal sound to an "oo" sound. This has the effect of moving the soft palate enough that sound can rise past it and begin to resonate in the correct place. This can help to eliminate the effects of the "invisible ceiling."

To get an idea of what it feels and sounds like when you move your soft palate, sing a sustained note while repeatedly pronouncing "nyuk nyuk" (you might sound like Curly from the Three Stooges). You'll probably be able to feel something near the roof of your mouth opening and closing or moving up and down—this is your soft palate moving in conjunction with your tongue. Singing an "oo" vowel causes the soft palate to move, making it easier to change the starting point of resonation of a note. You will want to practice this technique in the Vocal Power Workout exercises. It will then begin to happen automatically when you sing songs.

Beginners face a few challenges as they learn to use vowel modification:

Challenge 1: Figuring out when to modify a vowel before you find yourself "up against the ceiling." Many singers consciously or unconsciously wait until there's a very obvious sign that they're headed for trouble before modifying a vowel.

While you can easily wait too long to modify a vowel, you can never modify a vowel too early—so your best bet is to learn to do it before you realize you *have* to do it. If you get into the habit of transforming a vowel to an "oo" at the first hint of any change, you'll find that you can learn the technique more easily and more quickly and that you will automatically modify your vowels sooner. The key is to notice *anything* that makes whatever note you're singing more of a challenge to continue to sing. Are any of the notes getting louder? Harder to sing? Noisier? More unstable? It might be something you feel, hear, or sense in some other way. (Listen to track 8 of Listen and Learn now to get an idea of warning signs that a note needs to be modified.) If, as you're singing, you find yourself thinking, "I wonder if I should have modified that vowel?" it's probably because you've become aware of some challenge or change to the note as you're singing it.

Challenge 2: Getting over the misconception that modifying vowels is "cheating" and is a sign of an unskilled singer. Many of my students have confided to me that they thought the idea was to "go as high as possible" without "having to" modify vowels and that they believed the ability to do so was evidence of a more skilled singer. **Not at all.** Waiting to modify at the last instant only causes you to work harder than necessary, and you may end up making strained sounds. Think of vowel modification in the same way that you think of a shoehorn. A shoehorn is simply a useful tool to help you slip into a tight shoe more easily. In the same way, vowel modification is a useful technique that helps you to sing notes at the pitch you want more easily. Not having to use a shoehorn doesn't make you a better person, and not modifying vowels doesn't mean you're a better singer—it just means you're an overworked one. Practice using vowel modification as much as possible: like every other vocal skill I teach, the more you use it, the faster it will be programmed into muscle memory.

Challenge 3: Overcoming the tendency to modify vowels at the same point every time. As a singer, your instrument is the human body. Just as your car runs differently on different days, your body is constantly shifting and changing. Therefore, the point at which you need to modify a vowel can change frequently. Every time you sing an exercise, wipe the slate clean and notice where you begin to experience the ceiling *during that exercise.* Don't fall into the trap of memorizing where in the exercise you modified a vowel yesterday or at what point the singer on a Vocal Power Workout track modifies a vowel. What you did yesterday and what the singer does in the track are irrelevant in terms of you figuring out where you need to modify today. Instead, pay attention to your inner cues—you'll become a more "present" and powerful singer as a result.

Challenge 4: Learning to modify to an "oo" vowel without puckering the lips or closing the jaw. Each of us has muscles that indirectly connect the lips to the soft palate and the back of the throat. If you close the front of your mouth, you'll close the back of your mouth as well. This results in a smaller chamber for sound to resonate in, and it also allows less sound to pass through your mouth when you sing. Closing your jaw also allows your swallowing muscles to interfere during singing. These results are not what you want at all! It's difficult to make a pure "oo" vowel with the jaw and lips completely open, but you can come close enough.

As you practice modifying from an "oh" to an "oo" during the exercises without allowing your lips or jaw to become involved, you'll receive an added bonus: you'll begin to call on the back of the throat and tongue to work more in creating vowels. This makes for purer vowels than the ones you'll produce when you create vowels by primarily using your lips.

You may be asking yourself, "How will vowel modification work in a song? If I have to sing the word 'go' and I modify the vowel so that I instead sing 'goo,' people will think I've lost it." That's true—but remember that you'll be modifying your vowels in an exaggerated (and very noticeable) way when you sing the exercises simply so that your body becomes accustomed to using the technique; it won't be necessary to make such exaggerated modifications during your performances. With enough practice, you'll get so good at the process of vowel modification that you can use just enough "oo" vowel to move your soft palate and change the initial point of resonation without the audience being able to hear the process.

As you begin to transfer the techniques you'll learn from the exercises into your favorite songs, you'll find that vowel modification will work with any vowel.

Important Points to Remember

- Resonation involves changing the size and shape of the spaces in your head to affect the sound of your voice.

- Changing vowel color and vowel pronunciation are two ways in which you can affect your resonation to change the sound of your voice.

- The temporary use of an ultradark vowel color as you practice has four positive impacts on your vocal mechanism.

- By controlling vowel color, you can more easily sound authentic when you sing in different styles.

- Vowel modification allows you to more easily sing high and low notes.

6

Registration—The Two Gears of Your Voice

I first experienced both the joy and the heartache of singing when I was in a band called the Burnside Bombers. For the most part, we played danceable 1970s rock, country, and pop music, and I did a majority of the lead singing. At the time, I knew nothing about vocal mechanics, so I basically sang the only way I knew how. We followed the motto "If you can't be good, be loud." I sang a lot of high-energy, up-tempo songs, and I poured my heart (and probably parts of my throat) into every one of them. The joy I experienced as a part of the band came from making fun music with fun guys for fun audiences.

The heartache came each night we performed, usually about two hours into the gig. I could feel my throat getting roughed up; then I would start to get hoarse. By the end of the night I could barely hit high notes, and I would spend the rest of the next day trying to get my voice back to sounding halfway normal. I figured "that's just what singers have to go through." It's not— but, at the time, I didn't know that there was any alternative to pounding on my voice to sing everything in what's called pure "heavy register."

At one of my gigs, a friend came up to me and said, "You know, I have the sense that you could be a really good ballad singer if you wanted to be." Eventually, I did try to learn how to sing ballads. That's when I discovered that, in order to sing more softly—especially on high notes—I had to learn to use some of my "light register." Had I known how to access both "halves" of my voice back when I was belting out songs with the Burnside Bombers, I would have had more endurance, more options, more confidence, and even more fun during my performances with that band.

As it turns out, there are many people who don't know how to access their different registers; some people are not even aware that they possess two "halves of their voices." Frequently, when I demonstrate the two registers to students, I hear responses like, "Well, I can't sing like that—I don't have that kind of voice!" But the truth is that almost everyone has more "voice" than they are using. And one of the best ways to experience more power, passion, and confidence in your singing is to gain control over both of the registers that make up your vocal registration.

There's not a more hotly debated topic in singing than registration. In all of the voice books in my library, in teaching seminars I've attended, and in conversations I have had with other voice teachers and singers, this single subject brings out the most opposing viewpoints. The main point of contention is the number of registers there are in the human vocal registration system. Some say there's only one register; some say there are two; others say we have three to five; one music author claims there are thirteen; and still others say there is a register for every single note we sing.

In 1929 the renowned voice scientist Douglas Stanley, in his book *The Science of Voice*, emphatically stated, "There are two groups of muscles: the arytenoid and the cricothyroid groups, which act as tensors of the vocal cords. The preponderance of effect of one group over the other determines a register. There are consequently two and only two registers in the human voice." Basically, Stanley is saying that these two groups of muscles use the vocal folds to have a tug-of-war and that the winning "team" determines which register a note is sung in—therefore, there are only two registers.

You may be saying to yourself, "OK, I get that there are two registers—but I still don't understand what a register *is*!" Let's look at the ideas behind registration and registers a little more closely.

Registers and Registration Explained

Registers are groups of tones of the voice that each have their own distinctive sound quality. There are two registers in the human body: the light register and the heavy register. Registration is a term that is used to describe the body's system of these two registers.

It's thought that each register, or group of tones, is created by its own particular set of muscles that acts on the vocal folds in a specific way. Each of us has two registers (whether we know it or not). The main difference you may notice between the registers is that it takes more intense support (more power) to sing a note in heavy register than it does to sing the same note in light register.

Many people use confusing terms to describe the heavy and light registers. For instance, terms such as "regular voice," "full voice," "lower register," "modal voice," "speaking voice," "normal voice," "low voice," and "chest voice" are all used to describe the heavy register or the sensation we experience when singing in the heavy register.

Other terms are commonly used to describe the light register and various other aspects of our registration. "False voice," "falsetto," "high voice," "upper register," and "head voice" are sometimes used to describe the light register or the sensation we experience when singing in the light register.

It's worth noting that the commonly used terms "chest voice" and "head voice" can be very deceptive, leading singers to believe that the vibrations that are causing the vocal sound are actually happening in the chest or high up in the head. They aren't. *Every sound you produce is created by the vocal folds in the throat, and all sounds reverberate in one or more of the resonators, all of which are in your head and throat.* (See the illustration on page 73.)

Some people believe that there is a mysterious "third register" that lies between the light and heavy registers; this is sometimes referred to as the "middle register," "middle voice," "mixed voice," or "combination voice." In reality, this so-called third register is a combination of the two actual registers—the light register and the heavy register.

The term "break" is frequently used to describe the point at which a singer moves from one register to another (it's also used to describe the singer's sensation of moving from one register to another).

I think of registration as being much like the automatic transmission of a car, and I think of the registers as being like the gears that make up that transmission. If you drive a car that has automatic transmission, your vehicle automatically shifts gears as you increase or decrease your speed. However, if you wanted to, you could override that automatic action by using the shift selector to stay in a particular gear. For example, if you were about to climb a steep hill, you might override the automatic transmission and keep the car in a low gear to "help" your car make it up the incline. In much the same way, the body tends to use its vocal registration to automatically adjust to accommodate the pitch that's sung and the intensity with which it's sung. By learning to use "manual control" to override the body's tendency to automatically adjust, you can give yourself more options, dynamics, and style choices when it comes to singing.

Every person has a light register and a heavy register—and, whether they're used or not, both of them are available to every singer: male, female, bass, tenor, alto, or soprano.

Balanced Registration

To some extent, the two registers overlap. This allows you to sing some pitches in pure heavy register, in pure light register, or in a combination of the two. This combination is called "balanced registration." (See the following illustration.) This concept of singing in a combination of heavy and light registers may be foreign to many singers, but it opens up a lot of vocal real estate when you understand it and learn to use it. By developing the ability to change and control the degree to which you use each register, you will give yourself more options to choose from when singing any line of a song.

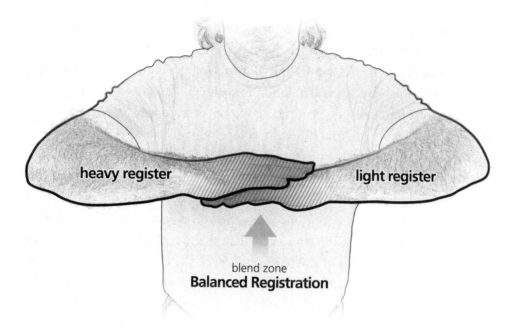

Having control over your registration is ultimately about having artistic control. Once you develop the ability to effectively use pure heavy register, pure light register, or a combination of the two, you can easily sing in the register (or combination of registers) that best matches the emotion and energy of your song. For example, you might normally sing a certain line in pure heavy register, using a strong, powerful delivery. For some singers (I used to be one of them), this is the only way the body can feel stable while singing. The song, however, might be better served by a more understated, softer, more emotional delivery—one that might be achieved by using, say, a balance of 50 percent heavy register and 50 percent light register. The challenge

125

is that singing while using a 50/50 ratio takes a different kind of strength and coordination, and you may not have access to that combination yet.

Or the opposite may be true: you may be a singer who has never sung higher notes in pure heavy register, but who has instead always used a softer, balanced registration. This sound serves some songs beautifully, but it may not deliver the emotion or energy that a powerful or up-tempo song requires. Still, it may feel dangerous or wrong for you to sing a high note in pure heavy register, and this may not be an option for you yet.

By learning to sing in different ratios of balanced registration, you develop the ability to use different colors of your vocal palette (yeah, I know—another pun) to paint with. This makes you a more interesting singer than you would be if you had only one way in which you could sing. Singing is much more fun and rewarding when you can sing a line five different ways. In addition, having options allows you to adjust for and sing around challenges you may encounter: you can change the registration to match your mood, the circumstances of the performance, or the condition of your voice.

If you think of pure heavy register as blue and pure light register as red, then balanced registration is all the shades of purple you can sing. *Any* sound you sing that is in neither pure heavy nor pure light register is called balanced registration, even if it's almost all one register or the other. Another way to look at balanced registration is to identify the power you use when singing. Let's say you determine that, when you sing a high note in pure heavy register, you use an 8 power to do so, and when you sing the same note in pure light register, you use a 2 power. If you sing the same note with a 5 power, you will probably be singing it in a 50/50 balance—50 percent heavy register and 50 percent light register.

This awareness will begin to enable you to sing a note blue, dark purple, medium purple, light purple, or red. You could describe the same thing with numbers: pure heavy register, an 80/20 balance, a 50/50 balance, a 20/80 balance, and pure light register. Intensity of support is the main way you will control registration when you sing.

Listen to track 10 of Listen and Learn (found on my website at www.SingFreeNow.com; see page 25 for instructions on accessing the audio tracks) to hear examples of a line sung using different ratios of heavy and light register.

Pure Heavy Register

I have found that the best way for a singer to develop his or her entire registration is to first work on establishing strength and stability in the pure heavy register, from the lowest note to the highest note a singer can sing without straining.

Remember—there's a difference between working hard and straining. You *will* have to work both your abs and your vocal folds with a lot of intensity in order to sing a high note in pure heavy register. Strain, however, is going beyond the point at which you can hold the note stably without noise.

This can be a challenge for those singers who think of themselves as having a quiet voice or who sing in light register or in a balanced registration that favors light register. For some, it may at first feel virtually impossible to even *find* their pure heavy register. The amount of lift and resistance needed to support singing in pure heavy register can seem so great that it feels dangerous—like you might hurt yourself. Or it may sound and feel like you're yelling or shouting. When I take students through the process of finding and using pure heavy register, many of them tell me that they thought good singing involved "relaxing everything." Perhaps you, too, have been told this—and, as a result, because singing a high note in pure heavy register feels far from being relaxed, it may seem wrong to you. Let me clear up this "relaxation" misconception right now:

Good singing does involve relaxing muscles that are not directly needed to create sound so that you don't waste energy tensing muscles that don't help you. But it does *not* involve relaxing the muscles that are used to actually produce sound. Think about it: if you relaxed those muscles, you wouldn't be able to make any sound at all! Remember: between "relaxed" and "strained" lies "controlled, purposeful effort"—and that's what you need in order to sing effectively.

There must be some tensing of the vocal folds in order for you to even be able to sing a note, and there must be some tensing of your abdominals to create the lift and the resistance that are needed to support that note. As you go through the process of singing in pure heavy register, you will learn the difference between necessary muscle tension that is required to efficiently make sound and unneeded muscle tension that sabotages good singing.

What is it that causes the anxiety that many singers feel when they try to sing high notes in pure heavy register? Part of the issue is that it takes a lot of work—especially as a singer is first learning how to do it. When this collides with the conscious or subconscious belief that good singing should sound and feel as though it takes little or no work, the brain and body may "decide" that singing high notes in heavy register is futile, wrong, or even threatening. Part of your development as a singer is to learn to recognize that these feelings are a result of your body's automatic attempt to protect itself from a perceived threat by using what I call your vocal defense mechanism. We'll explore this concept of the vocal defense mechanism further in the next chapter; for now, however, just realize that you have one—and that it takes its job pretty seriously, even when there is no real danger to defend against.

You might be saying to yourself, "Wouldn't it be easier to just forget the whole 'singing high notes in a heavy register' approach and to instead sing those notes in my light register, which I'm already used to doing?" Well, yes;

that would be easier—and that approach would work fine for many songs and styles. But that's a lot like favoring one leg while dancing. You would be a limited and less interesting dancer if you never started a turn with your left leg or planted your left leg to leap from; if you instead always relied on your right leg to carry you though. You wouldn't be able to accomplish nearly as much, and your style would be much more predictable. Favoring one "half" of your voice over the other "half" is similar. If you don't have the power of pure heavy register in your vocal arsenal, the softness and ease of your "balanced" registration and your light register can become predictable and stale.

Dynamic, artistic singing keeps the audience guessing, which keeps them interested. Predictable singing loses listeners' attention.

"Will you sing loudly on the next note, or will it be soft? Will it be sung in heavy or light register? Using a bright or dark vowel color?" These are the questions you want the audience to be asking (without knowing that they are) because it means they are engaged and interested. If you sing in only one register, you're painting with only a few of the colors that are available on your vast palette. The audience will begin to anticipate where you are going and how it will sound when you get there, and their minds may consciously or subconsciously wander or check out.

That's one reason to be courageous and to develop strength in your heavy register. Another is that it will allow you to step into your power both vocally and personally. For most singers, projecting a well-supported high note in heavy register for the first time is a liberating, exciting experience. Moving the amount of energy needed to create that much sound is exhilarating. When students in my classes and workshops begin to access their pure heavy register, I see their faces light up, and many singers tell me they haven't felt a thrill like that since they were little kids.

Here's a secret that most singers don't know and never experience: you need to have the use of a strong heavy register in order to be a truly confident singer.

Loud Is Natural

As children, many of us were subtly (or not-so-subtly) persuaded from owning and vocalizing our personal power. "Children should be seen and not heard." "Class, sit down and be quiet." "Ssshhh, this is the *library*." "Use your indoor voice." "You're too loud!" All of these reprimands had the effect of turning us down. Parents, teachers, religious leaders, and other elders of all sorts were constantly telling us to be quiet.

Acclaimed vocal coach Kristin Linklater, in her book *Freeing the Natural Voice*, talks about a huge shift that happens to all of us when we're young. One of the first experiences we have as babies is to cry loudly in order to get our needs met (we're hungry; our diapers need changing; we want to be held; and so forth). We soon figure out that crying works really well in that regard. *We make loud noises—we get what we want.* At some point, however, as we start walking and talking, we are suddenly told that crying, screaming, or yelling will *not* get us what we want (in fact, it will get us into trouble), and from that point on, we are taught to stop the impulse to use our voice loudly. We learn that "adult" communication—communicating quietly—will get us the results we want (in fact, people who use loud voices are often labeled "unreasonable" or "crazy" and are disregarded). On top of this are socialization differences for males and females. It's more accepted for boys to yell, shout, be rowdy, and play loudly. In contrast, girls are often reminded that it's more feminine to play quietly and to *be* softer and quieter. While some may suggest that these differences in expectations and ideals among the genders is in alignment with certain characteristics of masculine and feminine energy, they can negatively affect the ability of both females and males to sing effectively. This type of early socialization can tend to make it more difficult for a male singer to access his light register and for a female to sing in her heavy register. In addition, even though it's taught that it's "legal" for boys to be louder, I've found that most men and almost all women find it challenging at first to sing higher pitches in pure heavy register. However, the benefits of learning to do so definitely outweigh the challenge of overcoming the "norms" that society has instilled in us.

To sing with power, passion, and confidence, you need to learn that it's OK to return your voice to its natural state and to realize that expressing yourself in a voice that is at times loud, at times soft, and at times something in between is fun, safe, and, well, *natural*.

Developing the skills you need to be a better singer is just like building a house. You can't put up the walls or the roof without first laying a strong foundation. In your vocal "house" you'll build strength and coordination by singing in pure heavy register before moving to the light register. This applies to everybody—women as well as men—no matter their range or vocal classification.

There are three important elements of singing that will help you to access your heavy register on higher pitches:

1. **Strength.** Most singers are unaware of a simple fact: to free your voice and sing with power, passion, and confidence, you have to have a certain level of strength. By practicing the Vocal Power Workout exercises (found on my website at www.SingFreeNow.com; see page 25 for instructions on accessing the audio tracks) every day, you will build strength in your belly muscles and vocal folds so that you have the power you need to sing in pure heavy register.

2. **Support.** If your support system isn't developed or isn't work-ing well, you will sound and feel strained when you try to sing higher notes in pure heavy register.

3. **Vowel Color.** As pitches get higher, their natural vowel color becomes brighter which can make them harder to sing. If you sing higher pitches with a darker vowel color, it will be easier to keep them in pure heavy register.

Part of the challenge of singing in pure heavy register is recognizing what that sounds and feels like. Track 10 of Listen and Learn (found on my website at www.SingFreeNow.com; see page 25 for instructions on access-ing the audio tracks) offers examples of notes sung in pure heavy register and others that are sung in balanced registration. Study these carefully and prac-tice matching the examples. In this way, you'll begin to develop the aware-ness of the minimum amount of power needed to move a note from balanced registration into pure heavy register. Remember: balanced registration is not bad or wrong—it can be a great sound. It's just not the sound we're initially going to use to build the foundation of your voice.

Here's an exercise to start this process.

Exercise: Lay the Foundation

Select a note that is fairly high for you and sing it as loudly as you can in pure heavy register. On a scale of 1 to 10, how hard were you working to sing it (what was the intensity of the lifting/resisting action?) Now think about the vowel color of the note you sang. On a scale of 1 to 10 (with 1 being the darkest vowel color you can produce and 10 being the brightest), what number would you assign to the vowel color? Answering these two questions is critical when it comes to developing the upper end of your heavy register. Your success at singing a high note in pure heavy register greatly increases when you give your body specific instructions on how much power and what vowel color to use. A great way to do this is to assign a number, on a scale of 1 to 10, to each of these elements. If you don't give your body this kind of specific guidance, it will tend to underpower and overbrighten the note. This exercise has to do with something I said earlier: "Be an intentional singer, not a hopeful one."

Could you tell if the note you just sang *was* in pure heavy register? Refer often to track 10 of Listen and Learn to help you build your awareness of the use of heavy register, light register, and balanced registration.

Power and Registration

For each note you sing, there's a minimum amount of support (power) required to sing it the way you want to. When you practice, select the appropriate number, on the scale of 1 to 10, to tell your body how much power you want to use. Through repetitions, your body will begin to build this number into muscle memory; eventually, you'll only have to picture the sound you want in your mind, and your body will automatically respond with the right amount of power. You'll be in the driver's seat.

It's extremely helpful to record your voice in order to assist you in this exploration. Often you can more easily determine whether or not you're reaching your goal by hearing yourself on a recording than by trying to listen while you sing. You'll have a better idea of what your voice really sounds like when you don't have to split your attention between producing sound and listening to it. (See the Vocal Appraisal section of chapter 8 for more details.)

How Vowel Color Affects Registration

Vowel color is the other vocal element that's critical in singing higher notes in pure heavy register. When you sang the note loudly during the previous exercise, where was it on the vowel color scale? If it was much brighter than a 5, you were probably experiencing more difficulty singing the note than you have to.

As we sing higher notes, our vowel color tends to automatically become brighter. The way to compensate for this is to purposefully make the vowel color darker as you sing higher notes. This is especially important when it comes to singing higher notes in pure heavy register.

Attempting to sing a note with a brighter vowel color puts a different tension on the walls of the throat and tends to raise the larynx (voice box), which often results in a singer having more difficulty reaching the desired note and in keeping the vocal folds together. By darkening the vowel color, singers allow themselves to more easily produce the sound they *intend* to produce. Try this exercise to feel the differences involved when you sing a note with a bright and a dark vowel color.

Exercise: Darken Your Vowel Color

Sing a fairly high note using bright vowel color. (If the note is high enough, you'll probably automatically use bright vowel color.) Notice any strain this puts on your voice and the degree of difficulty you experience in trying to reach your target pitch. Now sing the same note again—but, this time, darken the vowel color by at least two numbers. Your larynx will lower and you should experience more ease in reaching and holding the note. If you don't, exaggerate the darkness of the vowel color even more. The note you produce may sound odd to you—but remember that this is not how you will sing during performances. It's just a technique to help your support system and the resonators figure out how to make the necessary adjustments so that you can reach higher notes using the heavy register.

As you gain more control and confidence in regard to singing higher pitches in pure heavy register, you can begin to brighten your vowel color until it is appropriate for the type of song you are singing.

Whenever you have to reach a note that seems too high to sing the way you want to, first make it ultradark; then begin to adjust your color as you gain more control.

I've found that this technique allows singers to expand their range and registration options much more quickly than they can if they try to achieve a performance sound they aren't yet able to make with stability.

Trusting the Process

Whenever I take singers through the process of learning to sing loudly or learning to sing high notes in their heavy registers, almost all of them tell me that it sounds like they're yelling or shouting instead of singing. If you measure your success by how you sound during this learning process, you may find yourself feeling disappointed. It takes trust to believe that what I'm asking you to sound like in the beginning is not what you will sound like once you've mastered the techniques of singing. Even if the sounds are strange to your ears, knowing that this is one step in the process can help you to trust that you'll achieve your goals.

It's one thing to gain the strength that you need to sing well; it is another thing to trust yourself to use it. You may be used to hearing songs sung in pure heavy register by other people, but you may not be used to hearing and *feeling* this sound coming from yourself. Oftentimes, singers who are learning to sing in pure heavy register on higher pitches interpret the sounds they produce as yelling—when, in reality, they're simply experiencing (perhaps for the first time) the sound of their own strength and power. However, if I played a recording of someone else singing a high note loudly in pure heavy register, most people would tell me it sounded good.

It's important to understand that your perception of the sounds you sing can be affected by the way your body feels when it's making them. What you may interpret as yelling as you sing a note might not sound like yelling to you at all if you listened to yourself sing via a recording. I invite you trust that the temporary use of a tone that may feel and sound strange to you now will get you where you want to go.

How to End Sustained Notes

There is another situation that registration can affect without a singer even being aware of it—ending notes. Most developing singers end sustained notes by trying to fade the volume. This is usually done subconsciously—and when I point it out to a singer, more often than not he or she doesn't like the sound of it. It is fairly difficult for even an advanced singer to fade a sustained note and make it sound musical. As the power decreases, the tension that holds the vocal folds together lessens, causing the folds to start pulling apart. This can cause glitches, wavering, or other instability in the sound. And, as the power decreases, the registration almost always changes, bringing more light register into the mix. For these reasons, fading volume is a difficult and inefficient way to end a note.

The best way to practice ending notes is to keep an even volume (which, theoretically, will keep an even registration) until you decide to end the note; then, using Bosnian Belly Breathing, simply expand the belly. Why does this work more efficiently? Because expanding causes you to inhale, and air can't exit and enter your body at the same time.

By expanding the abdomen, you'll place the job of ending the note on the muscles of your support system instead of on your vocal folds. Because they are larger and stronger than the folds, your belly muscles can be used to help you end notes much more efficiently.

At first, your efforts to end notes in this way will probably sound abrupt and unmusical. The note may end more quickly than you are used to. Over time, however, you will be able to produce a very quick and slight fade that will sound very musical. Again, you get to trust that making a temporary, non-performance sound is the quickest way to making the sound you *do* want.

From High to Low

When moving from a high note to a low note, singers' voices often become noisy, breathy, out of tune, or unstable. This may seem strange to you—after all, singing a low note should be easier that singing a high note, right? So why the trouble?

Here's what often happens: Let's say you're singing a good, solid high note in pure heavy register; you're lifting at, say, a 7, and your resistance to the lift is at about the same number (probably about a 6.5). You'll notice that, as you move to a lower note, the intensity of your workload goes down—let's say to a 3—because it takes less power to sing low notes in the same register. So far, so good. The problem is that, as you sing lower notes in your range, it's likely that you will also dial back your level of resistance too much—for example, if your lift is a 3, you might tend to sing with a resistance of a 1 or a 1.5. The difference between the level of intensity of the lift and that of the resistance is too great—and, as a result, you can end up underpowering and undersupporting the note. And lack of sufficient support can result in noise, instability, and pitch problems.

In order to produce a clean, stable sound, it's critical that your body maintains a level of intensity of resistance that is close to the level of intensity of your lift. Otherwise, you are likely to find your voice moving from pure heavy register to an unsupported balanced registration (I call this mixed registration). This can sound muddy or breathy.

When you use numbers (on a scale of 1 to 10) to set your intentions and direct your body's actions as you practice, you can dramatically shorten the amount time it takes your body to program itself (via muscle memory) to maintain the right balance of support and registration.

Singing Across the "Break"

Most singers that I work with complain about singing notes in the middle of their range—"You know, where my break is." First of all, I don't care much for the term "break"; it promotes the notion that some aspect of your vocal mechanism is broken. It's not—and I invite you to replace that word so that you don't negatively program yourself. The Italians call this the *passaggio*, or the passage between the registers. I call it the "register transition." Regardless of what you choose to call it, it's about what the voice does as it moves from one register to the other.

Why do most singers experience cracking, yodeling, and general instability in this area? The answer has to do with the strength (or lack of strength) of a singer's vocal folds and the two sets of muscles (one set for each register) that tense the folds—muscles that, in addition to being strong, also must work in coordination with the folds in order to be effective. In other words, the muscles must learn to "work well with others."

Here's an easy way to visualize this concept of the vocal folds and these muscles "working together": Picture a four-person, 400-meter relay race. Each person runs 100 meters and then has to smoothly pass the baton to the next runner. The runner receiving the baton starts moving just before the pass-off in order to be in sync with the passer. This makes for a smooth exchange of the baton. If one runner is moving at a different speed than the other, however, the baton is likely to be dropped. In singing, the equivalent of a dropped baton is the cracking, yodeling, or other instability that makes people use the word "break."

Making a smooth baton pass, or registration transition, takes a couple of conditions. First, both the light and heavy registers have to be strong. So far, I've coached you to begin your vocal exploration by developing the ability to sing high notes in pure heavy register in order to help you build the strength of your voice from the ground up. Once you can sing high notes in pure heavy register, you can move to singing songs that work your light register across all of its range. This will help you to build the strength you need in both registers in order to make a smooth transition from one to the other. If one register is weaker than the other, you'll always experience issues during the transition between them.

The other necessary condition is flexibility and coordination of both the vocal folds and the muscles that tense them. Exercise 7 of the Vocal Power Workout (available on my website at www.SingFreeNow.com; see page 25 for instructions on accessing the audio tracks) helps you practice moving through the register transition. Remember—don't worry about sounding good or being smooth. It's critical that you stay out of your own way on this exercise. That means not trying to manipulate your instrument to make the transition from one register to the other "sound better." You have to make friends with the cracking, yodeling, and other unwanted sounds until you've done enough repetitions of the exercise that the two sets of muscles that tense the vocal folds learn to work it out for themselves—and, trust me, they will! If you do anything to "help" the process, such as vary the volume or the vowel color as you transition between the registers, this will become your habit and your body will always require that assistance. You'll be stuck having to do that every time you transition from one register to the other when you sing.

Switching Registers Within a Line

What *can* help this process is finding some practice songs that require you to change registers within a single line. Your vocal defense mechanism "hates" doing this. Much as cowboys heed the old saying "don't change horses in the middle of the stream" (because the rider who tries this might fall off the horse and get swept away by the current), your body is very much aware of the potential for disaster should you switch registers within a phrase. As a result, your body will tell you that it's safer to stay in the same register in which you started the line, no matter where the melody goes. But this caution presents real problems for singers. If you begin singing a line in heavy register and the notes of that line go up quite high, you're going to have difficulty singing the whole line in heavy register. You may sound as though you're straining, or you might have to use so much power to reach the high notes that the resulting sound doesn't fit your artistic vision of the song. Your singing will sound more controlled and you will feel more confident in this situation when you can switch to a balanced registration that allows you to work more efficiently.

The same goes for a line that you begin to sing in a balanced registration that uses more light register than heavy. If the notes of the line go low and you try to sing the entire line in a balanced registration that emphasizes your light register, your voice will tend to sound weak, and it's likely that it won't project well. By developing the ability to switch to heavy register at the appropriate place, you can keep such lines sounding more musical and projected.

How do you know where that "appropriate place" is, specifically? Oftentimes, you have to experiment to find out. If you're transitioning from light register to heavy register, try switching registers on the highest possible note that you can reach in heavy register. Then try switching on the next-highest note, and then on the next. Once you are strong enough and in control enough to switch registers by choice, you can then decide where to switch based on what serves the song best. Does switching to heavy register on a higher note rather than on a lower one give the line the appropriate artistic power or is it too much for the song? Keep in mind that the "appropriate place" has as much to do with your artistic vision of the song as it does with your ease in making the switch.

The more you practice singing across the register transition, the stronger, more flexible, and more coordinated your vocal folds and the muscles that tense them will become. Eventually, your body will no longer resist changing registers and you'll be able to easily move from one register to the other according to wherever the melody goes. Then, one day, you'll "wake up" to find that you no longer even have a "break"; instead, you will have a voice that moves easily, seamlessly, and naturally from the lowest note of your range to the highest note of your range. This is a huge factor when it comes to singing with power, passion, and confidence.

The bottom line is that, while you're in the midst of developing your strength and skills, you have to make it OK for your voice to crack, yodel, or make other "bad" sounds while the vocal folds and the muscles that tense them get stronger and learn how the pass the baton.

This is another example of a temporary sound helping you to "graduate" to a performance sound. Become like Luke Skywalker and learn to trust "the force"; let yourself trust the process to get to the other side. It takes many repetitions of singing across the transition, but most singers report that, within a couple of months of practicing Exercise 7 of the Vocal Power Workout and singing songs that make them move between the registers, their register transitions become dramatically smoother and cleaner.

Important Points to Remember

- Registration is the system of the two vocal registers within the voice. A register is a particular series of tones that are of the same quality. We all possess a "light register" and a "heavy register."

- Many of the notes across the middle of the range can be sung in pure heavy register, pure light register, or balanced registration (a blend of the two registers).

- Registration is determined by the intensity of support (power) in relation to how high or low the note is. You control registration by changing the intensity of support.

- The ability to intentionally use either register, and to alternate from one to the other, gives you more artistic options.

- Singing a high note in heavy register may sound and feel like yelling at first. Learn to trust that this technique, which will be used only temporarily as you develop your abilities, is the quickest way to help you gain control of your heavy register.

- Most singers fade the volume to end a line or sustained note. Such fading is hard to control and usually sounds unstable. However, you can end a note with stability and control simply by expanding the belly. This puts the workload on the larger muscles of the belly instead of on the vocal folds.

- When moving from a high note to a low note, the quality of sound can change.

- On a scale of 1 to 10, the levels of intensity of your lift and resistance when you sing low notes will be lower than they are when you sing higher notes.

- Avoid breathy, unstable delivery of low notes by keeping your resistance at about the same level of intensity (within one number on a scale of 1 to 10) as your lift.

- Singing easily and smoothly across the register transition takes strong, flexible, and coordinated vocal folds.

7

Body Awareness—The "Inside" Scoop

In 1996 I recorded my first solo CD, *Shed My Skin*. I worked hard on it for months and, when it was finished, I scheduled a CD release concert at a great venue in Portland—the 600-seat Aladdin Theater. I'd hired many of my musician friends to perform with me that night, and as my eight-piece band took the stage, I felt a rush of excitement about sharing my music with the audience. But, almost from the moment I began to sing the first song, I realized that I was doing things I'd never done before in my career: I was scanning my body, noticing how my voice was working, and measuring how hard I was working against how hard I usually worked to sing that particular song. Was I able to sing the registration I intended? The vowel color I intended? How did everything sound and feel? Did I need to make any adjustments? It suddenly hit me—finally, I was using everything I'd learned about body awareness to monitor and adjust my performance.

Prior to that performance, I was more likely to sing songs exactly as I had rehearsed them, even if my voice was not working well. The idea of making adjustments "on the fly" would have been intimidating. Any awareness of the current condition of my instrument (my body) would have been too much to handle—I was too busy thinking about the lyrics, the melody, and the mechanics of playing my piano as I sang. Like most singers, I considered performing to be pretty much a "keep your fingers crossed and roll the dice" situation: you hope your voice is going to give you what you need, but you really don't know whether or not it will, and you have no "Plan B" in the event that your voice doesn't do what you want. This is where body awareness can change your life.

Being in touch with our bodies is important for all people in terms of our general health and well-being, but is critical for a singer. An awareness of any physical challenge, from muscle pain to tiredness to a stuffy nose, can help us to make adjustments as we sing and to achieve better results. This seems obvious, but so many of us ignore what is going on in our bodies. We may not want to acknowledge that our bodies are challenged in some way because that might mean we have to limit an activity—or, going deeper, it might force us to acknowledge that we *are* limited.

One of your biggest challenges as a singer is to come to terms with the fact that, on any given day, your voice may not work as well as it did the day before or even an hour earlier. This may not be due to anything you are doing wrong. Many factors can affect your body and, consequently, your voice.

There is a very big difference between singing and playing any other instrument. As a singer, not only do you need to be an artist, but you have to be a technician as well, usually without the help of a repair manual. No other instrument has the same constant need for adjustment as does the singer's instrument—the human body—so it is vitally important to learn about the factors that can affect your body. Only then can you identify what could be happening with your voice whenever it is challenged and make the necessary adjustments to overcome those challenges.

This will also help you to let go, as much as possible, of the fear that you're failing as a singer if your voice is not working perfectly at any given moment. Piano players usually don't fault themselves if a piano is out of tune or a key is sticking, but singers tend to feel inadequate if their sound is off by a few degrees. By becoming aware of what may be causing problems with your instrument, you can help yourself to let go of self-blame—an emotion that can, in turn, lead to a worse performance.

Let's take a look at some of the many factors that can affect your instrument.

Factors That Commonly Affect Singers' Voices

Diet. Many singers find that their voices become challenged when they consume certain types of foods or beverages. Common culprits include dairy (this food group tends to cause excessive mucus production), caffeine and alcohol (both cause drying), wheat and sugar (either of these may cause inflammation and other allergy-type symptoms), and spicy foods (these may produce symptoms of acid reflux or heartburn). Different foods affect individuals in different ways, so it's up to you to determine which foods and beverages create challenges for your voice. Keep a food log (write down what you eat and how it changes your voice) to identify those foods and beverages that affect you.

Smoke. Inhaled smoke (whether it's from tobacco, incense, or any other material) dries out the mucous membrane that covers the vocal folds and can cause noise and shrinkage of vocal range. This is true not only of smoke that is directly inhaled, but also of secondhand smoke, which has been proven to be just about as harmful.

Toxins. Paint fumes, insecticides, carbon monoxide, and other airborne toxins can cause a variety of problems, from noise in the voice to dizziness, nausea, and compromised lung capacity.

Stress. Arguing, worrying, feeling angry, anxious, or scared—all of these produce stress, restrict the movement of muscles, and alter your breathing. Because much of the vocal system consists of muscles, the effects of stress on the voice can include problems with range, clarity, pitch, tone, and volume.

Vocal Abuse. Yelling, talking over loud noise, extended loud whispering, and overuse of the vocal folds can cause hoarseness, tightness, and pain.

Lack of Sleep. Sleep deprivation and exhaustion can cause lower endurance and force singers to exert extra effort to produce sound.

Dehydration. The mucous membrane that covers the vocal folds doesn't function efficiently when it's dry. Water intake is critical to vocal range and flexibility of the vocal folds.

Menstruation. The hormonal changes that occur during monthly cycles can cause problems with endurance, vocal range, tone, and flexibility of the vocal folds.

Allergies. Foods to which we are sensitive, pollen, mold, and other allergens cause inflammation. This leads to stiffness of the vocal folds and it can cause problems with vocal range; singers may experience notes cracking or breaking.

Weather. Humidity and barometric changes can affect mucous membranes, causing problems with vocal range and flexibility of the vocal folds.

Body Clock. Vocal range, endurance, and flexibility of the vocal folds may all be affected when singing at a different time of the day than you are used to.

Cold Muscles. Singers who haven't sung for days or who have not warmed up their muscles can find that their ability to modify vowels and create support may be less than normal. Vocal range and endurance are also compromised by cold muscles.

Coughing. Intense or prolonged bouts of coughing can inflame the vocal folds, making the production of a clean sound and the ability to sing high notes very difficult.

Crying. The throat can tighten up during crying, especially if a singer tries to prevent herself or himself from truly "letting go." This can limit vocal range and endurance.

Depression. Anything that affects a singer's energy level can affect his or her voice. If your energy level is down, you will have to work much harder to make the sound you're used to making, and that is the opposite of what your body will want to do.

Prescription Drugs. Many prescription drugs dry out the vocal folds or cause jittery nerves, making artistic singing a significantly uphill battle.

As you can see, any one of these factors can get in the way of your voice working easily. Combinations of two or more can cause serious problems. So, the next time your voice isn't doing what you want it to do, stop and consider whether any of these factors exist. If you can identify any of these culprits, it won't necessarily make singing immediately easier, but it can help you to cope with the challenge. Knowing what is causing the problem is more than half the battle, as you can make more effective adjustments to your instrument if you know what's affecting it. By becoming aware of challenges your body faces and learning to adjust, you become more confident and can more easily experience the joy of singing.

It will serve you well to learn early on that your voice will be in different shape *every day* and that a big part of singing with power, passion, and confidence is to learn to adjust for whatever change occurs. (See Appendix B for more on this subject.) When you learn to let go of worrying or feeling guilty about the fact that your voice doesn't sound as good today as it has in the past, you are on your way to a freedom that makes singing much more enjoyable.

The truth is that your body is your instrument and it is constantly transforming. Unlike a piano or a trumpet, which sounds virtually the same every time you play it, the voice is likely to sound at least a little bit different every time you sing because it is created by a living, breathing, changing instrument.

By being in touch with your body, you'll have the perspective you need to make functional and artistic decisions when you sing. If you ignore what your body is telling you, you will make this job much more difficult.

Two Ways to Feel

Awareness of your body and how it works allows for greater control of the voice, and it is a huge factor when it comes to singing with power, passion, and confidence. I'm not talking about the physiology we've already touched on. Rather, I'm speaking now of being in touch with what your body is doing at any given moment and how particular parts of your body are moving and responding to the instructions you give it when you sing. These instructions may be conscious or subconscious; they may be productive or counterproductive. One of the ways to simultaneously free the voice and gain control of the singing process (this may sound like a contradiction, but it's not) is to sharpen your body awareness.

Two types of body awareness are kinesthesia and proprioception. Kinesthesia involves being aware of the sensations you are feeling during a certain circumstance or action (such as feeling a breeze or the sensation in your fingertips as you tap on a keyboard). Proprioception is defined as the ability to sense the position, location, orientation, and movement of the body and its parts (such as the ability to sense that your hand is raised or that you are hanging upside down). If the body is moving, proprioception also tells us the way in which it is moving and where parts of our body are in relation to other parts.

You may have an awareness of where, in relation to the rest of your body, your shoulder blades are as you sing (proprioception) as well as an awareness that there is an uncomfortable tensing of the muscles between them (kinesthesia). You will want to rely on both kinesthesia and proprioception to help you learn more about singing as well as to create a more connected performance. For the sake of ease, I lump both of these together by using the term "body awareness."

Body awareness can greatly speed up your learning curve when it comes to singing with power, passion, and confidence. For example, it is common to experience soreness or pain in the throat as you begin to work with your voice. But there are different types of throat pain, and it's important to be able to identify the type you're experiencing. One type of pain is caused by working the muscles in a different way than they are used to being worked. This is similar to what might happen when you start a new exercise program: if you are not used to lifting weights, you will probably feel some soreness when you start. Another type of pain in the throat is caused by oversinging— often the result of producing too much volume, not creating enough support on high, loud notes, or overextending periods of practice. This pain feels more like a sandblaster has scraped the back of your throat. Through experience, you will learn to differentiate between the two types of pain. The first type is not anything to worry about—in fact, it's often an indication that you are building strength in the muscles used to sing—but the second type is an indication that something needs to change. How will you know which pain you are experiencing? By using body awareness, you will be able to zero in on whether the pain is on the surface of the throat (a sign that you are oversinging) or in the underlying muscles (this is exercise soreness).

The Sound *and* Feel of Singing

Several years ago one of my teachers cautioned me not to teach singing "by feel." I believe what he meant was that too many people rely *solely* on feel to determine whether or not they are singing correctly. However, if you rely solely on *sound* when you are singing, your awareness of what is occurring is incomplete. This is why it's important to balance what you're feeling with how you sound when you sing.

Some singers find this to be a challenge because they have been taught that they should feel a certain way when they make a certain sound. The problem with this approach is that each singer's instrument is individual and unique. The size of the skull is different from person to person; the sizes of the resonation chambers and the tongue vary among individuals; bone and tissue densities vary. All of these can cause you to feel something slightly different than someone else when you're both singing exactly the same sound (and, of course, you'll never know exactly what others feel, anyway—just what they may report feeling).

I studied with a teacher who is nationally known and who works in theater arts. She tells her vocal students to pay no attention to the sound of their voices for the first six months that they study with her. This is the exact opposite of what I had been taught previously. I believe her thinking was that people focus too much on trying to achieve a finished performance sound as they are learning to sing, and that is not always possible to produce. I find that both of these approaches—learning to sing totally by feel and learning to sing totally by sound—are less valuable than learning to sing by using a combination of both.

Here's an example of how relying solely on either feel or sound may hurt a singer. I once worked with a student named Joel who told me about "blowing out" his voice at a performance because he couldn't hear himself singing. He was hoarse, he couldn't reach much of his range, his voice had a breathy quality, and he found it difficult to project. The problem was that he didn't know how to gauge his performance by feel; he only knew how to tell what was happening by hearing the sound his voice produced. As a result, when he found himself in a situation in which he couldn't hear his own voice, he was lost.

It's extremely important to able to hear yourself when you sing. However, based on my experience, that isn't always what happens in performance situations. If you're singing through a sound system, you may not have monitors, you may not be able to hear the monitors, or you may be trying to sing above music that is very loud. And there's always a possibility that, for whatever reason, the acoustics of the room may cause you to not be able to hear yourself.

The sensations you feel when you are making a certain sound can act as an anchor to help you find the sound again. This is a great use of body awareness.

It's critical to learn what it *feels* like when you're singing a certain sound. For example, you need to be aware of how much power you're using—in other words, how hard you are working the belly muscles and the vocal folds—to sing a word or line in a song. By assigning that amount of power a value (i.e., a number on a scale of 1 to 10), you can give yourself a way to use body awareness to help you sing with that same amount of power in the event that you find yourself in a situation where you can't hear your own voice. If you know that you use, say, a 6 power to sing a certain line, you can direct your body to use a 6 power every time you sing that line regardless of the environment in which you are singing. In contrast, problems can arise if you rely totally on sound and you cannot hear yourself very well—for example, you may work too hard (i.e., use too much power) in an effort to hear your own voice. This is one way that singers "blow out their voices."

A singer's reliance on the feel of his or her singing instead of on its sound when it's difficult to hear is similar to a pilot's reliance on the plane's instruments during instances of low visibility. When you can't hear well, "feel" is the only information stream left to you. You must rely on your instrument—the body—to help you navigate. Otherwise, you're flying blind.

The Lombard Effect

Body awareness can also help you to resist oversinging when you experience the Lombard effect, an automatic reaction in which a person uses more vocal force in an attempt to be heard over background noise. The higher the level of background noise, the more effort our bodies tend to exert to be heard. Most singers and public speakers fall victim to the Lombard effect, which obviously takes its toll on the vocal folds. It's important to learn to control this automatic response; otherwise, you could end up like some of the bird populations in London. In a study, some birds living in this bustling city were found to be singing more forcefully than Nature had ever intended them to in an effort to be heard over auto traffic and other background noise. It was causing strain on their vocal mechanisms and even damaging their hearing.

Some singers regularly perform in situations where background noise competes for the audience's attention. Think about a nightclub, a cruise ship lounge, or a bar, where a singer has to perform in the midst of people milling about, constant conversation, clinking glasses, and frequent outbursts of laughter. Choir singers often complain of not being able to hear themselves because of the sheer volume of all the other voices. In these situations, your natural inclination is to sing loudly. Learn to control that impulse and you will increase your stamina and decrease vocal abuse. This takes body awareness.

Experiments with speakers and singers who were told not to raise their energy levels when background noise was present showed that advanced vocalists could control the body's automatic inclination to exert more vocal force, at least in part. However, that same experiment showed that beginning or untrained vocalists had little or no success in controlling their responses. So, how do we adjust for the Lombard effect? By honing in on what it *feels* like when we sing. The challenge is that we want to hear the same level of sound coming from ourselves when there is background noise that we are used to hearing when we sing or speak in the absence of such noise. To achieve the same audio levels when competing with background sounds, the body is forced to exert more energy, which puts more of a load on our instrument. Oversinging is often the result.

Here's an exercise that will help you learn to become aware of your body's tendency to oversing when background noise increases.

Exercise: Learn to Identify the Lombard Effect in Action

1. Pick a note that's in the middle of your range and sing it at a 5 volume. Notice what your workload is on our scale of 1 to 10.

2. Create a fairly loud background noise level (you can turn on the television, the radio, or a noisy appliance such as a blender). Sing the same note and notice whether or not if feels as though your body is working harder.

The challenge is to focus on what it *feels* like to sing the note with no competing background noise and to then create the same *feel*, or workload, when there is noise. Learn to pay less attention to what your voice sounds like and more attention to what it feels like when you sing in noisy situations. For example, you might find yourself singing with a band that gets louder as the performance goes on, dealing with a monitor system that is not working well, or singing at an outdoor venue where there is little or no amplification.

The Lombard effect can also take a toll on your voice when you're simply speaking. Singers who are driving to a performance with fellow musicians often tire out their voices before they even arrive by speaking loudly in competition with road noise, background music, and each other. Also, singers who socialize with the audience during performance breaks and who try to be heard above the din of a nightclub, church, or music hall can tire out their voices.

The Lombard effect and its result—oversinging—can also occur simply by changing the room where you sing. For example, say you're used to singing in a room that has great acoustics, which allows you to get lot of sound back to your ears. If you then move into a room that is dead acoustically, you will not hear the same frequencies in your voice or the same volume when you use your normal workload. This is where you want to have a plan B. If you can't hear yourself well, you can rely on what your body is supposed to feel like when you're making a certain sound. This will provide you with a way to sing well no matter what circumstance you are in.

The Vocal Defense Mechanism

One of the major influences on your voice is something that most singers have never even heard of—the vocal defense mechanism. This is a system that, for the most part, reacts subconsciously to various types of information it receives during singing. The vocal defense mechanism developed in response to experiences that scared you, hurt you, or embarrassed you in the past, and its sole purpose is to protect you from further trauma.

The three main functions of the vocal defense mechanism are to:

- prevent you from injuring yourself
- prevent you from embarrassing yourself
- prevent you from overworking

The vocal defense mechanism is necessary because you *can* actually hurt yourself, embarrass yourself, and overwork during singing. However, it's a hypervigilant system, and it can easily kick in when there is no real, actual danger. Consequently, a singer may often find himself or herself experiencing a tug-of-war between the conscious mind, which knows what it *wants* to do during singing, and the body, which is directed by this subconscious defense mechanism to do something else instead.

Unfortunately, the vocal defense mechanism can put the brakes on your singing at the exact worst moment possible. For example, it may occur as you're singing a line that requires you to go from a relatively low note to one that is fairly high. In such a situation, your mind might send a subconscious (or even conscious) message to your body: "high note—here comes danger!" What danger, you may ask? Well, as far as your vocal defense mechanism perceives it, the note may be "so high" that it could potentially injure your vocal folds; if it's out of your "normal" range you might sing it out of tune or your voice may crack or warble, causing you embarrassment; and it may seem to your body that the note would take so much effort to sing that you'd be working too hard.

So what does your vocal defense mechanism do to "protect" you from such perceived dangers? It causes the body to automatically reduce the amount of lift and opposition you exert when you try to sing the note—exactly the opposite of what's needed in order to successfully sing it. Imagine a long hook and ladder fire truck—the kind with one steering wheel in the front and a second one that controls the rear wheels. No matter where the front driver intends for the truck to go, he alone is not in charge. The rear driver must steer in the same direction in order for the truck to safely reach its destination. Your challenge as a singer is to be the "front driver" of your body and to teach your vocal defense mechanism—the "rear-wheel driver" what is safe to allow you to do. This teaching job is an ongoing process: as you improve and expand your skills, you need to constantly "raise the bar" for your vocal defense mechanism by teaching it that you can safely achieve more and more.

Your "Limit" Note

Let's say that right now you can sing an F above middle C before you run into difficulty. This information is imprinted on your vocal defense mechanism. As you make friends with your belly, begin to use the vocal principles, and improve your mechanics, you may find yourself able to hit a note that's a whole step higher, to the G above middle C. However, your vocal defense mechanism may still hold the belief that the F is as far as it is safe to go. In order to reach your potential with minimal interference from your vocal defense mechanism, you need to reprogram that mechanism to understand that you are now able to safely sing higher notes.

The process of reprogramming the limit of the vocal defense mechanism involves two steps:

1. Become aware of when the vocal defense mechanism is being triggered. Can you feel the brakes being put on? This can show up as less lift and opposition or as your voice flipping into balanced registration when your intention was to stay in heavy register. If the line of a song has a note that's higher than your previous "limit," the vocal defense mechanism will probably be triggered when you begin to sing that line. Observe what happens. Can you notice an involuntary drop in power or a change in registration? Does it happen on the approach to the note or just as you reach it? The first step to

reprogramming your limit, or ceiling, is to become conscious of the point at which your vocal defense mechanism perceives danger and kicks in to "protect" you from it.

2. Sing the note that your vocal defense mechanism currently perceives to be your "limit note" in pure heavy register and place a value on the level of power used to sing it. Let's say that your current limit note is an F and that you use an 8 power to sing it. You will need a little more power to sing a step higher and remain in pure heavy register. If you have a musical instrument such as a piano or a guitar, play a G on it and then sing that note using an 8.5 power. (If you don't have a musical instrument available, consider purchasing a pitch pipe—it's fairly inexpensive, and you can buy one at most music stores.)

I have taken thousands of people through the process of learning to sing high notes loudly in pure heavy register. The process is a very powerful one, but it is also tricky at first. The vocal defense mechanism is very good at doing its job. It doesn't easily let go of old limits and habits (to many of us, that's a pretty familiar tune). If you find it impossible to stay in pure heavy register on your new target note, here's an exercise that can help.

Exercise:
Teach Your Vocal Defense Mechanism a New "Limit"

Pretend that you are watching a small child cross the street and that she is unaware of a car that is speeding toward her. Yell a warning "hey!" as if her life depended on it. Really yell it out. (Check out track 22 of Listen and Learn for examples of "hey!" in pure heavy register and balanced registration.) Feel and listen to the sound. Notice how it feels in your belly and what your support system muscles are doing when you make a sound in pure heavy register. Now go back to your new target note and use your body in the same way to sing the note at an 8.5 power. This can show your vocal defense mechanism that it's safe to make this much sound.

A cautionary note: you should not start this reprogramming process until your skill level has improved enough so that you are able to support the new note. How will you know when you're ready? Many singers, after just a few weeks of using this program, report to me that it is easier to sing high notes than it used to be and that they feel an overall improvement in their vocal strength and stability. If you have reached this point, you may be ready. Be careful not to try to change the limit of your range until you notice strength improvements. Also, as you start the reprogramming process, be careful not sing your new target note too many times in a row. A few repetitions sung a few times each day is much more productive and safer than singing many repetitions at one sitting.

Be aware of another challenge during this process. Remember that almost all singers experience a negative reaction to the sounds they produce as they begin sing higher notes in pure heavy register. I hear comments such as "it doesn't sound like singing; it sounds like yelling" and "it doesn't sound musical; it's just shouting." As you begin to reprogram your vocal defense mechanism, it's more than likely that you'll also feel this way about singing new, higher notes in pure heavy register. What usually happens is that the *feel* of singing this way colors your perception of how your voice *sounds*. Because it takes so much power to sing these new notes, it *feels* as though it "must sound like" yelling instead of singing. Yet, if you were to listen to a recording of someone else singing those high notes in pure heavy register, it would almost certainly sound musical to you.

Be Strong

This is a process that takes trust. The sounds you produce that seem less than musical now will become new colors on your palette in time. As you become stronger and are able to sing higher, your vocal defense mechanism will learn that those new notes are now part of your safe, usable range. You will then be able to use less power to sing them and to bring more nuance and expression to your performance. In the beginning stages of this process, however, *you must remove artistry from your practice.* Don't try to make a performance-quality sound and don't try to put expression or dynamics into your practice. As you become stronger and you find it easier to sing higher notes in pure heavy register, you can then sing with artistry. We will discuss how to do that later.

Strength is an important, yet often overlooked, element of singing. It is especially important when it comes to singing higher notes in pure heavy register. You must have the mind-set of an athlete to develop your singing strength. This is a foreign concept to most developing singers. Going to the "vocal gym" by doing the exercises found in the Vocal Power Workout (available at www.SingFreeNow.com; see page 25 for instructions on accessing the audio tracks) every day and singing one to three challenging songs as part of your practice routine will help you to build the strength you need to sing with power and confidence. My experience is that most singers believe that, in order to become a better singer, they must master certain skills and techniques—but they are basically unaware of how many muscles are involved in making sound and how strong these muscles must become. As you begin to build more strength in both your abdominals muscles and your vocal folds, singing with power and confidence becomes a reality.

One issue that tends to surface as you get stronger is that you may need to change the workload that you use when singing. For instance, say that you're accustomed to singing a certain high note of a song using an 8 power but that you now find that the note sounds too loud or noisy. What may be happening is that you've gotten stronger. An 8 power is now "overblowing" the folds, and they may not be able to hold together. Even if they can, the volume will be greater and the color may also be brighter. With each increase in strength you achieve, you'll be able to decrease the amount of power you use to achieve the same results in terms of volume, color, registration, and so forth.

Muscle memory can be very strong. Once a power level is memorized, your body will tend to use this same setting even if your strength or skill has changed. It's important that you listen for these changes as you develop so you can then "recalibrate yourself," or adjust for strength increases. If you stay clear on your intentions for volume, color, and registration, you will be more likely to hear changes in the sound and become aware that you've gotten stronger. This is another way in which body awareness can make you a more confident singer.

By noticing what it feels like when you are singing, you will have a clearer picture of how and what your instrument is doing at any given moment. The streams of information available to you while you are singing can help you make adjustments whenever they're needed. This information is made up of what you are hearing, what you are feeling, and, occasionally, what you are seeing as you sing. Many singers are aware of only one of these streams and are therefore missing out on important information.

(Don't) Shut Your Mouth!

When you hold the jaw and occasionally observe yourself in a mirror as you sing the exercises in the Vocal Power Workout (available at www.SingFreeNow.com; see page 25 for instructions on accessing the audio tracks), you'll easily be able to tell if your jaw and lips are staying open in order to keep the throat open and the soft palate in its proper place. It's not quite so easy when you're performing a song—you're not holding your jaw or looking at yourself in a mirror, so you can't get immediate feedback on the position of your mouth from your hand or your reflection. You have to learn what to feel and listen for in order to keep an open jaw and mouth.

Many singers do have a tendency to "close down" their mouths and jaws when singing. Why does this happen? There are two main reasons:

It tricks the body into thinking it's doing less work. By closing down, you create a smaller opening to move air through when singing. This increases the air pressure (much as partially covering the end of a garden hose with your finger increases pressure), which causes you to feel more opposition. Your body reacts to this by letting up on some of the workload in the belly when creating support. On paper this seems to be a good idea—"work smarter, not harder." Your vocal defense mechanism loves this idea. Unfortunately, closing the mouth actually sabotages the process because we *want* the abdominals do to the heavy lifting. You get better support and better sound when the belly muscles do the work.

When both the throat and the mouth close, the sound has a smaller opening to come through, less sound actually is produced, the sound is dampened by the lips, and the frequencies that give the sound its sparkle are muffled. If you sing a line of a song with the mouth held open at a comfortable position and then sing the line with the mouth partially closed, you will probably be able to hear and feel the difference. It is similar to the difference in the sound a trumpet makes when blown wide open and when the trumpet player adds a mute. The music is still interesting and fun to listen to, but there is a drastic difference in the sound the instrument is able to make. This is due to the size of the opening that the air passes through and the resonation that is created.

An open mouth and jaw creates a feeling of vulnerability. The more open the mouth is, the more sound comes out and the more *real* you come across. This can feel very threatening. For one thing, mistakes will be more noticeable if your mouth is more open. The biggest reason that most singers feel vulnerable when singing with an open mouth, however, is psychological: it has to do with the belief that "if people don't like your voice, they're basically saying they don't like you." That can be scary. You can overcome this fear by creating performance opportunities with "safe" audiences made up of friends, family members, and others who love and support you. This will help you to develop the confidence you need to feel comfortable singing in front of total strangers.

It is critical to experience making mistakes in public so that you become less focused on singing "perfectly." Does that mean you should *try* to make mistakes or take a totally casual attitude toward them? No. You don't have to try to make mistakes—you're human, they will happen. Not caring at all about mistakes won't serve you, either; you do want your mechanics to be as good as you can make them. However, if you focus only on perfect mechanics, you lose the point of singing—to tell the story of the song, to bring the emotion of the song to the audience, and to *feel* what you are singing. You are setting yourself up to fail if you always demand perfection from yourself. We all make mistakes onstage, just as we all make silly blunders in other areas of our lives.

Most singers don't consciously close their mouths in an attempt to make mistakes less obvious; the vocal defense mechanism does it for us. However:

The very experience of making mistakes is what will help you realize that they don't have to have a negative impact on your singing.

Performance mistakes can feel like a threat to your very existence. I've seen singers cry, get dizzy, or run from the stage just because they felt they'd "blown it" by making a mistake. It is a very strong and very real fear for many, if not most, singers. And it can definitely trigger the mouth closing down. Singing in front of one safe person can help you to experience making mistakes, continuing the song, and realizing that the world has not ended. Then, by learning what to listen and feel for, you can practice keeping the mouth open until it is habit.

With enough repetitions of the Vocal Power Workout exercises, you will fine-tune your radar and be more likely to hear and feel the mouth closing down. (Obviously, when we sing words, some consonants will cause a momentary closure of the mouth. What I've been referring to is the overall average size of the mouth opening.) Self-monitoring also comes into play by helping you to know whether you are sustaining vowels or consonants when you sing. The idea is to sustain the vowels, not the consonants. For example, if you sustain the consonants of the word "valentine" as you sing it, the jaw and mouth will close to make the "l" and "n" sounds, and the word will come out sounding like "vallllll—ennnnnn—tinnnne." The audience will hear less sound and feel less energy from you than it would if you sustained the vowels instead as you sing the word: "vaaaa—lehhhh—ntiiiine." In order to sustain the vowels, you have to keep the jaw and mouth open—and that keeps your energy and personality coming through.

There are many benefits to be gained by developing your self-monitoring skills. Believe me—they will make a huge impact when it comes to your singing.

Stance

I have seen singers stand in almost every possible way while singing. Few people really understand that this can work against them, but it can. In fact, some stances can actually restrict the free flow of a singer's voice. One of the worst stances a singer can adopt is to stand rigidly erect with the knees and thighs pressed together and the hands held tightly against his or her sides. Although this may look proper and ladylike (whatever that is), it doesn't work well for singing. Why? Well, stand in this position and have a friend gently push on your shoulder—you'll probably find that your balance is easily thrown off. Even if you manage to stand your ground, the fact is that, because you *are* fairly unbalanced in this position, your abdominal muscles have to work extra hard to help hold you up. This prevents them from having the freedom to expand and lift properly to create support.

Poor posture or a bad stance can also cause shallow breathing. Lock your knees and notice your breath. Do you find yourself struggling more with your breathing? Now lift your shoulders and notice the results. You will probably experience shallow breathing whenever your knees are locked or your shoulders are lifted. This can sabotage your projection, starve your brain of oxygen, and cause you to forget lyrics. And, occasionally, it can cause the tall kid on the back row of the risers to keel over in a dead faint during the high school winter concert.

A better stance is the position you would be in if you were pretending to box with someone—knees slightly bent, one foot a little in front of the other, and hands held above your waist. This position makes you look more relaxed, for one thing, but it also makes you much more steady on your feet—if your friend were to push your shoulder, you would not be easily thrown off balance. When you have proper balance, your belly muscles do not have to work overtime to hold you upright and they can more easily do their job of creating support. Your Bosnian Belly Breathing will be freer and easier.

There is another common stance that can actually sabotage your support system and make it harder for you to sing. (I once recorded the lead vocals for an entire CD while standing like this, and I always wondered why I was working harder than usual.) It is the position in which your hands are clasped behind you and are resting against your tailbone. This tends to move your pelvis forward and shift your weight onto your heels, making it harder to expand and lift your abdomen. It also stretches your shoulders back, tightening the ribcage and making it more challenging to expand the lungs.

An important part of your stance is where your weight is resting on your feet. Stand comfortably and determine whether your weight is mostly on the balls of your feet or on your heels. Many singers lean backward slightly as they sing; this can seriously hamper the singer's performance. When your weight is on your heels, you tend to move the pelvis forward and tuck in the tailbone. This restricts your ability to expand, lift, and create support.

My first voice teacher was a director for a Sweet Adelines chorus. He used to have all of his singers wear shoes with two-inch heels, which caused each singer's body weight to rest on the balls of her feet. I heard recordings of the chorus singing while wearing flat shoes and then singing while wearing the two-inch heels, and the difference was amazing. High notes sounded stronger and the choir's intonation was better when the singers' weights were more on the balls of their feet. You don't have to wear high heels to sing better (but you certainly can if you want to!). Instead, you can just train yourself to check in with your body and determine where your weight is resting. With practice, you can make your weight shift to the balls of the feet automatically when you sing.

Circadian Rhythms

Circadian rhythms are cycles of physical, mental, and behavioral changes that we experience approximately every 24 hours. There is a definite connection between circadian rhythms and singing. For example, you may find that if you're used to singing early in the morning (say, in a church choir), your body has learned how to physically and emotionally prepare to sing at this time of day. Your body gets used to this cycle and it develops certain expectations about when you sing and how it will feel. It basically tells itself, "This is when we sing, and this is what we do to make that happen." These singers may find that they have a much more difficult time singing at some other time of the day (say, later in the evening).

The same is true of many people who are used to singing in the evening (say, in bars or nightclubs). If they are then suddenly faced with an early morning gig, their bodies may not be prepared to respond in the way they need to. It takes practice and awareness to be able sing at a different time than your body is used to. It is certainly not impossible, and it should not prevent you from choosing to perform at a time of day that is not normal for you. But you'll want to do extra work to prepare for a performance at the new time.

I coach singers to begin "stretching their voices out" well in advance of a performance. This may mean getting up quite early to warm up if your performance is in the morning. More than anything, you must develop an awareness of your body in relation to singing that will help you through a performance at a different time of day. Many of the factors that can challenge singers in general can also affect a singer's vocal ability when he or she sings at a different time of day than is customary. Hydration, sleep, diet, warming up, and so forth all need to be taken into account. The more you become aware of what works for you and what does not work for you in terms of performing, the more positive an experience you will have when you are singing at a time that's outside your comfort zone.

How Your Speaking Voice Can Affect Your Singing

You may not know it, but there are issues that you may have with your speaking voice that can cause your singing to suffer. Dr. L. Arick Forrest, a leading voice specialist and vice chairman of the Ohio State University Medical Center's department of otolaryngology, says this about singers: "They rarely get into trouble as a result of something they're doing when they're singing—they get into trouble because of something they're doing when they're speaking. So, they have to alter what they're doing when they're not performing in order to avoid injuries to the voice."

Your Natural Pitch

There are two main elements to focus on. The first is the pitch of your speaking voice. Many people speak at a lower-than-natural pitch, which can cause stress and irritation to the vocal folds. On track 11 of Listen and Learn (available on my website at www.SingFreeNow.com; see page 25 for instructions on accessing the audio tracks) you can hear an example of a voice at lower-than-natural pitch. Does it sound familiar? If this sounds at all like your speaking voice, you're going to want to change your voice's pitch.

The problem with speaking below your natural pitch is that you are lowering the tension on the folds—that's how you make the pitch lower. With less tension, the folds can slap or scrape against each other, irritating themselves. This can lead to hoarseness, stiffness, and thickening of the folds. It's very difficult to sing clean high notes when you've been speaking with an unnaturally low pitch. In the extreme, a lowered pitch becomes what is called *glottal fry* (you can hear examples of both spoken and sung glottal fry on track 12 of Listen and Learn). Some singers use this sound as an artistic tool. Used intentionally for brief periods of time, it can be interesting. When it's done unintentionally for extended periods of time, however, it can lead to vocal trouble.

So, how do you know if the pitch of your speaking voice is in the right place? You may never have thought that your speaking voice even *had* a pitch. If someone were to tell you something interesting and you responded, "Hmmm," you would most likely be making that sound at the natural pitch of your speaking voice. Make the "hmmm" sound and immediately count to 10 at the same pitch. Could you keep the pitch from dropping? Does it sound too high? Most people find that the natural pitch of their speaking voice sounds strange at first. Did you notice your voice sounding cleaner at the higher pitch? With practice, you can become used to speaking (and to hearing your voice) at this pitch. Because it takes more tension to raise the pitch, the slapping or scraping of the folds is reduced and both your speaking and singing voices will stay cleaner and more flexible.

Another issue that can cause problems with your singing voice is never varying the registration and pitch of your speaking voice. If you always speak aggressively in pure heavy register or you always speak softly in light register, you are not changing the workload of your folds, and they can stiffen and lose range. Read a few sentences from a book or magazine and see if you can move between the registers, varying the pitch at the same time. Not only does this help keep your voice flexible, but it also makes your speaking voice more interesting and your verbal communication more powerful.

Over/Under

The other element that can affect your singing is overuse or underuse of your speaking voice. Overusers tend to be loud, passionate talkers who have jobs that require a good deal of speaking. They are usually outgoing, and they tend to engage in conversation easily. They may belong to many organizations or groups (which promotes more talking), and they generally use their speaking voices a great deal. In addition, they may frequently be in situations in which they must be heard over noise (think about stockbrokers shouting out orders on the floor of the U.S. Stock Exchange or coaches who shout to their players from the sidelines during games), which tends to make them frequent victims of the Lombard effect (see page 154). This overuse of the speaking voice can tire out or even injure the voice, causing problems that will impact their singing.

By learning to speak with less power and side-stepping the Lombard effect, singers can help themselves avoid overuse of their voices and keep their voices healthier.

On the other side of this issue are the underusers. These are people who don't use their speaking voices much during the course of a normal day. Shy, quiet people who don't interact verbally very often in their lives fall into this category. Because the voice goes unused for long periods of time, when an underuser sings he or she may find that the folds are tight and stiff. Warming up, regular vocalizing of the exercises found in the Vocal Power Workout, and singing songs every day are the keys to keeping an underuser's voice healthy.

Important Points to Remember

- Many factors that have nothing to do with your skill as a singer can affect your voice. By becoming aware of these factors, you can learn to adjust the way in which you sing to achieve better results when your voice is working less than perfectly.

- Body awareness involves sensing what you feel in your body and where you feel it. By learning to sing by assessing how it feels as well as how it sounds, you will become a more confident singer.

- You can use body awareness to sing more confidently in situations where you cannot hear your voice as well as you would like.

- Each of us has a vocal defense mechanism that subconsciously protects us from hurting ourselves, embarrassing ourselves, and overworking while we are singing.

- Oftentimes the vocal defense mechanism can hinder our ability to use newfound levels of strength and vocal skill in our singing.

- In order to sing with power, passion, and confidence, we must know how to override the vocal defense mechanism when it perceives a threat that doesn't actually exist.

- The way you stand when you sing can greatly affect how you sing.

- Circadian rhythms—natural, 24-hour cycles of physical, mental, and behavioral changes that we experience every day—can affect your singing in a variety of ways.

- Everyone has a time of day at which it seems easiest to sing.

- By becoming aware of how your circadian rhythms affect your singing throughout the day, you will be better able to prepare for and adjust to singing at *any* time of the day.

- Issues with the speaking voice can negatively affect your singing.

- It is critical to speak at your natural pitch and to vary the registration of your speaking voice in order to prevent your singing voice from being harmed.

- Overuse or underuse of the speaking voice can make singing more difficult.

8

Vocal Exercises and Audio Examples

When I was 10 years old my father told our family that we were going to spend the day at Jack LaLanne's house. "Cool, huh!" he exclaimed. LaLanne was an icon of the fitness world whose TV exercise show aired from 1951 until 1985, and he is considered by some to have single-handedly started the fitness industry. My brother and I looked at each other, wondering how we could possibly be invited to the house of "that exercise guy on TV." "Your grandfather knows him, and he wants us to come swim in his pool," my dad explained.

I spent one of the most interesting days of my youth watching Jack—he insisted we call him Jack, not Mr. LaLanne—jumping off the roof of his house into the swimming pool, doing push-ups, and thoroughly amazing us kids with his feats of strength. As we got ready to leave his house, I asked him the secret to being so strong and coordinated. (I really was hoping for a pill or something quick and easy I could do that would make me look and *be* like him.) He said, "Mark—you have to exercise every day. It's as simple as that."

In the same way, the strength and coordination you need to sing well doesn't develop magically or overnight. It comes in large part from doing daily vocal exercises. I've designed the exercises in this chapter to help you in a number of ways as you progress in developing your instrument. In the beginning, your main focus will be on building strength and coordination. Eventually, as your strength and coordination reach a higher level, you will find that these exercises are a great way to maintain what you've built. All the while, you'll be using them to stretch and warm up all the muscles involved in breathing and making sound.

Make a Clean Sound

The number one priority when doing your exercises is to make a clean sound. This may seem too obvious to mention, but so many singers are not aware of noise in their voices. This noise can creep in when singers don't really pay attention to what they're doing. You may reach a point, once you have done the exercises a number of times, that you find yourself simply going through the motions of singing them—that the exercises seem to "sing themselves" without any real direction from you. Whenever this happens, it's easy for bad habits to creep in. The key is to stay conscious and really *listen* to your voice instead of just hearing it.

In his book *The Mozart Effect*, author and music educator Don Campbell defines hearing as taking in auditory impulses. In contrast, he defines *listening* as processing, identifying, selecting, and remembering information about those impulses. The difference between merely hearing and really listening is akin to the difference between just looking at something and truly "seeing" it—or, as Sherlock Holmes memorably chastised his partner, Watson, "You see but you do not observe." It's critical that you really listen to your voice when you sing your exercises because this is the time and place to diagnose the shape of your voice. Do you really want your first glimpse of how your voice is working that day to be on stage in front of an audience? If not, it's essential to analyze the state of your voice as you sing your exercises.

Understanding the Reverse Ratio

In many of these exercises, you'll be using both the high and the low ends of your range. To maintain a constant volume and vowel color, you should be aware of the relationship between the way in which you are controlling an element from inside your body and the way it sounds outside your body. This is called the *reverse ratio*, and most singers are not conscious of how it works. In the case of volume, for example, it has to do with changing the amount of power you use to sing various notes in order to maintain a steady volume. Lower notes require less power than higher notes to achieve the same volume. Therefore, in order to sing all the notes of an exercise (or a song) at, say, a level-5 volume, you'd use less power on the low notes and more power on the high notes.

By changing what's happening on the inside—the amount of power you are using—you can keep what's happening on the outside—the volume—at a consistent level. If you sing using the same amount of power as you move from low notes to high notes, the volume of the notes will change. What's happening on the inside is the reverse of what's happening on the outside. This phenomenon occurs with all vocal elements. For instance, vowel color tends to change as notes get higher and lower. If you want to maintain a 5 vowel color throughout an exercise, you will have to sing darker on high notes and brighter on low notes to keep the color line even. In other words, you need to change some aspect of what's happening inside your body in order to prevent the sound that comes out of your body from changing. By being aware of this reverse ratio and understanding how to use it, you can have more control over your voice and you can sing with more power and confidence.

Important Exercise Tips

Before you begin to explore the Vocal Power Workout exercises, it's a good idea to remind yourself of the following points:

- As you sing these exercises, your jaw should be held open with an easy downward pull. This limits the action of the swallowing muscles and helps to keep the throat open.

- In the beginning, sing the exercises with an ultradark vowel color—at a 2 (with 10 being the brightest and 1 being the darkest you could sing). Pretend you are doing an exaggerated impression of an opera singer. Once you've been singing the exercises daily for about a month, switch to singing the exercises at a 5 vowel color.

- Keep the volume at about 5 as you sing all of the exercises (except Exercise 3 for Females, which should be sung at a 2 volume, and Exercise 8 for Females, which should be sung at a 4 volume). Add power on high notes and decrease power on low notes in order to maintain a consistent 5 volume.

- When you expand your belly to take in a breath, make sure to expand it as far as you can. At the end of each vocal line, make sure that you have lifted in and up about seven-eighths of the way, leaving a small supply of air at your disposal. This ensures that you're using enough of your air to make a fully resonant sound and that you have a little extra air on hand should you decide to improvise at the end of a line in a song.

- If you sing your first set of exercises in the morning, your vocal folds may be in *mourning*—they didn't necessarily want to get up either! Because the folds have been inactive all night, it may be harder to sing, and your voice may be noisier than it would be later in the day. This is completely normal. Always strive for a clean performance sound—but don't be upset if you don't get it first thing in the morning.

The Vocal Power Workout

The exercises in the Vocal Power Workout are designed to build strength, coordination, and flexibility in your voice. You will achieve greater results and have more fun if you keep the following points in mind as you do your workout.

- Always sing at your level. Many of these exercises may go higher or lower than you can reach without straining. Resist the temptation to sing beyond a comfortable stretch. Remember, you are working muscles—if they become overstretched, they may actually begin to contract and stiffen (this is called the "stretch reflex").

- Spend all the time you need between exercises. I encourage you to turn off your audio player and rest whenever you feel tired or out of breath. If you race through the exercises, you'll often get poor results. Take your time with the workout and you will be more productive.

- Modify the vowel to "oo" as you sing higher notes. Listen and feel for changes in the pronunciation of vowels or in your ability to hit notes easily as indications of when to modify. Vowel modification is like a shoehorn—it's a tool to make the task at hand easier. Don't forget to use it!

- Stay focused as you sing the exercises. If your mind wanders, you may not pick up on signals that you need to make adjustments. Good singing requires awareness. If you find that you are not truly present during the exercises, stop your workout and try it again later. Make sure that you reinforce the correct principles during each of your workouts. Remember—practice makes permanent!

- Have fun! The Vocal Power Workout gives you the chance to exercise while making music—so be as musical as you can. The more you put into your workout, the more you will get out of it.

There are four sets of exercises for both males and females:

Set 1 (includes guide vocals): The exercises are slower and lower in pitch; they are designed to warm you up and to allow you to stretch and begin to build strength.

Set 2 (includes guide vocals): These exercises have faster tempos and greater range; they allow you to progress even further in terms of strength building.

Set 3 (does not include guide vocals): The exercises are slower and lower in pitch; they are designed to warm you up and to allow you to stretch and begin to build strength.

Set 4 (does not include guide vocals): These exercises have faster tempos and greater range; they allow you to progress even further in terms of strength building.

Sets 1 and 2 feature guide vocals that allow you to hear the melodies of each exercise as you perform it. Use these sets until you have learned the melodies. (This might take a day; it might take two or three days.) Once you have learned the vocal melodies of the exercises, stop using sets 1 and 2 and move on to using sets 3 and 4 exclusively. This will allow you to hear what's working and what's not working as you sing the exercises and to make the necessary adjustments to move forward more quickly. (It is much easier to hear your own voice accurately when it is not being masked by the guide vocals.)

The optimal approach is to sing both sets (sets 1 and 2 as you're learning the vocal melodies; sets 3 and 4 once you've learned them) each day, giving yourself at least 90 minutes of rest between the sets. (You can wait hours before you do the second set if that's more convenient for you; just make sure to do both sets each day.) Take extra time after any exercise if you feel tired. Again, you are working muscles. Take care not to overdo it.

Last, enjoy the process. Any day that we are able to make music is a gift. Don't lose sight of the talents you already possess. I wish you all the joy of singing!

To access the Vocal Power Workout exercises and the Listen and Learn audio tracks, go to my website: www.SingFreeNow.com. See page 25 for instructions on accessing the audio tracks.

Exercises for Females

Exercise 1 (syllables: "yoh-oh"). This exercise is intended to turn on the vocal mechanism and warm up the vocal folds and the muscles of the support system. Expand the abdominal wall before each "yoh-oh," especially after the second one. At the end of each "yoh-oh," the abdominal wall should be lifted in and up seven-eighths of the way. Be sure to sing all notes in pure heavy register.

Exercise 2 (syllables: "yoh-oh"). This exercise is intended to further warm up and stretch the vocal folds by incorporating changes in pitch (remember, in order to sing different notes, you must change the length of the vocal folds). It should be sung with one continuous lift. Pace the speed of the lift so that you do not run out of air before the end of the line. Be sure to sing all notes in pure heavy register.

Exercise 3 (syllables: "nyoo-oo"). This exercise uses the same melody as exercise 2, but it isolates and works the muscles of your light register. Sing it with a flute-like sound at very low volume—about a 2 on a scale of 1 to 10. As in exercise 2, sing it with one continuous lift. Be sure to sing all notes in pure light register.

Exercise 4 (syllables: "yoh" on the ascending line; "oh" on the descending line). This exercise is intended to work the muscles of the support system by creating opposition. The support system should be expanded before the ascending line as well as before the descending line. This exercise also enhances your ability to sing different intervals (the distance between two notes): a second, a third, a fourth, and a fifth. These terms refer to common intervals that you encounter whenever you sing songs. So, not only are you working on mechanics with this exercise, but you're getting some ear training practice, as well. Be sure to sing all notes in pure heavy register.

Exercise 5 (syllables: "yoo-oo"). This exercise builds strength in the support system muscles and promotes the ability to sing a staccato line efficiently. Staccato means short separate notes—it comes from the Italian word for "detached." Sing the first eight notes staccato and the last three notes legato (tied together). If you sing the first note more loudly than the rest, it will be easier to create the lift and resistance you need to make sure your abs, and not your throat muscles, are doing the work of separating the notes. You will know this is happening efficiently if you can feel your belly bouncing as you sing the staccato notes, as if you were making an "ooh ooh ooh" sound like a monkey. If your throat tries to do the majority of the work of making the notes staccato, you will make a sound like that of a chicken squawking. (Check out track 23 of Listen and Learn for examples of these.) Be sure to sing all notes except the first one using pure light register; you'll want to sing the first note using balanced registration.

Exercise 6 (syllables: "yoh-oh"). This exercise promotes flexibility of the support system by requiring rapid expansion. This comes in handy when you have two long lines to sing in a song and only a short time between them in which to take a breath. Expand as quickly as possible before each of the three lines (in the context of these exercises, a line is whatever you sing between two breaths) while still completing each lift. Don't sabotage yourself by partially expanding or lifting. Be sure to sing all notes in pure heavy register.

Exercise 7 (syllables: "yay-ay-nyoo-oo"). This exercise builds fluidity in the light register and helps you to practice maintaining an even vowel color line when changing vowels. The "ay" vowel is naturally brighter than the "oo" vowel—make sure to match the color of the "ay" to the "oo." Expand the support system before each "yay-ay." Be sure to sing all notes in pure light register.

Exercise 8 (syllables: "yoh-oh"). This exercise is the only one in which you move from one register to the other. Because it is longer than the others, this exercise promotes pacing of the lift, vowel modification, and register transition. It is to be sung with one continuous lift. Sing this exercise at a 4 volume—you will notice that, in order to keep the higher notes at the same volume as the lower notes, you will change registers. As you move from the heavy register to the light register and back again, do not try to smooth out the transitions. Allow this to happen at its own pace. Keep all of the notes at a consistent volume.

Level 1 Female Exercises

Exercises for Males

Exercise 1 (syllables: "yoh-oh"). This exercise is intended to turn on the vocal mechanism and warm up the vocal folds and the muscles of the support system. Expand the abdominal wall before each "yoh-oh," especially after the second one. At the end of each "yoh-oh," the abdominal wall should be lifted in and up seven-eighths of the way. Be sure to sing all notes in pure heavy register.

Exercise 2 (syllables: "yoh-oh"). This exercise is intended to further warm up and stretch the vocal folds by incorporating changes in pitch (remember, in order to sing different notes, you must change the length of the vocal folds). It should be sung with one continuous lift. Pace the speed of the lift so that you do not run out of air before the end of the line. Be sure to sing all notes in pure heavy register.

Exercise 3 (syllables: "yoh" on the ascending line; "oh" on the descending line). This exercise is intended to work the muscles of the support system by creating opposition. The support system should be expanded before the ascending line as well as before the descending line. This exercise also enhances your ability to sing different intervals (the distance between two notes): a second, a third, a fourth, and a fifth. These terms refer to common intervals that you encounter whenever you sing songs. So, not only are you working on mechanics with this exercise, but you're getting some ear training practice, as well. Be sure to sing all notes in pure heavy register.

Exercise 4 (syllables: "nyoo-oh"). This exercise stretches the range of the heavy register. It is sung on one continuous lift. Move from the "oo" vowel of the first syllable to the "oh" vowel of the second syllable without moving your open jaw or lips. Focus on matching the vowel color of the "oo" and the "oh." Be sure to sing all notes in pure heavy register.

Exercise 5 (syllables: "yoh-oh"). This exercise promotes flexibility of the support system by requiring rapid expansion. This comes in handy when you have two long lines to sing in a song and only a short time between them in which to take a breath. Expand as quickly as possible before each of the three lines (in the context of these exercises, a line is whatever you sing between two breaths) while still completing each lift. Don't sabotage yourself by partially expanding or lifting. Be sure to sing all notes in pure heavy register.

Exercise 6 (syllables: "nyoo-oh-oh"). This is an advanced version of Exercise 5. It encourages stability in the lift and helps to build strength by having you sing a descending line, an ascending line, and then a final descending line. As you ascend to the highest note the second time, be sure to modify the vowel to an "oo." Sing the exercise with one continuous lift and focus on maintaining a consistent vowel color and volume. Be sure to sing all notes in pure heavy register.

Exercise 7 (syllables: "yoh-oh"). Because it's longer than the others, this exercise promotes pacing of the lift, vowel modification, and register transition. It should be sung with one continuous lift. Sing this exercise at a 4 volume—you will notice that, in order to keep the higher notes at the same volume as the lower notes, you will change registers. As you move from the heavy register to the light register and back again, don't try to smooth out the transitions. Allow this to happen at its own pace. Keep all the notes at a consistent volume.

The Glide

The glide is an exercise that is very useful before doing a set of vocal warm-ups, as well as before, during (yes, during; I'll explain how in chapter 12), and after a performance. In fact, you can do it whenever you want to—just be sure that you do it correctly. It is simply singing a "yoh," starting at the lowest note you can sing and gliding all the way up to the highest note you can sing, then gliding back down to your starting note. Keep the volume at around a 2—this is the key to this exercise. If you do the glide at a volume that's louder than that, you will put enough of a workload on the folds that they could begin to contract and stiffen. What we want is a safe volume that allows the folds to extend as far as they can and loosen as much as possible.

Level 1 Male Exercises

As you get higher in pitch, you may begin to hear noise in the voice, and you might even experience what feels like an "air pocket," where you can't make any sound at all. This happens because the folds are too stiff or thick to make a small-enough glottis for sound to be created. Your body will want to sing louder because it knows that more air pressure can force the folds to close tighter and you might be able to sing through the "air pocket." The problem with this approach is that you will be pounding on muscles that are already stiff or thick, and singing louder can stiffen up the folds even more.

A better approach is to find an "air pocket" and start singing just below it. Keep the power low and sing past the "air pocket" by a few notes. Do this three or four times in a row, even if you are getting no sound or just the sound of air. By using low power, you are safely stretching the folds and you will more quickly get them to stretch out and make sound than if you sang loudly.

Listen and Learn

Here is a list of the tracks that are available in the Listen and Learn section of my website:

1. Supported sound/Yoh-oh exercise
2. Unsupported sound
3. Bright vowel color
4. Dark vowel color
5. Dull, muddy sound
6. Diphthongs
7. Vowel integrity (good pronunciation versus bad pronunciation)
8. Modifying the vowel
9. Advanced modification
10. Different ratios of registration
11. Speaking voice that is too low in pitch
12. Glottal fry

13. Dynamics: volume
14. Dynamics: vowel color
15. Dynamics: phrasing
16. Dynamics: articulation
17. Dynamics: clarity
18. Dynamics: registration
19. Dynamics: ornamentation
20. Dynamics: melody
21. Vibrato exercises
22. "Hey!" sung in pure heavy register and in balanced registration
23. Examples of efficient and inefficient staccato
24. Different weights of voices

Step 2

Passion

Make It Your Own

9

Dynamics—The Roller Coaster Ride

It's a sunny day and I'm so excited I can hardly stand it. My family's station wagon pulls into a parking lot that's bigger than some towns, and we are directed to space K18. I have to run to keep up with my brother and sister as they dash for the tram that drops us off at the front gate. As we enter the park it finally hits me—"I'm in *Disneyland*!" We wind our way to the center of Tomorrowland and take our place in line for the ride I've dreamed about for a whole year—Space Mountain.

Forty-five minutes later I am ushered into a "rocket car" with seven other squealing kids. As we lurch forward I shout, "This is going to be so cool!" Just as we are about to enter the darkness, a sign saying "Main Ride Closed" appears and we detour onto a side track. Our car winds lazily around the building for the next three and a half minutes—never speeding up or slowing down; never rising or falling. As we exit, my brother blurts out, "That was about as much fun as cruisin' around Gramma's mobile home park in her golf cart!"

Unfortunately, this is the type of "ride" that most singers take us on— safe, even, predictable, and often not very exciting. Many singers are so pre- occupied with mechanics and trying to sing without making mistakes that they sacrifice feeling and style. Their performances lack dynamics.

Understanding Dynamics

Singing with dynamics is one of the best ways to create interest and excitement in your singing. Let's look at the elements that make up dynamics and how you can use them.

The term "dynamics" refers to the result of changing any element in singing. Unfortunately, it's a term that many singers mistakenly associate only with volume. I actually heard a singer once say, "Oh, you want more dynamics—sure, I can make it louder!" But it's the use of a *variety* of dynamics elements that makes the difference, in large part, between a so-so performance and a great one. By using dynamics, you can bring out the storytelling aspect of the performance by varying your delivery of the song. This, in turn, keeps the listener interested and engaged. If you were sitting around a campfire telling a ghost story, you wouldn't be likely to build much interest or create the fear that makes a ghost story fun if you told the whole thing using a monotone voice. However, if you changed the inflection of your voice, spoke more loudly or quietly in appropriate places, and varied the tone of your voice, you could really take the audience on a journey.

To some people, the word "monotone" means a boring, low-key, uninflected voice. However, the real definition of monotone is simply "one note." Remember—an unchanging loud voice is as much monotone as one that is consistently soft and breathy. Dynamics involves the use of a *variety* of vocal elements to create interest and energy.

Your singing can also fall prey to being monotone. If all of the elements—from volume to vowel color to registration and other elements—are exactly the same throughout the song, chances are good that your delivery will be pretty boring. In other words, if all of your vocal elements are on a flat line, your song flatlines (it dies).

You will want to practice changing vocal elements so that you can do it on the fly during your performance. This is what will create the dynamics that make for a memorable vocal experience. Doing this can be a challenge; for most singers, it tends to be counterintuitive. Your body usually finds it much safer to continue down the path it's on with as little variation as possible. Changing an element in the middle of singing a line tends to trigger the defense mechanism.

The following figure and exercise will help you learn to create dynamics. These are by no means all of the vocal elements that you can change—but command of these eight elements will help you to bring power, passion, and confidence to your singing.

Figure 3
Eight Vocal Elements That Can Be Changed to Create Dynamics in Your Singing

1. Volume	Soft	1 ⇨ 5 ⇨ 10	Loud
2. Vowel Color	Dark	1 ⇨ 5 ⇨ 10	Bright
3. Phrasing	Behind	1 ⇨ 5 ⇨ 10	Ahead
4. Articulation	Legato	1 ⇨ 5 ⇨ 10	Staccato
5. Clarity	Clean	1 ⇨ 5 ⇨ 10	Noisy
6. Registration	Heavy	1 ⇨ 5 ⇨ 10	Light
7. Ornamentation	Straight	1 ⇨ 5 ⇨ 10	Embellished
8. Melody	Original	1 ⇨ 5 ⇨ 10	Altered

Let's do an exercise that can help you get a handle on what each of these elements is and how you can change each one in order to have better dynamics.

Creating Dynamics Using Volume

Most singers find it relatively easy to incorporate dynamics into their singing by changing the volume of their singing during a song. To hear examples of a song sung at different volume levels, listen to track 13 of Listen and Learn (available on my website at www.SingFreeNow.com; see page 25 for instructions on accessing the audio tracks).

Exercise: Use Volume to Create Dynamics

This exercise will help you get a feel for what you can create when you change things up. We'll begin by changing volume.

1. Choose a song that is in a comfortable range for you and sing the first two lines the way you normally would. Now consider the first vocal element listed in the figure above—volume. On a scale of 1 to 10, how loudly did you sing the lines? Make a note of the number.

2. When it comes to mastering volume as a vocal element, it helps to start by working at the extremes—very soft and very loud. Let's start with loud. Sing the same lines again, but this time at an 8 volume (with 10 being as loud as you can sing). Could you do it? This will be easy for some people and with some songs, and harder for others. You may find that you are able to start loud, only to have your defense mechanism trigger and cause your volume to drop.

Sing the lines until you can hold a steady 8 volume all the way through. (Please note that this will probably not sound artistic at all. Don't worry—that's not the intention at this point. Here, again, you are making a temporary sound to learn a new skill.)

3. Now sing the same lines at a 2 volume. Whether this is easy for you or not, keep at it until you can sing the lines at a steady 2 volume throughout.

4. Now comes the real payoff of this exercise. Choose a few words in the lines to sing at an 8 volume, some to sing at a 2 volume, and some to sing right in between, at a 5 volume. Keep at it until you can sing the lines using different volumes for the words.

How did you do? Did it sound or feel strange? Remember—exaggeration is a great learning tool. Yes, your singing will probably sound mechanical and "un-artistic" at first—but, by singing the words at different volumes, you can begin to experience dynamics.

What will ultimately transform your mastery of dynamics into a usable, artistic tool is *where* and *when* you choose to change an element. Did any of the words that you sang at an 8 or a 2 volume "make sense" or "feel right" at that volume to you? If they did, remember what they were and sing them that way again. If they didn't, choose different volume levels and sing the lines once more. Change words you sang as a 2 to an 8 and vice versa. Experiment until you notice that the dynamic changes in volume you've made fit well with the lyrics, melody, and mood of the song.

Don't be afraid to experiment in assigning volume levels to words. One way to do this is to sing the first word in a line as an 8 and everything else at a lesser volume. Then sing the line again with the second word at an 8 volume and everything else, including the first word, at a lesser volume. Repeat the exercise until you've sung each word at an 8. Did any of the words sound good at this volume?

If you find that none of the words make sense when you sing them at an 8 volume, repeat the exercise using a 7 and then a 6. The idea here is to find the high and low dynamic point of each line. Variation is the key to dynamics, even if sometimes your changes aren't more than one number on a scale of 1 to 10. It's so easy to sing everything with little or no change in the vocal elements—but taking the easy route here isn't going to make you a confident singer or ensure that your performance is engaging.

Creating Dynamics Using Vowel Color

Let's move on to the next vocal element that can be used to create dynamics: vowel color.

Exercise: Use Vowel Color to Create Dynamics

Sing the two lines you sang in the previous exercise again and notice the variations of vowel color you use when singing them. Assign each variation a number on our 1-to-10 scale (1 being ultradark and 10 being ultrabright). Then sing the lines at an 8 vowel color (very bright), and then at a 2 (very dark), as you did with volume. Continue the steps of the previous exercise, using vowel color instead of volume to create the dynamics. Listen to the examples found on track 14 of Listen and Learn to check your progress.

Go through the previous exercise using each of the eight vocal elements listed in Figure 3. The Listen and Learn section of my website features examples of each of these vocal elements in action (see tracks 13 through 20). Remember—with each of these elements, the key is to begin by exaggerating your use of the far ends of the 1-to-10 scale (or close to the far ends), move on to incorporating the middle of the scale, and then learn to dance all along it.

Creating Dynamics Using Phrasing, Melody, and Ornamentation

When it comes to creating dynamics, the three vocal elements that are the most challenging for the majority of singers are phrasing, melody, and ornamentation. Let's start with phrasing. This refers to the rhythm of the melody and where the notes fall in relation to the beat of the song. Many singers experience a very strong subconscious resistance when they attempt to sing in front of or behind the beat. For those of us who were taught very early in our lives not to color outside the lines, changing the phrasing will immediately trigger our defense mechanism. The key to loosening up phrasing is to know where the word you are singing falls in relation to the count of the song. For help with phrasing, listen to the examples of the song "Swing Low, Sweet Chariot") that are found on track 15 of Listen and Learn (available on my website at www.SingFreeNow.com; see page 25 for instructions on accessing the audio tracks) for help with phrasing.

It's important to note, however, that, in order to be able to change phrasing, you first need to be able to sing exactly on the beat. It is very easy to be slightly behind the beat at any given moment unless you're aware of an important point: If you sing the first consonant of a word right on the beat, the word will probably sound a little bit *behind* the beat. That is because the first vowel of the word—not the first consonant—needs to be sung on the beat. If you sing "Swing Low, Sweet Chariot," for example, and you sing the "sw" of the word "swing" on the beat, then the "i" vowel will come slightly after the beat, causing the word to sound late. Sing the "sw" slightly ahead of the beat, and the vowel will line up correctly.

Exercise: Sing on the Beat

A good way to practice singing on the beat is to sing without the initial consonants: For example, "Swing Low, Sweet Chariot" becomes "ing ow, eet ariot." Once you can feel the vowels lining up on the beats, put the initial consonants back in and keep the vowels where they were. This will become automatic after enough repetitions.

You may also experience a strong feeling of resistance when you attempt to change the melody—another serious "color outside the lines" activity for many singers. By experimenting, you can find other notes that still fit musically but that may not be precisely the same as those found in the original melody. To hear examples of melody changes, listen to track 20 of Listen and Learn.

Keep in mind that, when it comes to changing phrasing and melody, a little usually goes a long way. If you're singing a jazz song, changing both these elements is not only encouraged, but also expected. But with any other style, if you change either element too much you run the risk of sounding too "jazzy" or of not sounding stylistically authentic. However, it's important to exaggerate both elements at first in order to learn to change them. Only then can you get a sense of the "right" amount of change for the song you are singing. The ability to change each of these elements will go a long way toward helping you to "own" a song and to create your style, and it is one of the main ways to build passion and confidence in your singing.

Ornamentation refers to the embellishment (or lack of it) that is present in a note. Ornamentation, which is also called "riffing," "adding frills," and "runs," is the art of singing trills or other movements on notes (to hear examples of this, listen to track 19 of Listen and Learn). It is not so much changing the melody as adding to it. The musical term for this is "melisma," which means the singing of more than one note on a syllable. Often associated with gospel, R&B, Middle Eastern, and Irish styles, you can use it when singing in almost any style. As a way of learning this element, I highly recommend listening to a recording of someone who uses a lot of ornamentation in a song. (Mariah Carey and Christina Aguilera are two singers who are known for their heavy use of ornamentation.) It's very helpful to slow down the track so that it becomes easier to hear the movement of the ornamentation. There are CD players and software programs that allow users to do this. (One such software program, which is reasonably priced and which does a great job, is called the Amazing Slow Downer; it's available at www.SingFreeNow.com).

Again, the best way to learn how to ornament your singing is to exaggerate (detect a theme here?). Practice singing a riff slowly until you can easily sing it. Then you can experiment with actually inserting it into a song. (It may take many repetitions before you feel brave enough to try *any* change to your dynamics while you are actually performing. However, my experience has been that, once you do, you will notice a positive impact immediately. Changing dynamics "on the fly" makes songs more fun and more meaningful and brings more joy to your singing.

Creating Dynamics Using Clarity

Clarity is the next vocal element. It involves reducing or increasing the amount of noise that's in your voice as you sing a song. Singers who have noise in their voices all of the time may find it tricky to incorporate this element into their vocal dynamics. On the other end of the spectrum are singers who find it challenging to *add* noise to their voices (such singers are often initially skeptical that this could even be desirable—"Why would I want *noise* in my voice?"). If you have noise in your voice all of the time, the first thing

I would suggest is that you visit an otolaryngologist (an ear, nose, and throat doctor) to make sure that there is nothing physically wrong with your vocal folds. This is the first thing to rule out. My next suggestion is to check out Appendix B for tips on how to clean up your voice.

If being able to *make* noise is a challenge to you, part of the issue could be an unconscious resistance to creating a sound that you don't think is "right." But moving your voice from clean to noisy can be a dynamic way to convey emotion. I've been told by quite a few singers that noise was only for genres like blues or heavy metal. Not true. Rock, pop, reggae, soul, gospel, and country singers routinely use noise as a way to create dynamics in their singing. Listen to how artists you like use noise in songs in order find approaches that appeal to you and that can be models for this dynamic element.

Noise can be described in many ways—raspy; gritty; smoky—and it might be found in a scream or in a breathy note. Regardless of the way in which it is described, it's all distortion of some kind that's made by the sound of air moving through the folds.

There are two main ways to create noise:

1. Overpower the folds, blowing them slightly apart. They still need to be pulled tight and you need a lot of resistance to the lift in order for this approach to work. This approach is well suited to screams and raspier sounds, and it is easier to make on higher notes and on louder notes. (To hear examples of this, check out track 17 of Listen and Learn.) The key to safely generating noise while singing in this manner is to have your support system as engaged as possible in order to reduce the trauma to your throat. The more your belly is working, the longer you can make noise without wearing yourself out.

2. Underpower the folds, loosening them so that air leaks through. This is achieved by lowering the resistance to the

lift of the belly. This can make for a breathy, smoky type of sound. It is easier to use this approach on quieter notes and on lower notes. In the extreme, it is also the method you use to create glottal fry (check out track 12 of Listen and Learn).

Both of these approaches can be challenging for the developing singer, as they go against what feels "right" in singing—having the appropriate support to make a clean sound. With practice, you can learn where the support-tension threshold is and be able to make the noise you choose whenever you want. Please be aware, however, that, no matter how much your support system is engaged when you make a noisy sound, it will eventually wear you out. Ideally, noise is an element that you will use sporadically to vary your sound, not as a permanent part of your sound. It's like cooking with a strong spice—a little goes a long way.

Creating Dynamics Using Registration

As with all the other vocal elements, the key to creating dynamics with registration is to make a change. If you sing an entire song in pure heavy register, in a 50/50 balance, or in any other particular ratio of balanced registration, the audience will soon be able to predict exactly what you will sound like for the rest of the song. This can make your performance less interesting than it could be. Notice where your comfort zone is in relation to registration and bravely go where you usually don't go. Make yourself sing some notes in pure heavy register and some notes in different balances, finding new possibilities that serve the mood and meaning of the song. Listen and Learn track 18 will give you examples of changing the registration.

Creating Dynamics Using Articulation

Articulation is an often-overlooked element that can really spice up a song. If you normally sing with an easy flow that leans toward legato, a few staccato notes will grab the listener's attention. If you're singing an upbeat, energetic song that "wants" to be sung staccato, try singing a few words with legato articulation. Changing articulation is a great way to accent a word or phrase. Be sensitive to the fact that you don't need to make a lot of changes to make a big impact. To hear how articulation can be changed, refer to Listen and Learn track 16.

After experimenting with all eight vocal elements individually, you can move on to the final piece of the dynamics exercise: experiment with changing two or more vocal elements at the same time. For example, you may want to move from loud to soft *while* getting brighter and more staccato. As you experiment, notice your habits and comfort zones. If you tend to routinely change the same two or three vocal elements to add dynamics, you can stretch your comfort zone (and raise your skill level) by picking two or three different vocal elements to experiment with. Practice to the point that you can change all eight vocal elements in the course of singing a single song. When you can do this, you are ready to use them all in a performance.

One of the keys to learning to change vocal elements is to know that, as you are experimenting, you are going to sing lines that don't sound "good" to you. **Please make this OK.** It is virtually impossible to learn how to improvise (and making unrehearsed changes to your dynamics is a form of improvisation) without making "mistakes." I put the word mistakes in quotes because often something unplanned or unintentional will turn out to sound great and be effective. This is one of the ways that most of us create our style. We start by copying something we like; then, intentionally or unintentionally, we make changes to it that take us down a new road. If you make it safe to sound "goofy" and "over the top" when doing your dynamics exercises, you will actually master dynamics more quickly.

"Good" Stress

Stressing, or accenting, key words in a phrase is also an important piece of creating dynamics. Knowing which words to stress will make your singing more artistic. One way to gain awareness of which words of a song to accent is to read them out loud as if you were reciting a dramatic poem. Notice where the accents fall. If you don't stress any of the words in a line, you'll end up with a pretty boring reading. The same thing is true when you sing a line of a song. Accents are used to give added meaning or impact to the words.

For example, if you say, "I really love you" without placing any accent, or emphasis, on any of the words, it may not sound as though you're sincere. If you say, "*I* really love you," you're saying, "It's me, as opposed to someone else, who loves you." "I *really* love you" speaks to how strong your feeling is. "I really *love* you" shows that your emotion goes beyond merely liking the person. "I really love *you*" means the person you're singing to is "the one." As you can see, the specific word or words you choose to accent can radically add or change meaning to a spoken line.

The same is true in singing. If you take the lines you sang for the dynamics exercise and experiment with accenting different words, you will find new meaning in them. Look at the lyrics and decide what the key words are in each line. Which words really deliver the message? Which words "feel" as though they should be sung more strongly? Once you have decided on the words you want to accent, you can then experiment with *how* to accent them. Volume is the easiest and most obvious vocal element to use but try all the others in the dynamics exercise as well. You may find one or more that really make a line interesting.

Creating a Dynamics Map

To help you get a better feel for using dynamics, I'm going to ask you to create what is called a "dynamics map" of a song you are working on. A dynamics map is a visual reference tool that allows you to see, make changes to, and document the ways in which any vocal element is used to create dynamics in a particular song. Since volume is the most obvious vocal element and the one that most singers think of when they hear the word "dynamics," we'll use that in our example. Then, using the process described below, you can go on to create dynamics maps for any vocal element you want to work on.

Select a recording of a song that you want to work on (it can be a recording of you singing or of someone else singing). Write or type out the lyrics on a piece of paper. Be sure to allow for enough space between the lines so that you can write above each word in the lyrics. Make several copies of your written or typed lyrics (you'll need at least three copies for each vocal element you work on).

Listen to the recording of your song as you mark up one copy of the lyrics. Starting with the very first word, write a number (on a scale of 1 to 10) above it that indicates the volume the word is sung at. Continue to listen to the song and, whenever the singer changes his or her volume, write that volume number above the first word that is sung more quietly or loudly. (If the volume stays the same for a few words, you don't need to write the same number over every word.) When you finish the song, you will have a volume dynamics map. This serves as a visual image of the rise and fall of the volume that's used by the singer.

Using your volume dynamics map as a visual guide, practice singing the song using the same volume dynamics that the singer uses in his or her recording. (If you're using a recording of your own voice, skip to the next step.) Pay close attention to any word or phrase where you have difficulty matching the singer's volume. It may be an area that is triggering resistance from the defense mechanism. Oftentimes this occurs with words that are sung loudly—your body may feel vulnerable when you try to match the volume and compensate by lowering the power. By using the dynamics map you created, you can easily see where your body is likely to "bail on you" and then take the necessary steps to overcome that. This will help you to convey the same intensity of feeling that was created by the singer in the recording and to connect strongly with your audience.

Next, use a separate copy of the lyrics to create a second volume dynamics map. This time, instead of mimicking the vocal dynamics of the singer in the recording, just randomly change the volume numbers that you assigned to the words in the first map. If the singer sang a word at a 6 volume, assign some other number to that word. The purpose of this step of the exercise is not to sound artistic; it's to loosen up any restrictions your body may be trying to impose upon itself when it comes to changing the volume. By using different dynamics than the singer uses on the recording, you'll begin to "make it OK" for your brain and body to create your own dynamics. Sing the song following your random volume dynamics map until it's easy to do.

Last, create your own volume dynamics map of the song as you want to perform it. During the previous step, when you randomly assigned volume numbers to words, did you notice any places where it felt right for you to sing at a different volume than the singer did on the recording? You can use those places as starting points to create a volume dynamics map that incorporates your own personal style. Open yourself up to being influenced by both the lyrics and the melody. It often makes sense to sing higher notes more loudly and lower notes more quietly, but don't necessarily make this a habit. Experiment. Use volume (either high or low) to accent key words.

When you are satisfied with the results, sing the entire song and observe your volume dynamics. Have you, for the most part, just copied the recording and stuck to the singer's volume choices, or have you really "made the song your own"? Sing through the song again and notice what works and what doesn't. Are there areas that still need to be tweaked? Are you conveying the emotions you want to get across throughout the song? Keep adjusting your volume dynamics map until you are happy with every volume choice in your song.

Changing dynamics is really about looking at things differently. I once heard a story about a young girl and her little brother who were riding an elevator. He was eating an ice cream cone while standing next to a very elegantly dressed woman. At one point the old elevator lurched and jostled everyone, causing the little boy to bump his ice cream into the woman's mink coat. In a very reprimanding tone, his sister shouted, "Johnny, be careful—you just got fur on your ice cream!" There is always more than one way to look at something.

Eventually you'll get to a stage where you can simply improvise your vocal dynamics as you sing to match your mood and intention. To me, one of the most rewarding experiences in singing is the ability to allow myself the freedom to sing a song as I feel it *at that moment*. It doesn't have to be exactly as I'd rehearsed it or even as I had planned to sing it. This is the freedom that many of us yearn to experience through singing. But this freedom won't just magically happen one day—you have to practice changing dynamics in order to be confident enough to do it in front of an audience. Ultimately, this is an aspect of trust in singing. You have to trust that spontaneously changing the dynamics is not only permissible, but also is a major aspect of creating art, singing with power, passion, and confidence, and experiencing the joy of singing. If you want to truly develop your own style, you have to be willing—and able—to move outside preset lines.

Developing Your Personal Style

I will never forget an experience I had one summer night when I was singing with my band in a downtown nightclub. I was the lead singer and front man of Boystown, a pop-funk-rock band that, for the most part, played songs that I had written. On this particular night we were really feeling it, and we had the crowd dancing and hollering into the wee hours. During a break, a guy came up to me and asked if he could talk to me for a minute.

"Sure—what's going on?" I'd seen this guy in the audience during my performances at various places that I played regularly, but I didn't really know him. "I just wanted to tell you that I've seen you perform around town quite a bit and I don't think I've ever heard your voice sound as good as it does tonight!" he exclaimed. "Well, thanks!" I said to my new best friend, puffing out my chest a bit. "But," he continued, "it sounds like you're singing from sheet music."

I felt as though I'd been punched in the gut. My new ex-best friend went on to describe what he meant. "All the verses sound the same; all of the choruses sound the same. It sure would be more interesting if you changed things up now and then." Then he just walked off. I spent the rest of the night fuming—the audacity of this guy! But on the drive home it hit me like a ton of bricks: he was *right*.

I had become used to spending most of my rehearsal time figuring out how I was going to sing a song and then I would wrench it into place, practicing it the same way every time. In retrospect, I realize that I was sticking to the safest approach to singing that I could have taken: First, determine how I want to sing a song. Second, stick to that approach no matter what. Third, sing all the verses using the same phrasing, volume, and so forth throughout the entire song in order to make things as easy on myself as possible. The problem with singing this way is that, although it's easier in the short run—there's less to think about; there's less possibility of making mistakes—in the long run it makes for a very stale and boring performance.

This "gift from the Universe" (that's what I call that guy now) was, of course, talking about dynamics. But what he was *really* getting at was the concept of *using (or not using) dynamics to create a personal style.*

As you develop as a singer, you may be faced with the questions, "Do I have a style? And if so, what is it?" Most singers can't really define style—they just know they want one.

Style is created by the choices you make when you sing. All of the vocal elements you use can be combined in different ways. How you choose to use them at any given moment defines your style. If I sent 10 people into your closet, one at a time, and asked them to get dressed, they would each come out wearing different combinations of your clothes and accessories. This is style, and it's the biggest part of "owning a song"—putting your stamp on it.

If 10 of us were to sing the same song, each of us would use volume, vowel color, registration, and every other vocal element in different ways.

I'm often asked, "How do I create my own style?" The answer is to start by identifying what moves you when it comes to *other* singers' styles or performances. I once had a student who told me she didn't want to listen to other singers or sing any songs she hadn't written herself—she wanted to create her own "unique" style. She felt that, if she was going to be "an original," she shouldn't allow herself to be swayed by anyone else. The problem with this approach is that it forces singers to "reinvent the wheel." You will work much harder than you have to if you try to create something from scratch than you will if you give yourself a starting point from which to branch out.

The truth is, it's unlikely that you'll use every single vocal element in a way that's totally different from the way in which anyone else has ever used it. In fact, singers who feel the need to do this may spend a lot of time and effort trying to be different just for the sake of being different—and they may overlook the possibility that those differences are actually hampering their ability to perform well or to connect with an audience What is possible, however, is to develop your own unique style by *combining* elements that others have used.

Here's an exercise that will help you start the process of creating your unique style.

Exercise: Begin to Create Your Personal Style

Listen to a recording of a singer you really like. Make written notes of every choice that artist makes that you can pinpoint. Start with support, resonation (specifically, vowel color), and registration—the Big Three Vocal Principles. If there is a particular spot in a song that you especially enjoy, analyze it. Figure out what the singer is doing in terms of the vocal elements. It may be the way he or she pronounces a vowel or changes vowel color or registration. It could be the way the singer ornaments a word or how he or she phrases the lyrics.

Your next step is to copy what that singer is doing. The intention is not to turn you into a clone of someone else. When you are able to absorb the best parts of others' good singing, you can then recombine those parts into your own style.

A great way to learn what someone else is doing is to chart that singer's performance using a dynamics map. That way, you have a baseline from which you can begin to create your own "take" on the song. When you get to the point that you can copy an element of good singing from another singer and use it in a different song, you'll be well on your way toward building the foundation of your personal, unique style. Eventually, you will have a collection of choices you can use that will be different from anyone else's collection.

The great thing about style is that, like you, it's constantly changing. If you listen to the recordings that span any good singer's career, from that singer's earliest efforts to his or her most recent releases, you will hear the evolution of the choices the singer has made. As you continue to be affected by both your musical and non-musical environment, your style will change and evolve. This is healthy, and it's necessary in order for you to continue to make a song your own, to sing in the moment, to be confident, and to experience the joy of singing.

Another aspect of style that singers tell me they want is their own unique sound. They want something that is recognizable as their voice; something that sets them apart from the crowd. You may be surprised to learn that you already have this—your singing voiceprint. The term "voiceprint" has been used primarily in identifying the speaking voice. It is generally defined as a set of measurable characteristics of a human voice that uniquely identifies an individual. These characteristics, which are based on the size and shape of a speaker's mouth and throat, stay the same no matter what sounds the individual makes with his or her voice.

This concept of voiceprints applies to the singing voice as well as to the speaking voice. The size and shape of each person's skull, mouth, throat, resonators, and other characteristics make for a unique singing voice that is as personal and identifiable as a fingerprint. If you feel as though you don't have a unique voice, understand that your perception may be based more on how you've chosen to *use* your voice—how you've let your natural uniqueness come through (or, perhaps more to the point, how you've attempted to prevent it from coming through)—than on any missing unique tonal quality. For that reason, I use the term "enhance" instead of "create" when I talk about a singer's unique sound. *You don't have to create a unique voice—that's already been done for you.* Instead, you get to learn what *makes* it unique and how to build on that. Let's start that process by further exploring dynamics.

The Vocal Appraisal

One of the most important tools you can use to develop dynamics and create artistry in your singing is a vocal appraisal. This is a simple method of quickly and easily determining how a singer is using his or her voice in a particular song. This goes beyond deciding whether or not you like the performance or whether or not you think the singer is good. It gives you a way to zero in on the nuts and bolts of the performance so that, if you decide you want to reproduce what a singer is doing, you'll know exactly how to do so. This is handy when you want to "borrow" something you like from another singer to enhance your own style. It's equally useful when you want to make sure you're not inadvertently using your voice in the same way as a singer you don't like.

Using a vocal appraisal involves analyzing a performance in relation to the Big Three Vocal Principles. You can use it on another artist's recording, a live performance, or even on a recording of yourself when you want to check your progress or work on a specific challenge.

A vocal appraisal involves 3 steps:

Step 1: Select a recording of a song that you enjoy and analyze the intensity of support that the singer is using. ("Power" and "workload" are other terms that describe intensity of support. How much power is the singer using? How big is the workload? What is the intensity of singer's support? Use whichever term works best for you.) Come up with a number on a scale of 1 to 10 and write it down. A singer's intensity of support may change many times over the course of the song, so select a number that best represents the average workload just to get you started. You can then change that number as needed.

Step 2: Repeat step 1, this time focusing on vowel color. Where, on a scale of 1 to 10, is the singer generally hanging out (if 1 is as dark as the singer could possibly sing and 10 is as bright as he or she could sing)? Choose a number that best represents the average vowel color that's used by the singer throughout the song and write it down.

Step 3: Now do the same thing for registration. Is the singer performing in 100 percent heavy register, in 100 percent light register, or in a balance of the two registers? If it's balanced registration, what is the ratio? Write down the percentage that is heavy register first. For example, you might write "60/40," meaning that 60 percent is heavy register and 40 percent is light register.

If you're not sure what number to go with for any of the Big Three Vocal Principles in the track you're listening to, trying singing a line using an extreme of the scale. For example, if you are listening for vowel color, sing a line along with the singer and go for a 10 (as bright as you can possibly sing the line). Don't worry about how "good" it sounds—focus on hitting your target. Then sing the line again, this time going for a 1 (as dark as you can possibly sing the line). Once you've heard yourself sing the line at both a 1 and a 10, it will probably be easier for you to identify the number at which the singer is performing. No matter what element you are working on, knowing where the ends of the scale are makes it easier to find everything in between.

With practice, you'll be able to do vocal appraisals more easily and quickly. Eventually, you will be able to instantly identify numbers for each of the Big Three Vocal Principles in any song you listen to. When you find a performance that really moves you, doing a vocal appraisal will allow you to expand your style by "taking what you want and leaving the rest" from the singer. You will be able to do this because you'll know how much support is needed, what vowel color to sing, and what registration to use to get the same sound as the vocal performance you enjoy. You can then use those same parameters to sing along with that recording and to get a feel for how the singer is making the sounds you like. Then, sing the same sounds in a differ-ent song, being careful to use the same settings. When you can identify what is being done by a singer to make a sound you enjoy, and can then replicate the same effect in another song, you know have that sound as part of your repertoire. The more ammunition you stockpile by borrowing from those singers you connect with, the easier it is to vary your singing, with the ulti-mate purpose being to keep the listener interested and engaged. You can also do vocal appraisals of your own singing to check your mechanics and style.

In my experience, almost all of the problems you could encounter in your singing have to do with one of the Big Three Vocal Principles (see also Appendix B). If something is not working, you will have a way to identify the issue and change your approach. If you record yourself, you can then ana-lyze your support, vowel color, and registration. Let's say you're consistently cracking on a high note. You can analyze your support intensity and then change it one number at a time on a scale of 1 to 10. You may find you were underpowering or overpowering the note and that the cracking may clear up as you change your support intensity. Or you may hear on the recording that your high note is very bright; by darkening the vowel color, you can make the cracking disappear. You might notice that the registration is not where you need it to be in order to sing the high note stably. You may need more heavy register to hold the note in place. Or the note may be to high to sing in pure heavy register; it may stop cracking when you switch to balanced registration. The key to finding what works is to experiment by making changes to each of the Big Three Principles. Eventually you will get faster at identifying what is causing vocal problems and be able to make changes quickly. This makes it so much easier to consistently sing with confidence and joy.

A bonus to learning how to do a vocal appraisal is that it gives you a way to critique other singers that doesn't shame them. I have heard far too many horror stories from singers who were dumped on by "friends" or family as they critiqued the singer's performance. Doing a vocal appraisal of someone's singing allows you to identify specific elements that worked and didn't work in a way that comes across as helpful rather than judgmental and that gives the singer concrete information about something he or she might want to consider changing. Always start an appraisal by first talking about what worked in the performance. ("John, the registration you used seemed appropriate to the style of the song and worked well")—then you can gently suggest ways in which a singer could adjust one or more elements to improve his or her performance ("I did notice that some of your high notes were sung using a much brighter vowel color than the other notes of the song. If you evened out the vowel color line, you'd create a more controlled, consistent performance.") Put yourself in the singer's shoes and try to deliver your vocal appraisal in a way that's as useful, supportive, and nonjudgmental as possible.

Choosing the Correct Key

Most of the singers I've worked with believe that whatever key a recorded song is sung in is "the key" of the song. Period. When a singer works from sheet music, the same thing happens: the singer thinks that he or she has to sing that piece in the key in which it was written. The problem with this assumption is that it often forces you to sing in a key that just doesn't fit your range or to sing in a way that doesn't match your artistic vision of the song. Let's look at both of these challenges and how they affect your key choice for a song.

First and foremost, choose a key that allows you to deliver the best vocal performance you can create for each song you sing. I make this point because singers in bands and other groups often report to me that, when they suggest changing keys to instrumentalists, they often come up against resistance. "Just sing it in the same key as the recording—that's the right key" is a common reaction. Or, "I already learned the song in the original key. Why do we have to change it?" Much of this resistance comes from players not wanting to put in extra work to accompany you, the singer. In addition, changing the key to one that works better for your voice may mean that the instrumentalists have to play their parts in keys that they're not used to or that are more difficult for them.

The bottom line, however, is this:

It rarely makes sense to perform a song in a key that is easier for an instrumentalist but harder for the singer. Your performance will suffer if you are overworking to reach notes that are too high for you. The same goes for singing in a key that causes you to hang out in the basement of your range, where notes are so low that they're hard to hear.

The "original" key is usually just the key the recording artist chose based on his or her range and on the kind of energy it imparted on that artist's rendition. It's no "holier" than any of the other 11 keys the song could be sung in. What I mean is that no key is more "right" for a song than any other. When it comes to deciding the key in which to sing a particular song, it's always best to base that decision on what works best for *your* voice and performance, not on what others have done or on what's easiest for the instrumentalists that are performing with you.

How can you tell whether or not a certain key is good for a particular song? There are three main factors to consider.

Key Choice Factor 1: Workload

If you want to generally sound like the singer on a recording of a song, decide how hard that singer is working to sing it. Let's say that the singer is using a 6 workload. If you sing the song in the same key and you have to work at an 8 to reach the notes in the same registration, your performance won't have the same feel as that of the recorded version of the song. If you want to match the feel of that recorded version, you should lower the key until you find the one that allows you to sing the song at the same 6 workload as the artist. This would be the key for you to use. But if you want to alter the song to make it your own, sing it using a workload that's different from the workload the recording artist used. Regardless of whether the workload you choose is more or less intense, you will always wind up changing the feel of the song.

You may be wondering, "How in the heck can I figure out how to sing a song in a different key than the one that's used in a recording or that's indicated in the sheet music?" On page 201 I talked about the Amazing Slow Downer software. Not only does it slow down or speed up a track, but it can also play it in a different key. There are many other pieces of software and hardware that allow you to change the key of a song. Then all you have to do is sing along until you've learned the song in the new key. Or, if you have access to a musical instrument and the sheet music of your song, you can simply play the song (or have someone else play it) in the key you want and sing along. Changing the key of a song is called transposing. If you have access to an electric keyboard, you can simply use the transpose function to raise or lower the key. If you have a guitar, you can use a capo (a movable bar) to raise the key by half steps. If neither of these options is available, you can transpose the song yourself, or have someone do it for you, by rewriting the chords or notes of a song in a different key.

Key Choice Factor 2: Song Range

The next factor to consider when choosing a good key is the overall range of the song. The U.S. national anthem, "The Star Spangled Banner," is an example of a song that features a big range—it includes a couple of very high notes and some very low notes. If you moved the key of this song too far in one direction, you'd make one end of the range easier to negotiate, but the other end of the range even more difficult. Fortunately, most songs don't have this extreme range, and you can usually change keys to either make high notes or low notes more reachable and effective. Try different keys to decide whether the low notes or high notes need more help.

An additional option is available to you whenever you sing a song in a key that is great for you except that one note is too high or too low: you can slightly change the melody by singing a different note. This will usually go unnoticed unless that note is a signature part of the song—like the high note at the end of the national anthem. Further, changing one note in the melody can be a bonus—it's another way to make the song your own.

Key Choice Factor 3: Your Artistic Vision of the Song

When you first give yourself permission to change keys, your next thought might be to lower the key of every song enough so that they are all really easy to sing. The problem with this approach is that, if you are singing a song that you want to be energetic and you've lowered the key too much, you won't be working very hard to sing it, and the result will be that your energy won't match your intention. The opposite is true if you want a song to have a soft, ballad-like energy. If the key is too high, you will have to work too hard to hit the notes and the energy will not match your intention for the song.

Vibrato

We've talked about eight vocal elements that can be used to create a dynamic performance. Vibrato is yet another vocal element that you can use in this way, and it's a characteristic of the voice that almost all singers want to have. Most of my students, at some point in their development, ask me if they are ever going to have control of this vocal element and if there's anything they can do to help develop it more quickly. Let's examine what vibrato is, what it is not, and what, if anything, you can do to make vibrato a part of your singing repertoire.

If you've ever seen a violin player or guitar player rapidly move a finger back and forth on a string while playing a sustained note, you've witnessed that musician create vibrato. In singing, vibrato is a controlled, pulsing change in pitch that is almost always accompanied by small fluctuations in volume. It shows up when your support system is strong enough and efficient enough to create it. It's made by sending pulsing nerve signals, which are initiated by the opposition of your belly muscles, to your vocal folds. To turn vibrato on, you engage the abdominal muscles with enough resistance that pulsing takes place. It is similar to lifting something that is heavy enough to cause your biceps and triceps to tremble. At the same time, you must maintain an even amount of air pressure against the vocal folds to create vibrato, so it is important to have a steady in-and-up lift of the belly. When it's created properly, you can place a finger against your belly and feel the support mechanism that's working to create these pulses. That sensation in your belly won't be noticeable if you are trying to create vibrato in your throat or with your jaw. An enemy of vibrato is tension in the neck and the throat muscles that are not directly related to making sound. If neck muscles are visibly working, there is too much tension.

If you use it correctly, vibrato can add depth to the sound of your voice and give sustained notes a sense of forward motion. Where, when, and how you use vibrato can go a long way toward determining how effective it can be—but before you learn how to use it in a strategic way, it's important that you learn how to create it the *correct* way.

If you don't have vibrato in your voice yet, please be patient. Everyone can develop vibrato; it's mostly about building strength and coordination. The same factors that create good support—strength, abdominal resistance, and an even lift—will eventually create vibrato. If you sing the two sets of exercises in the Vocal Power Workout daily, you will eventually notice vibrato starting to appear in your voice. In the meantime, there are some vibrato-specific exercises you can do to help it along. These are on track 21 of Listen and Learn (available on my website at www.SingFreeNow.com; see page 25 for instructions on accessing the audio tracks).

The first vibrato exercise is intended to make you sound like you are trying to start the engine of an old car. It will help your support system to get the idea of creating the pulsing that will become vibrato.

The second and third vibrato exercises have you trill from a target note to a half step below that note, and then from the target note to a half step above it. Both of these exercises start slowly and then increase in tempo, helping your system to create the rapid pitch change that will eventually become a pleasing vibrato.

The last exercise uses a three-note trill that starts on the target note, drops a half step, returns to the target note, and then goes up a half step. All of these exercises will help you create vibrato as quickly as possible.

A singer once asked me a great question: "Is any vibrato better than no vibrato?" Not necessarily. First of all, the speed of your vibrato must be at a certain rate in order to sound musical. If it's too fast, you can create a subconscious nervous tension in your audience (probably not something you want). The same result can happen if your vibrato is too slow (this is sometimes called a wobble). What's the magical rate for sounding musical? Between about six and eight pulses per second. This was discovered early in the last century by analyzing the recordings of many of the great singers of the day. All of them had vibrato rates of six to eight pulses a second!

Continued research has shown that most of us don't tend to like the sound of vibrato that is faster or slower than this rate.

If your support system is doing most of the heavy lifting and your throat is open, you will almost always sing a vibrato that sounds musical. A vibrato that is not pleasing to the ear is often the result of singing with unwanted tension in the throat or singing without support. The best way to help your vibrato sound better if it's too fast, too slow, or stuck in the "on" position is to practice singing an entire song with a straight tone (no vibrato). This may sound easy, but you may find it quite challenging at first, especially if you are used to singing all notes with vibrato. Like any other element, if vibrato never changes—if it's always "on"—it becomes boring and it can lose its impact; everyone will be so used to hearing it that, without hearing any straight tones to compare it to, they won't perceive that it adds anything to your singing. This is where singing an entire song using a straight tone comes in. By learning to do this first, you will gain control of your instrument, become intentional about using vibrato, and develop better strength and coordination by using your support system more efficiently—all of which translates into your ability to produce a more musical vibrato rate.

Singing with constant vibrato can be a problem for another reason, as well. It can allow your support system to work with less accuracy. Your body is often looking for the easiest way to work, and vibrato can sometimes cover up a note that is off pitch, allowing your body to work more easily than it would have to in order to hold the note in tune. This is an example of how vibrato is *not* to be used—as a way to cover up being out of tune. In the long run, this just doesn't help you to be a better or more confident singer. Like any other element in singing, vibrato is something that you must use correctly— and that you must be able to *choose* to use. If you are using it unintentionally, you're doing so out of habit, and your singing may suffer because of it.

Where and when should you use vibrato? As is the case with any other vocal element, this is ultimately up to you. However, there are some general guidelines that might help. The higher the pitch, the more it makes sense to use vibrato. The same is true of volume: the louder the note, the more vibrato you can use. Low notes can be a challenge because they are already vibrating more slowly than high notes; that's what makes them sound lower. If you add the pulsing of vibrato to a slower vibrating low note, you may end up with so much wavering that it sounds out of tune.

A rule of thumb is to use "terminal vibrato" on a sustained note. This means singing the first half of the note with a straight tone and bringing the vibrato in at the end. In this way, you can create a nice feeling of forward motion for the note that you won't get if you start off the note with vibrato or sing the entire note with no vibrato at all. I suggest you experiment to find where and when to use vibrato, and I recommend that you listen to recordings of yourself to help you choose wisely. When it comes to using vibrato, like many of the vocal elements, sometimes less is more.

Important Points to Remember

- Dynamics are the result of varying any vocal element—not just volume.

- Dynamics help you to create feeling, energy, and interest in your singing.

- Your style is created by the choices you make to combine the different elements of singing.

- Style is what allows you to "own" a song.

- A vocal appraisal is a way to determine what a singer is doing in relation to the Big Three Vocal Principles.

- Vocal appraisals can help you to identify anything that isn't working well in your own singing, to enhance your style, and to keep your audience interested in your performance.

- In order to sing a song in the key that's right for your voice, you may need to sing in a key that's different from the one that's used on a recording or on the sheet music.

- Vibrato is an effect that is caused by singing while making small, pulsing pitch changes.

- Everyone can develop and use vibrato. A pleasing vibrato is created by having strength and coordination in your support system, not by manipulating your throat or jaw.

10

The Zen of Singing

The first time my wife, Tracy, heard me sing, I was at the Last Hurrah night-club performing the Van Morrison song "Moondance." It is one of her favor-ite songs, and she really enjoyed the performance (she had to say that—we had just started dating!). One day years later, after she had taken voice classes and private lessons in my studio, she asked me why the song sounds different when I sing it to her than when I sing it in public. "Are you using some vocal elements differently, or changing your support or something?" I love it when singers start thinking this way.

I answered that I wasn't really aware that I was singing it differently, but I decided to find out what was going on. When I sat down to sing the song to her, I noticed that I was feeling different than I do when I sing the song in public. Because of how I feel about Tracy, and because I know how much she likes my rendition of the song, I can't help but put tenderness and love into my singing when I do it for her. This changes the mechanics and the impact of the song.

Singers often tell me that they want to sing with more emotion but that they don't really know what is involved in learning this skill. That is both a great self-observation and an excellent issue to consider.

The very first step in singing with emotion is to know *what* emotion or emotions you want to experience and express in your song. The best way to answer this question is to create a song overview (like a book report) of each song you sing. In my experience, song overviews are more powerful and useful when they are written down instead of just hashed out verbally.

Exercise: Create a Song Overview

I invite you to write down your own song overview. First, choose a song for the exercise. Now think about who is singing the song—not the artist, but the character that you imagine the song and the artist are trying to portray. Is the character a teenage girl in the throes of her first love? An elderly man reflecting on his misspent youth? A lost soul who's crying out for help? What is the point of view of the character singing? Is the character a male or a female? Does the song deal with a particular character's personal experience, or does it involve more of a universal theme, with the character singing as an impersonal narrator? Whatever the case may be, have a clear idea of who is doing the singing. Then write down an answer for each of the following: who, what, when, where, and why. If you can't tell about one of these elements from the lyrics, either skip it or make up something for yourself that helps you to set the stage for the story.

For example, let's look at Bonnie Raitt's recording of the song "I Can't Make You Love Me." We could say that the singing character is a woman remarking to herself, in a poignant moment with her lover, that he will never be in the relationship the way that she is and that her heart will undoubtedly be broken, but that she wants one more night with him anyway. The *who* is a woman and her lover, the *what* is that she fears she's about to get her heart broken, the *when* is at night (we can assume this because of the lyrics "turn down the lights" and "here in the dark"). The *where* is probably a bedroom ("turn down the bed"), and the *why* is he's not in love with her in the way that she is with him. By answering each of the who, what, when, where, and why questions, you have created a song overview.

Now that you have an overview, the next step is to identify what *you* feel about the story and what emotions you want to express while you are singing the song. I ask singers to condense these feelings into a couple of one-word emotional tags, such as elation, sadness, joy, envy, and so forth. When you're singing, you'll find it easier to remember these tags than whole sentences that explain the feelings. In our example we might choose the word sadness because her heart is breaking; the word bittersweet because she loves him anyway; and the word longing because she yearns for things to be different.

Now focus on the words sad, bittersweet, and longing as you record yourself singing the song. Listen to your recorded performance. Can you hear these three emotions? Oftentimes, just being aware of what you want to express and what you want the audience to feel while you are singing will change the way you use mechanics to reflect those feelings.

Sometimes, though, we need a little help in knowing what to do to express a certain emotion. One way to get this help is to analyze recordings that make you feel a certain way. If you have a track of someone singing something that makes you feel sad, pinpoint what it is that the singer is doing that makes you feel sad. More often than not, he or she will be singing fairly softly, in balanced registration, with a vowel color on the darker side. Usually, the articulation will be legato (smooth and connected), not staccato (short and separated). Compare this to a recording of a song that makes you feel happy. The singer's volume will probably be louder, the vowel color will probably be brighter, and the articulation will probably be less legato. Angry usually sounds even louder, brighter, and more staccato. Obviously, these are not hard-and-fast rules, but they will help you become aware that the way you use mechanics directly affects the emotional impact of your singing, and vice versa.

When the Beatles recorded "I Want to Hold Your Hand," they used an upbeat arrangement, fairly loud vocals sung in pure heavy register with bright vowel color, and a staccato articulation. The result was a fun, danceable track that feels happy. The version in the movie *Across the Universe* (a similar version was also featured in the TV series *Glee*) was performed at a slower tempo with mostly balanced registration, a darker vowel color, and a legato articulation. As a result, this version is more poignant, and it borders on portraying sadness. By having different emotions in mind and using vocal elements in a way that supports those emotions, the performers of the slower versions of "I Want to Hold Your Hand" deliver what almost seems like a completely different song.

One way to practice this is to record yourself singing a line from a song several times, each time with a different emotion. Sing the line as though you are angry, sad, wistful, happy, bitter, frightened, ecstatic, heartbroken, bored—any emotion you can think of. Experiment with volume, vowel color, and all of the other vocal elements. As you listen to your recordings, take notes. Keep a file of which specific mechanics tend to create which emotions. These notes will be valuable in helping you to sing with emotion and to create your own style. Table 2 (below) lists some emotions that you can practice with, or you can come up with your own.

Table 2
Emotions

Negative Emotions	Positive Emotions
Anger	Cheerfulness
Annoyance	Compassion
Anxiety	Contentment
Contempt	Excitement

Despair	Gratitude
Envy	Happiness
Fear	Hopefulness
Guilt	Joy
Shame	Love
Shock	Pride

Once you've done this, it should be clear to you that it is very difficult to inject emotion into your singing without using dynamics. It's extremely challenging to make your audience feel what you want them to if all the vocal elements are constant through the entire song. Remember: if the vocal elements are on a flat line, your song has "flatlined." Even if sad is the emotion you're going for, you can accent certain words by singing them with more volume. If joy is your goal emotion, you can sing an occasional word quietly to make louder words stand out. Without some variation, your singing can seem stale—and that is one quality that most singers *don't* want to convey.

Your Ideal Voice Model

An important tool in the development of singing with power, passion, and confidence is your Ideal Voice Model (IVM). It involves creating an image of your ideal voice, learning to recognize the state of your voice in relation to that image, and building a singer's toolbox that contains the tools you need to adjust your voice so that it matches your vocal image as closely as possible.

If I had a magic wand, tapped you on the head, and said, "You've now got the singing voice you've always wanted!" what would your voice sound like? By having an image of how you want to sound, you give yourself a target to aim for as you do your exercises and work your voice in practice songs. This image is your Ideal Voice Model.

The first step in creating your IVM is to determine the type of voice that you have. One of the main factors in typing voices is what is called the *weight* of the voice. The weight of the voice is actually the most accurate tool to use to determine whether a singer is a bass, a baritone, a tenor, an alto, a soprano, and so forth. The common misconception is that these classifications are made by how high and how low you can sing—your range. The weight of your voice, however, is determined by how deep your voice is and the range of its "comfort zone." The musical term for the comfort zone is *tessitura*. In other words, if your voice falls into the "baritone" category but you learn to sing a high C, this does not suddenly make you a tenor. It simply means that you are a baritone who is able to sing high notes. You will not, however, sound the same as a tenor singing a high C because the note is not in your comfort zone. You will have to work harder to reach the note and, when you do hit it, your voice will have a deeper sound than the voice of a tenor. (To hear examples of different weights of voices, listen to track 24 of Listen and Learn.)

Remember—we are not referring to strength when we speak about different weights of voice; it's more about how deep the voice is and about the range in which a singer can comfortably sing. A bass has a deeper voice, a baritone a less deep voice, a tenor an even less deep voice, and on up through alto, mezzo, and soprano.

If you want to sing classical or operatic material or sing in a choir, you will undoubtedly be "classified" as a tenor, a soprano, or what have you for the purpose of repertoire. For most other types of singing, it's not important to know your classification. It does help, however, when it comes to creating your IVM, to be able to hear different weights of voices.

Listen to recordings of your own voice and to the voices of other singers until you have identified three or four singers that you like and whose voice weight is similar to yours. This comparison can be very challenging for many singers because they feel that comparing their voice weight to that of another artist means they are saying that their skill level is the same as that of the artist's. Don't focus on whether or not you are "as good" as a singer you listen to—only on whether or not the weight sounds similar. It may help you to also listen to some voices that have very different weights than yours—the contrast can sometimes help you to pick up on similarities in your voice and other artists' voices more clearly.

Make a recording of snippets of songs sung by each singer you choose for your IVM—just a line or two of each song that really moves you from each singer. By listening to these snippets over and over, you can extract the best aspects of voices that are similar in weight to yours and that sound good to you—like your voice would if it worked just the way you wanted it to. You'll begin to notice how these singers use support, vowel color, and registration. You'll also be able to study and absorb how they pronounce vowels, how they move from low notes to high ones, and how they use other vocal elements and principles. Keep in mind that the IVM is not intended to teach you to imitate someone, but to help you to be able to add to your own repertoire the best qualities of singers you admire. (Obviously, you want to choose singers for your model who not only have a similar voice weight to yours, but who also have high skill levels.)

The next step in using this model is to listen to one of the snippets and then record yourself singing the same section. This will speed up the process of imprinting your IVM into your voice. If you have a tough time matching a vocal element of another singer, use numbers on our scale of 1 to 10. For instance, figure out the vowel color the singer is using, put a number on it, and use that number to help your body sing the same vowel color. If you listen to yourself on the recording and it doesn't match up, rerecord yourself using a different number until it does match. Again, this is not about impersonating another singer—it's about using the principles in the same ways that these professional singers do to increase your skill level.

The next step in creating your IVM is to record yourself singing a line or two when your voice is working really well. Here, you're using yourself as your own ideal model! This can help you learn to adjust your voice when it feels or sounds less than perfect. By noticing where your voice is in relation to an example of yourself singing well, you can more easily diagnose the current shape of your voice. This can be really helpful on days when it feels like something is wrong. Record yourself and compare it to your model. What do you need to do or change to get closer to your ideal sound? When you are having a day where your instrument is not working as well as it can and doesn't match your IVM, you may find that you have to work harder and make more adjustments, but it doesn't mean the sound has to suffer.

While learning to sing you have to balance three things: your habits—the factors that determined the voice of your past; your Ideal Voice Model—the voice of your future; and what you are focusing on in your practice right now—the voice of your present. By staying aware of each of these things, you can more easily navigate this balance and experience much more joy in your singing.

Visualize the Ideal Sound

One of the bonuses of creating your Ideal Voice Model is that you will develop the ability to visualize exactly how you want to sound while singing a line in a song, even if you can't yet make that sound. By visualizing the emotions you want your voice to express, you direct your body to use mechanics in a way that supports those emotions.

How does visualization help you to attain your vocal goals? Let's say, for example, that you face a challenging high note in a particular line. It's critical that you can "hear," in your mind, exactly how you want it to sound, even though you may not yet be able to produce that sound. If you visualize singing a 7 vowel color and a 6 volume using a 60/40 registration, your support system muscles and the walls of your throat will attempt to create this combination. You may not *yet* be strong enough or have the fine muscle coordination to achieve the desired result—but, by sending these instructions to your body, you are laying the groundwork to increase your skill level. Because we are working with complex muscle systems in singing, changes don't usually occur overnight. However, the process can be accelerated by visualizing the sound you want.

How does this work? In his article "The Power of Visualization for Achieving Your Goals," John Assaraf, a noted spiritual advisor who is featured in the bestselling book *The Secret*, explains: "The reason athletes practice visualization is because they want to condition their minds in such a way that the body automatically behaves the way they want it to without effort. It is the only way to become 'unconsciously competent.'"

Because singing is a lot like an athletic activity, in which you are vigorously using muscles, having the desired mechanics built into muscle memory makes everything easier when you sing. The main reason that visualization affects the sound you create during singing is that you are using intention to direct your instrument. Most singers unconsciously cross their fingers and hope they sound good when they start to sing; they don't direct the body by using any clear instructions because they have no clear intentions about the desired sound. By not telling the body what you want it to create, you will often get a sound that you don't want or like. This is where using numbers on a scale of 1 to 10 can be so powerful. You can have a way to tell your instrument exactly what you want it to do—and that's a lot better than telling it, simply, "Please sound good—*please*!" Visualization not only helps your body learn new skills, but it also trains your body to automatically use those skills without you having to micromanage the process.

The Comparison Game

When building your Ideal Voice Model, you have to walk a fine line between observing where you are in relation to another voice and comparing yourself to that singer. It's easy, tempting, and part of human nature to compare yourself to others, and it is no different when it comes to singing. I can think of nothing more damaging to your progress, however, than to stack yourself up "against" someone else. There will always be singers who are more skilled and less skilled than you, and where you are in this line is unimportant.

You might find yourself comparing your skill or talent to those of other singers in a conscious way by listening to a recording of yourself and judging your voice in relation to another. You might do this subconsciously by telling yourself you don't sound good, when you are really thinking, "Not like *so and so* sounds." These judgments will only serve to sabotage your development. Remember—you will be making some temporary sounds as you work through certain vocal principles, and it's apples and oranges to compare your voice during this process to the voice of some other singer.

If you compare yourself to someone on the radio or on a recording, you are telling yourself that you "should" already be an advanced singer. If what you hear in your voice doesn't sound as good to you, you may be tempted to think that you don't really have a voice to work with or that you don't have what it takes to be a singer.

Each of us has a voice. That is true both literally and figuratively. Each of us has an original story—a view of the world around us—that is shaped by what we sing and how we sing it, and it is worth sharing with others. Don't set yourself up for needless disappointment by comparing yourself to someone else. Give yourself—and the world—the gift of experiencing the uniqueness that is you.

Where comparisons *can* be useful is in comparing your own singing in relation to what you intended to sing. Questions like, "Did I sing the vowel color that I wanted to sing?" or, "Did I sing in the registration that I intended to?" can be useful. It is valuable to be able to identify specific elements in your singing that are not working for you.

When we compare ourselves to others, however, we tend to throw the baby out with the bathwater and tell ourselves things like "I don't sound good" or "my voice sounds terrible." If we don't find out what *does* work as well as what doesn't, we feed our fears. I'm reminded of a story that Julia Cameron, the author of *The Artist's Way*, tells of director Martin Scorsese and the discoveries he made when he spoke to college film students. Many of them had an unrealistic assumption that his genius had shown up, right from the start, as perfection in everything that he did.

Scorsese found that most of the freshmen expected their first efforts to be masterpieces. From then on, he began his lectures to film students by showing them his very first movie, which was awful. This gave the students a glimpse of how he had progressed over the years. It also allowed them to see that everyone must develop their skills, that there are very few instant successes in any field.

Singing Without Attachment

One of my yoga teachers once gave a great talk on karma yoga (karma means action). Basically, the concept refers to the performance of selfless service for others. This is very relevant to singing because it speaks to the heart of our motivation to sing. We can be obsessed with the outcome of our performance or we can let it unfold without attachment. "Without attachment" means giving your gift through your song and letting go of how it is received. This may feel almost impossible to you at first, but as you begin to realize that you have no control over how others think about your singing, you may actually feel liberated. You can stop laboring to "make everyone like your singing" (because that's impossible) and focus on allowing as much of your unique personality, life experience, and view of the world to come through your voice as you can. We really have two choices when we perform: we can sing to *get* something or we can sing to *give* something. In other words, we can sing in the hopes of receiving adulation, fame, riches, or even just a smile—or we can sing to give something of ourselves, whether it's our voice, our emotions, or our desire to connect to another human being.

When I was in my 20s I sang as much to meet girls, impress my friends, and live as a "rock star" as I did to experience my love of music and the joy I derived from performing. The more I sang, the more I wanted validation, attention, and glory. I became very frustrated because, even though I received positive feedback, it was never enough. I wanted everyone to *love* what I did. I wanted everyone to appreciate my singing. But you know what? That will never happen. It's such a cliché, but it's so true: you cannot please all of the people all of the time. You free yourself to *be* yourself as soon as you get in touch with the fact that, at every performance you give, there will probably be someone in the audience who doesn't love what you do. As saxophonist Joshua Redman once said, "If everyone liked what I did, I probably wouldn't be playing anything of depth."

It is difficult to truly be yourself if you are trying to achieve perfection and please everyone. Often this is our motivation in singing. I once asked a student about her goals as a singer. She replied, "I want to have a perfect performance." When I asked her what she meant by that, she said that, in a perfect performance, she would sing all the notes in tune, she would remember all the lyrics, she would look comfortable on the stage, and *everyone* would love her.

Folks, that last part is *not* going to happen. You can't control others and their reactions; you can only have an opportunity to control yourself. We are spiritual beings in human form, and what defines that human form is glorious imperfection. Allowing for that imperfection frees us to improvise, to take chances, and to blaze new trails that we wouldn't dare allow to happen if we were attached to being perfect. In fact, being attached to perfection makes it almost impossible to learn to sing with power, passion, and confidence.

At a recent performance I was singing one of my original songs. When I got to the first chorus, I sang the first two lines—and then I completely forgot the third line. I stopped, looked out at the audience as if it were a trusted friend, and sheepishly admitted that there was a really a great lyric that was supposed to go in that spot but that I couldn't remember it. Everyone laughed, and I went back to the beginning of the chorus, assuming that singing it again would jar my memory. No deal. I ended up singing the entire song, complete with all three choruses—each time singing "something cool goes right here" when I hit the spot where the line I couldn't remember was supposed to be.

When I finished the song I got a standing ovation, and that day I sold all the CDs I had brought with me. One guy even asked me, after the performance, if I had staged the whole thing so that he would have to buy my CD to hear the missing lyric! (Hmmm . . . there's a marketing idea.) People loved the fact that I was human onstage—that I was imperfect—and that I didn't (couldn't) try to hide it. Because I didn't freak out, the whole thing felt very lighthearted and fun. I got to remember and experience what I tell singers all the time—it's not about singing perfectly. A good performance is about connecting with the audience and telling the story of the song.

Learning to improvise, experimenting with style, and exploring the vocal principles requires that you allow "imperfections" to occur along the way. No one can immediately move from the place they are to the place they want to be without stumbling along the way. It's part of the journey of learning. My friend Mark Fountain says, "The only people who don't hit bad notes are the people who don't sing."

There is a Japanese aesthetic system called wabi-sabi (I love that word). Wabi-sabi is all about recognizing and embracing the beauty in the imperfect. From Wikipedia comes this definition: "At the core of wabi-sabi is the importance of transcending ways of looking and thinking about things [and] existence."

Here are the principles of wabi-sabi:
- All things are impermanent
- All things are imperfect
- All things are incomplete

Wabi-sabi is characterized by the following terms:
- Suggestion of natural process
- Irregular
- Intimate
- Unpretentious
- Earthy
- Simple

I love looking at singing in this light. It's much more real than having expectations of perfection in a performance. When I sing, the more I observe without attachment what, in the past, I would have called "mistakes," the more I experience the joy of singing. The great jazz pianist Thelonious Monk once said to a fellow musician, "You play too perfect. You've got to make a mistake to discover the new stuff." To that sentiment you can add the words of the legendary jazz trumpeter Miles Davis, who said, "Do not fear mistakes; there are none." I look at mistakes as merely unplanned events. They might work; they might not—and it's (usually) OK either way.

Kathy, a friend of mine who studies singing with me, was about to audition to sing the national anthem at a sporting event. At one of her lessons she confided to me that she was having trouble getting rid of a nagging memory of having "flubbed up" singing in public in the past. She was afraid she would do it again at the audition. She compared it to striking out at a baseball game and having to come to bat again a few innings later, afraid she would strike out again. I reminded her that, in Major League Baseball, a great hitter is one who has a batting average over .300. That means that three out of ten times he gets a base hit—which means that seven out of ten times he doesn't. In other words, you don't have to hit perfectly every time in order to be considered a good hitter. The same goes with singing. It's not how perfectly you sing the notes—it's how willing you are to turn yourself "inside out."

What I mean by that is your willingness to take everything you keep inside you—your thoughts, feelings, experience, and personality—and share it through your singing. Yes, you will probably feel vulnerable. Yes, it can be scary. And no, everything won't be perfect. But once you truly turn yourself inside out, you can experience the joy of singing. This is where making art happens, this is what will free your voice, and this is what allows you to sing with power, passion, and confidence.

When I first decided to start writing my own songs, I spent years—literally—composing my first one. I would write a line, measure it to see if it was "hit worthy" (perfect), and throw it out because it wasn't. Only when I got so frustrated with never finishing anything did I finally let go of editing every line as it came out and allow myself to write something that I knew wasn't perfect. My first few songs weren't great, but they were finished pieces of art and I was able to learn from them. I began to see that I had something to say, something to give, and this became my motivation to sing. When you realize that every one of us has a gift to give and has our own singing voice-print—one that is absolutely unique—it can become easier to let go of any attachment to being perfect. Doing good work and making art is much more fun than trying to be perfect. Once you embrace this idea, you'll have taken a major step toward turning your fear into joy and creating confidence in your singing.

Important Points to Remember

- In order to sing with emotion, you must be aware of *which* emotions you want to express in your performance and you must sing with the conscious intention of expressing them.

- You can create a song overview to help you to identify the emotions you want to convey in the song.

- Specific choices in vocal mechanics can help you to express different emotions during singing.

- Your Ideal Voice Model (IVM) is your perception of all the attributes that make up your ideal voice.

- Your IVM can help you to recognize the state of your voice at any given moment.

- Visualize the sound you want, even if you can't make it—yet. Visualization helps your body to figure out the mechanics needed to create your target sound.

- Comparing yourself to another singer is a no-win proposition.

- Comparisons of your singing to what you have done previously and to what you intended to do are the only comparisons that are of value.

- "Singing to give," not "singing to get," will help you focus on sharing your gift and you'll more easily experience joy when you sing.

- Perfect mechanics are not what make for great singing. Great singing happens when you are not obsessed with the outcome but instead allow the singing to unfold in its own way.

- Remember the principles of wabi-sabi when you sing: nothing is perfect; nothing is ever complete; we are all works in progress.

Step 3

Confidence
Make a Move, Make a Connection

11

Practice Makes Permanent—How to Integrate What You've Been Learning

In the early 1980s I was in a band called Puzzle. One day our manager told us he had a surprise for us. He knew someone who knew someone and, as a result, was able to hire as our band consultant Dick Nicklaus (who was also credited on albums as Dick Peterson). Dick is the drummer for the Kingsmen, whose recording of the classic song "Louie Louie" was one of the biggest hits of the '60s. (Thanks to its practically unintelligible lyrics and the establishment's general suspicion of all things rock 'n' roll at the time, the recording was also was the target of an FBI investigation on obscenity. After much ado about nothing, the case was dropped for lack of evidence. Later in my career I played a few gigs with Jack Ely, the lead singer on the recording, who told me that he had braces on his teeth when he sang the vocal— something that certainly couldn't have helped in terms of his diction. Say . . . perhaps there *is* something to be said for less-than-perfect vocal mechanics!)

At any rate, my bandmates and I were pretty excited to be working with Dick, and we set up our equipment in our manager's garage for a rehearsal. Dick listened to us play a song we'd been working on, then took a metronome out of his bag. He had us put a microphone close to it so we could hear it through the sound system, and he asked us to practice with it for a few minutes while he talked to our manager. Every time we came to the chorus of the song, the metronome began to slow down. Finally, we couldn't stand it anymore and we turned the thing off.

When Dick came back and asked us how it went, we told him about the defective metronome. Smiling, he replied gently, "No, you guys are actually speeding up every time you get to the chorus." We didn't want to argue with such an icon of the music business, but we knew he was wrong. After much coaxing on Dick's part, we agreed to try an experiment: we'd go ahead and play the entire song, including the chorus, at the speed of the "defective" metronome. Yet, even though we deliberately tried to keep pace with it throughout the entire song, we once again found ourselves speeding up as we hit the chorus. We had to admit that the problem was ours, not the metronome's—and we were shocked at how difficult it was for us to play the chorus at the right speed. By that point, we were so used to playing the song incorrectly that speeding up had become an ingrained habit, and it took a lot of hard work and focus to break ourselves of it.

The old saying "practice makes perfect" is not true at all. In reality, practice makes *permanent*. Whatever you practice becomes a habit. What you put your focused attention on while practicing becomes burned into muscle memory. Researchers have determined that behaviors are not learned simply by performing repetitions of those behaviors. New brain connections are created and learning occurs only when full, focused attention is used. That's why it is very important that you become intentional about not only *what* you practice, but also *when*, *where*, and *how* you practice.

While there is no such thing as "perfect" when it comes to singing, the right method of practicing can help you to deliver sparkling performances. In this chapter we will look at all the factors that make for productive practice.

Your Learning Style

No one learns to sing in exactly the same way as anyone else. It can be very valuable to discover how you best learn something new.

There are three main ways in which we take in and process information. While no one exclusively uses one method—there is a lot of overlap among these methods—when it comes to learning, each of us favors one of these three approaches. One works best for some people, while one of the other methods work best for others.

1. Visual learners like to see demonstrations, read directions, see pictures, graphs, and charts, and create images in their minds.

2. Auditory learners prefer to hear instructions, samples, and models.

3. Kinesthetic learners like to learn through touch and other forms of sensation; they prefer hands-on interaction and instructions about what to experience internally while learning.

If you find yourself using words like "seeing where the song is going" or picturing the lift and resistance of support as two hands opposing each other, you are probably more of a visual learner. If you use words like "I hear what you mean" and you find that listening to an audio example is more useful than reading a description, you are probably more of an auditory learner. If you use words like "I can feel the difference" and you find that placing your hands on different parts of your body really helps you to focus while singing, you are likely more of a kinesthetic learner.

By discovering the style of learning that suits you best, you can make learning to sing much easier, more streamlined, and more fun. You can directly go to the information that you can more quickly take in and process.

In both this book and the Vocal Power Workout and Listen and Learn sections of my website, I have provided information in each of the three ways whenever possible in order to help you progress no matter which learning style you prefer. It's important to remember, however, that while each of us favors one style of learning over the others, almost all of us learn faster and better retain and access information that is learned through a combination of all three methods.

How good are we at retaining the information we take in? It depends on how we take in and process that information.

Table 3
Retaining Information

You retain:

10% of what you read.

(Dark vowel color is the sound used by opera singers)

20% of what you hear.

(Track 4 of Listen and Learn is an example of dark vowel color)

30% of what you see.

(There is an opera singer on TV widely opening her jaw and singing a dark vowel color)

50% of what you hear and see.

(I can hear how dark that opera singer on TV is singing)

70% of what you say and write.

(I will say "open the jaw to sing dark" as I write it)

90% of what you say as you do something.

(I will say "open the jaw to sing dark" and then sing with a dark vowel color)

While the percentages noted above may not be absolutely true for all people (as each person has his or her own favored learning style), it is clear that everyone can retain *more* information by combining all three types of learning styles—visual, auditory, and kinesthetic. For example, if you write down your intention (visual), then say it out loud (auditory) before you begin your practice (kinesthetic), you can really help to speed up the learning curve.

It is also important to determine whether you are a "linear" or a "holistic" learner. Linear learners like step-by-step instructions, and they like to take in information in small chunks that they eventually piece together in a logical progression. In contrast, holistic learners like to see the big picture, know the overall strategy, and experiment with the different steps of the process, sometimes doing them out of order. Knowing which of these approaches you tend to use can help you learn to sing more efficiently.

Where to Practice

Where you practice singing is incredibly important. Ideally, your practice space will contain some type of equipment that allows you to record yourself so that you can listen to, analyze, and re-record your singing as part of your practice. Select a place that is safe to sing loudly—one where you won't be heard by anyone who might "volunteer" to analyze your approach or give you unwanted feedback. If you live in an apartment or a condo or with family members or roommates, your home can make for a challenging practice environment, and you may have to negotiate with neighbors or others in your home in order to make this work for everyone involved so that you don't bother others with your singing and they don't bother you with unsolicited feedback or advice. No matter what your circumstances are, it's important to create the best, safest practice environment that you can.

Part of your practice will involve singing in pure heavy register. This involves singing with quite a bit of power, often fairly loudly. If you don't feel safe singing loudly in your practice space, you'll find it very difficult to master the basic skills you need to be a good singer. So what do you do if you live in an apartment or a condo, or with friends and family? One of the easiest ways to solve this issue is to make your car (or your family's car) your practice studio. If it feels safe to be parked in front of your house or in a driveway, practice there. If not, you can drive a couple of blocks away or to a parking lot and practice there.

An additional option is to soundproof a room or garage. For years, teenagers have tacked empty egg cartons to garage walls to cut down the volume of band rehearsals. Thick curtains or blankets can also help, as can foam padding. Experiment by playing a stereo loudly in your practice space while walking the perimeter. If you can barely hear the music, it should be a safe environment for vocalizing. The bottom line is this: Do whatever you need to do in order to have a safe place to practice. It's critical to your development as a singer.

Keep It Under Your Hat

Even though family members or friends may be interested in your pursuit of singing, be very careful about who you allow to actively listen to your practice sessions. The sounds you'll be making in exercises and practice songs can be very confusing to someone who's not aware of the process. Having to constantly explain why you're making certain sounds, why songs sound a certain way, what your overall strategy is, and so forth can be very tiring and may even cause you to question your own process. Choose wisely who you let into your "inner circle" as you develop your singing. You can be in a vulnerable place emotionally during practice, so it may be very easy for someone on the outside to upset your balance—even if that person has good intentions.

In her book *The Artist's Way*, Julia Cameron cautions readers to be very careful about who they allow to witness their flowering as an artist. People can be envious, afraid of change, afraid of losing their friend, or threatened by the fact that someone is pursuing his or her dream and they aren't. It's not uncommon for friends, family members, or other people to lash out at singers as they explore their own voices and artistry. In addition, some people seem to get a kick out of witnessing others fail or struggle as they pursue their goals. (The German word for this is *schadenfreude*, which means to take pleasure in someone else's hardship or misfortune.) Instead of working to improve their own abilities or lives, these people prefer to drag others down in order to "level the playing field."

The opposite of schadenfreude is a Buddhist concept called *mudita*, which is loosely translated as "experiencing joy in another's good fortune." As much as you can during the beginning of your "vocal exploration" and when you try out new sounds or methods, share your singing with only those people who embrace this concept (whether or not they know its name) and who are emotionally healthy enough to support you on your path. Many people struggle with their own, self-sabotaging inner voices as they go through this process. Focus on getting rid of any internal negativity you may have and avoid exposing yourself to negativity from those around you. Trust me—there's no advantage to getting "help" from a doubting Thomas when you're learning something new.

How to Learn a New Song

On the surface, this might seem to be a subject that needs no explanation. You have a new song to learn, so you just start singing it, and you go over and over the whole song each time until you've got it down, right? Not exactly. That is a recipe for wasted time and having to undo mistakes you may have already programmed into the song.

If, as you're working a new song, you sing all the way through it each time, you'll likely notice things that aren't correct. This could be a wrong melody note or a rhythm that's not quite right. You might notice that you're not entering a line in the correct place. Or you might be having difficulty phrasing the lyrics correctly. There could be any number of mechanics issues when it comes to singing the vowel color, registration, or note that you want.

Most singers observe these occurrences as they go by, vowing to do better the next time they sing the song. The problem is that, if you continue to sing the entire song each time, it will be a little while before you arrive at those problem areas again. By the time you do reach those problem areas, odds are good that you will have forgotten what you wanted to change, and you will then experience the same problems again. In reality, by repeating them each time, you are more deeply programming these problems into your singing—and it will take much longer for you to learn to "undo" the problems than it would if you simply worked through each problem as you came to it.

Here's a more productive way to learn a song. By following the steps outlined below, you can build sections of the song correctly instead of repeating an entire song that's full of problems.

1. Listen to the song a couple of times in order to "get the big picture."

2. Starting at the beginning of the song, sing until you run into the first snag. Stop, figure out what the issue is—melody, timing, mechanics, lyrics, or whatever it may be—and determine how to fix it.

3. Then sing through the same part again. Were you able to change the problem? If not, continue to sing the same part, adjusting how you are singing until you get what you want. It is very helpful to isolate a line or even just a few words or notes so that you can sing a few repetitions of the same part in a short time. In this way you can focus on what you want to change and what you have to do to make the change, and you can then program in what you want to be singing at that spot in the song.

4. Once you have cleaned up the first issue, sing until another issue appears, and repeat the process.

One challenge with this method is that, for many people, it is more fun to sing the entire song every time than it is to work on one small part at a time. As a way to stay engaged and have fun as you're working on a song, you can reward yourself by singing the entire thing every few minutes. As long as you don't do this too frequently, and as long as you balance it with actual practice to work through the song, you won't have to worry about programming in mistakes. This is also a good way to gauge what you have left to work on when you go back to cleaning up each problem as it comes up. Just don't let yourself lose sight of the reason you're practicing in the first place. If all the singing you do is practice singing and none of it is for fun—done just to experience the joy of singing—you will quickly lose sight of what you're practicing for. Make sure you have a balance of "work" and "play" in your singing time.

Practicing While Sitting or Standing

I was recently working in my studio with one of my students, Stephen, who is a jazz singer and a guitar player. We were exploring the differences he feels when singing his exercises while standing, sitting, and holding his guitar.

In theory, it's easier to create support when you're sitting than it is when you're standing. When you stand, the major abdominal muscle, which is called the rectus abdominis, tightens and holds the other abdominal muscles in place. This makes it more difficult to move your belly in and out and to create support, and it's why I recommend that you sit to sing your exercises whenever possible. When you're sitting, the rectus abdominis relaxes, allowing the other abdominal muscles to help with lifting and resisting. Then, if you stand while practicing *songs*, your abdominal muscles will get used to the extra workload needed to create support and will automatically adjust during performances.

Some singers, however, find it easier to sing when standing than when sitting. Stephen discovered that, when he stands, the tightening of his belly muscles helps him to develop a feeling of resistance, as if he's creating support just by standing up. When Stephen sits, he has to work much more consciously and actively to create support than he does when he stands.

I want to pass on to you the method that Stephen found to encourage lift and resistance when he sings his exercises in the car. It's similar to the exercise of lifting against an immovable object that I had you experiment with in chapter 4, and it may help some of you to more easily create support when you're sitting.

Do not attempt the following when you're behind the wheel of a car that is in motion or that is temporarily stopped (say, at a traffic signal). Use this technique only when the car is parked and the engine is turned off.

If the seat of your car is high enough, you can lift against the steering wheel with either your knees or your thighs and cause your abdominals to tighten. This creates the same resistance that's needed for support. It may not be to the same degree that you'll use during a performance, but it is still a good way to exercise your support muscles. By periodically lifting against the wheel, you can help the support action stay firmly programmed in muscle memory.

Recording and Analyzing Your Voice

One of the most powerful ways to develop both your voice and your ears is to record yourself singing. While there are some challenges to recording yourself, I believe that these are outweighed by the results you can achieve.

Selecting a Recording Device

When it comes to recording your voice, the first challenge is to get the best audio quality possible. There are all kinds of recording devices out there, and some offer better audio quality than others.

At the bottom is the microcassette recorder, which is often used for dictation. It's better than nothing, but it's not going to inspire you to record yourself on a regular basis because the sound quality isn't very good.

The next step up is the small, handheld digital recorder. Its sound quality is better than that of a microcassette recorder, but its tiny speakers produce tinny sound that's not as accurate as it could be. A way to improve the sound quality of these recorders is to plug them into a system with better speakers (such as a computer, a home stereo system, or a musical instrument amplifier). With the proper cable and adapters, the sound of your voice can come out of the headphone jack on the recorder and into an amplification system. Stores such as RadioShack can help you with this.

Cassette recorders do a pretty good job of capturing and reproducing sound, but these devices are quickly becoming a thing of the past. Pawn shops and second-hand stores are good sources for older, used cassette recorders.

There are dozens of computer software programs on the market that allow you to record your singing and download your recordings to your computer for burning to a CD or MP3 audio file, which can then be loaded onto an iPod or other MP3 player. If you search online for "free recording software," you'll find a number of basic programs that you can use at no charge. Many Mac computers come with the software program GarageBand already loaded; it works well for this purpose, but there's a small learning curve involved in using it. In addition, you'll need a USB microphone that you can plug into your computer's USB port. You can purchase fairly inexpensive USB microphones at stores such as RadioShack, Best Buy, and OfficeMax.

One of my favorite recording devices is the portable digital recorder that can record directly onto its own internal disk drive or memory card. With this type of recorder, it's easy to record anywhere. The audio quality is phenomenal, the device is easy to use, and you can easily transfer your recordings to your computer or MP3 player. The manufacturer Zoom makes a line of good-quality, relatively inexpensive portable digital recorders; these can be found at Amazon.com and other stores.

That's Not Me!

Whichever recording device you choose, your next challenge is to stay disciplined about recording yourself on a regular basis. This can be difficult at first if, like many other singers, you find that your recorded voice does not sound as good to you as the voice you hear inside your head when you're singing. I've heard singers describe their recorded voices as sounding thin, brittle, shallow, tinny, high-pitched, childlike—the list goes on and on.

There are physiological reasons that your voice sounds different on a recording than it does in your head. When I hear you sing, my auditory nerves are stimulated by one sound source—the vibrations that travel out of your mouth, through the air, and into my ears. When you hear yourself sing, you're receiving two sound sources—the vibrations that travel out of your mouth and into your ears; and the vibrations that travel inside your body through the bones and the cavities of your skull, directly striking the inner ear without first going through the outer ear. The effect of the bones and spaces of the skull on vocal vibration is to add a deeper, richer tone to the sound. Unfortunately, at least at first, the rest of the world doesn't hear the effect that you hear thanks to the second sound source. But you can learn how to make what *we* hear sound like what *you* hear by making your voice fully resonant—and the best way to do that is to record yourself singing.

The more you hear your recorded voice, the sooner your voice will become fully resonant. Part of this process may involve a conscious change in the sound you make, but your body will also begin to help the process without your being aware of it. As you hear a more accurate representation of your voice by listening to recordings of it, your "mind's ear" begins to hear this inside your head when you sing. This is why it is so important to record and listen to yourself often. It is much easier to work on a specific element, such as vowel color, registration, vibrato, and so forth, when you can listen to your voice on a recording instead of having to rely on what you hear as you are singing.

One of the best ways to learn how to control a vocal element is to make a uniform vocal line—say, with no vibrato, or with a certain vowel color all the way through. By recording yourself as you sing, you can immediately tell whether or not your intention was achieved. If it wasn't, immediately re-record the line and see if you can make the necessary adjustment. This is much more effective than singing all the way through a song and trying to remember to adjust something the next time you sing it.

Rehearsing with a Group

It frequently happens that singers have more problems with their voices while rehearsing than they ever do at a performance. By knowing what to focus on at a rehearsal, especially a group rehearsal, you can help to avoid these problems and make practice sessions more productive.

Whether you're practicing with a band, other vocalists, or both, you have to be able to hear yourself when you sing during rehearsals. I can't stress this point too much. More singers have "blown out their voices" (made themselves temporarily hoarse from oversinging, straining, or not singing with support for extended periods) because they weren't able to hear themselves at a rehearsal than almost all other reasons combined. If you are working with a band, you may be up against the age-old battle of singers versus instrumentalists when it comes to volume. Please let your bandmates know if you experience difficulty hearing yourself. If they can't hear themselves play, they're probably not going to hurt themselves—but if you can't hear your voice, you can easily trash it. The same goes if you are in a choir and your own voice is being drowned out by a louder voice nearby. If this is the case, ask to trade places with someone else in your section or talk to the director about changing your placement in the group.

Being able to hear your voice may involve moving speakers so that they don't produce feedback (a squealing noise) when you turn up the volume. It can also involve turning down instruments, playing with more dynamics, or simply getting everyone in the band clear on the fact that, whenever the singer is singing, his or her instrument takes priority over all others.

Here's a tip if you are rehearsing with a group: Try setting up in a circle. When everyone is facing each other, it can be easier to hear both yourself and all of the others than it is when you set up in a straight line, as you might when you're onstage. Also, when you rehearse in a circle, you may find that you don't have to practice with as much volume as you would otherwise.

If you've tried everything and you still can't hear yourself well, rely as much as possible on feel to help you use the appropriate power and reduce the stress to your voice (see chapter 3).

A great way to reduce stress to your voice during rehearsal is to sing at a lower volume than you would during a performance. Another great way is to sing everything an octave lower while the band or the vocal group is learning parts or experimenting with arrangements. In the worlds of opera and theater, this is called "blocking" the vocals. There is no reason to sing with performance power while one of the instrumentalists tries different ways of playing the song. Wait until all of the parts and the arrangement have been decided on before you sing with the same power you would onstage. Your group may find this a little odd at first, but they will get used to it, and you will reduce the amount of fatigue and stress that's placed on your vocal folds.

You can make your voice last longer and your rehearsals more efficient by working on two songs at a time. Sing song A once or twice; then switch to song B and rehearse it a couple of times. Different melodies and dynamics work the vocal folds in different ways. By alternating between songs, you won't wear out your voice as quickly. The bonus is that, by rehearsing song A, switching to song B, then going back to A, you will more quickly find out whether or not parts and arrangements are being retained by the group and you will know what needs more work.

When rehearsing with a group—whether it's a band, a vocal ensemble, or a choir—the bottom line is to "conserve it for when you need it." In other words, don't work your instrument as hard during regular rehearsals as you would during a final pre-performance run-through, a dress rehearsal, or an actual performance. This will go a long way toward making rehearsals fun, productive, and easy on your voice.

Warming Up and Cooling Down

Singing involves the active, extended use of muscles, and these must be warmed up before being used and cooled down afterward to help prevent stiffening. The main reasons to warm up and stretch out muscles are as follows:

1. **To prevent injury.** This can show up as hoarseness or pain.

2. **To increase endurance.** By warming up first, you will be able to sing longer before becoming tired or hoarse.

3. **To increase vocal range.** Warm-ups enable you to sing higher and lower notes.

Too many singers do too little warming up before singing and then are disappointed in their results. A proper warm-up involves more than merely singing a couple of scales or running through a song lightly before a performance.

On the day of a performance, plan to spend more time warming up your voice than you would on a non-performance day (see Preparing for a Performance in chapter 12). Stretch your vocal folds so that you can reach all of the notes in your range easily, and "power up" your voice by singing, in pure heavy register, the highest notes that you will be singing in your performance. Once you can do that, pull back the power so that you can reach those notes in a balanced registration with less heavy register. This allows the vocal folds to stretch even farther.

The advantage to warming up the voice in this way is that, regardless of whether or not you actually plan to sing the highest notes in pure heavy register, you will be prepared and able to do so if you choose to. You will also have the option of singing the high notes using a balanced registration, which allows you to work less strenuously and, therefore, to have more endurance. An 80/20 balance of heavy and light register often works well in this situation. Obviously, the specific amount of heavy register you use in your balanced registration will be determined by your artistic intention for the song.

How much time should you allow between your warm-up and a performance? I suggest that you experiment to find out what works best for you. Many singers find that ending their warm-ups at least an hour before a performance allows the voice to rest without stiffening up. If you are working your voice too hard right before a performance, it may not have time to rebound before you start singing for your audience.

I discovered this fact the hard way. During one stretch where I had nine performances in five days, I experienced an alarming drop in my endurance. I couldn't figure out what was happening, so I brought it up during my next voice lesson. When my teacher asked me about my pre-performance exercise routine, I told him that I did my last set of exercises on the drive to the gig, often only 15 or 20 minutes before I hit the stage. I figured I would be good and warm by doing this. What I found out is that this routine just made my voice good and *tired*. When I changed my routine so that my warm-ups ended an hour or so before I was to start performing, my endurance increased dramatically.

After you've finished your pre-performance warm-up (either right after you finish warming up or sometime later during the day or night), you can use the glide exercise to keep your voice warm. The glide will also become your good friend after the performance.

The glide, an exercise that is described in chapter 8, is one of the best ways to both warm up and cool down the voice. It stretches the vocal folds all the way out without using enough of a workload to cause them to be overworked or to stiffen up. Remember: When singing the glide, never get louder than a 2.

> Both during your pre-performance warm-up and on the way home from a performance, sing glides until you can move through most, if not all, of your range without hitting any air pockets or stiff points.

If you are singing on consecutive days, it's critical that you cool down your voice between performances. This will make it much easier for you to "fire it up" the next day and to efficiently sing with power and control over the course of several consecutive days' performances.

Performing for a Challenge Person

You may find that, on occasion, you will be singing in front of what I call a "challenge person." This can be someone who seems supportive but whose opinion means a lot to you (such as a colleague, a friend, a relative, or a mentor), someone who may be neutral in terms of support but who could benefit your singing career (such as a choir director, a booking agent, a bandleader, or an audition director), or someone who tends to intimidate you by being negative or unsupportive. If you know that a challenge person will be listening to you sing, it can lead to extra tension and anxiety.

Martial arts experts know that the best way to prepare themselves for actual high-stress encounters is to practice defending against attack. Singers, too, need to practice dealing with threatening people or situations, as this will help immensely whenever a challenge person shows up at your performance.

What many singers experience when singing in front of a challenge person is a loss of focus. Remember: your attention should be on telling the story of your song. By staying focused and "climbing inside" the story, you may be able to let go of worrying about mechanics, whether or not you are good enough to impress the challenge person, or any other sabotaging thoughts that your ego can throw in your path.

The process of changing your experience when this happens is very much like the practice of meditation. While you are singing, you may notice a negative thought rise to your awareness—"Oh, great: so-and-so is here and I have to hit a really high note in this song." Simply observe the thought, release it, and move your focus back to the story of the song. With intention and practice, this will become easier and easier to do and, eventually, it will become second nature. It's the perfect opportunity to practice singing in the moment. If you practice singing for a challenge person of your choosing, you will become comfortable with performing in front of others whose presence may cause you to feel insecure. As a result, you'll actually make yourself a better, more confident singer overall—even when you're performing in front of a fully appreciative audience.

You can use the following techniques even if you don't have a designated challenge person: when you are practicing, just think of whoever you might dread suddenly appearing in the audience.

Regardless of whether you practice with a real or an imagined challenge person, notice what you feel as you sing—and how it affects your voice and your body.

- Does your throat begin to feel dry? This is a reminder of how important proper hydration is for singers.

- Are your shoulders lifting up? Is your head tilting back? Unwanted movements get in the way of creating and maintaining efficient support.

- Do you feel tightness or butterflies in your belly? When this occurs, the support system tends to break down and the old, less-efficient way of breathing can re-establish itself.

Here's a simple technique that will help your body to stay focused on maintaining proper support: Lightly place your fingertips on your belly (you can probably find a way to make this gesture fit into your singing without anyone being the wiser). This will bring your focus back to your support system and help your body to regain its balance through Bosnian Belly Breathing. (Note: you may need to exaggerate the expanding and lifting motion of the belly to get yourself back on track.) This one movement—placing the fingertips on the belly—can really ground you and help you to align your mechanics. Again, practice this often in front of your designated challenge person or while visualizing a challenge person appearing where you will be singing. With enough repetitions, it will become an automatic response.

It is important to realize that any fear you have about singing in front of a challenge person can be a symbol of your fears about singing in general. Most of us have feelings of vulnerability during the performance process. We're unsure if it is safe to open ourselves up—we are putting ourselves in a position where we could be ridiculed and have a negative experience. There's an important cliché to remember here: "You can't please everyone." I used to hear that a lot and think to myself, "Yeah, I know that." But I wasn't really living like I understood the concept. I had an unconscious expectation (actually, more of a hope) that everyone would love my singing. It's important to remember that there will always be people in an audience who don't love what you're doing. If you spend most of your energy trying to win everyone over and worrying that someone's not appreciating your performance, you'll find it difficult to sing in the moment.

Each time you sing, you have an opportunity to create art by revealing yourself. **You can't achieve this if you are focusing on trying to please everyone or worrying about someone not liking you.** We all get to learn to trust our own gifts and give them without attachment to an outcome. This is the unique opportunity you have when you sing in public, or even to just one other person.

Singing in a "Strong-Emotion" Situation

I got a call one night from a voice student of mine who is a minister. Someone at Jack's church needed the services of a singer for a funeral. Could I do it with two days' notice? "Sure," I told him—I'd sung at plenty of funerals, often on short notice. He told me the names of the two songs that the family had requested for their daughter's service, and I learned and rehearsed them. When I got to the church, I saw that the front of the sanctuary had been decorated like the girl's bedroom, with stuffed animals, posters, photos, and other items a child might cherish. It was only then that I discovered that the service was for a 13-year-old girl who had died on the operating table during a heart transplant operation, just before her new heart was to be implanted.

This was what I call a "strong-emotion" situation, or an "SES." I could feel tears welling up as I watched the family file into the first row. "What they must be going through," I thought. But I knew that, if I burst into tears during my singing, I wouldn't be able to continue and I wouldn't be able to serve the family in their time of need. Fortunately, I had already learned what I needed to do to get through an emotional situation such as this: I had to focus on the melody and lyrics of the song in such a way that I could put emotion into the singing without allowing any visual images to enter my consciousness.

What I mean by this is that, if I'd pictured that little girl on the operating table while I was singing, tears would have welled up. If I looked at the sanctuary and saw her bedroom in my mind, the same thing would have happened. The same went for looking at the family as I sang.

If you don't allow yourself to see or imagine visual images that create strong emotion, you will be much more able to focus on your singing and to do your best to meet others' needs. The practice of letting go of emotional images is much like meditation.

If you see or begin to think of an emotionally charged image, simply notice it, let it pass through your mind, and immediately return your focus to the song. I visualize that I'm underwater and that the image is a bubble that rises to the surface and gently bursts.

With practice, this technique will serve you well. This is what I used to "hold it together" so I could sing at that little girl's funeral. Because I had practiced the technique many times before I ever stepped into that church, I was able to move my attention away from any emotionally charged visual and back to telling the story of the song.

If you have enough time before singing in an SES, there is another technique you can use as well. When you are in a safe practice situation, allow your mind's eye to focus on a visual image that could cause you to experience strong emotion. You may find yourself getting choked up or crying every time you sing a certain song. If you make that OK, oftentimes after a few repetitions the energy of the emotion will begin to fade enough so that you can sing the song the way you would like to. Practice singing the song until you have moved through the strong emotion and have reached a point where you can tell the story of the song without losing your focus.

These techniques will work whether you are singing at a funeral, a wedding, a commencement ceremony, a retirement party, or in any other SES—even those where it's the song itself that causes you to feel strong emotions.

If you find yourself in a situation where you are very unsure that you can hold it together during a performance, you might also consider recording yourself singing the song beforehand for playback at an SES. While this may not be what you'd want in an ideal world, it is a way to have your vocals present at the event without having to worry about falling apart in a demanding situation. When my dad died, I decided that I would sing two songs that I had written about him at his funeral. I performed the first song at the beginning of the service and it went fine. The second song, however, came at the end of the service, and halfway through it I began crying and had to stop singing. I now wish I had recorded my performance beforehand to play there—a recording would have been much easier and less stressful for everyone—but I didn't know these techniques at the time, and the thought never occurred to me.

Memorizing Lyrics

Without a doubt, one of the biggest fears most singers have is that they'll forget the words of a song they're singing. Many singers have confided to me that they have poor memorization skills. My experience leads me to believe that it's not so much skill that they lack, but an awareness of *how* to memorize lyrics and the realization that it often takes real *work* to make it happen. Merely singing a song multiple times won't automatically burn the lyrics into your memory.

I've found four different memorization techniques that work well for many singers.

Memorization Technique 1: Write out, in longhand, the lyrics of the song. Yes, I know that takes time—but that's exactly why this works. The lyrics can take firmer root in your mind because you are slowly going over each word during the process. As you're writing, make a note of any story line or plot element in the lyric. This can make the order of the lyrics more obvious. After you write out the entire song, set aside your written lyrics and sing the song from memory. How did you do? If you had any trouble, write out the entire song again, then set aside the written lyrics and sing the song once more. If you are now able to remember all the words of the song, you know that this technique is well-suited to your personal learning style. If you still have difficulty, try one of the other techniques listed here.

Memorization Technique 2: Temporarily enlist the aid of a lyric sheet as you sing. Have a lyric sheet (a piece of paper on which the words of the song are written) available. Place the lyric sheet face down and sing the song. At the first point that you can't remember the words, turn the lyric sheet over and find the missing words.

The next step is very important. Start the song over and see if you can sing through the part that just caused you a problem. If you can't, turn your lyric sheet over again and look at the words. Is there some connection you can make between the last line you remember and the line you keep forgetting—some way that will make it stick in your mind? Don't move on in the song until you can get past the first challenge point. Then move to the next challenge point, repeating the process until you are all the way through the song.

Memorization Technique 3: Write a cheat sheet that contains just the first few words of each line or section of the song. Oftentimes, seeing the first words of a line or section triggers your memory of the rest of the lyrics. If this technique suits your personal learning style and allows you to remember the lyrics of the song, you can then turn over your cheat sheet and use Memorization Technique 2 to wean yourself from using any help at all.

Memorization Technique 4: Listen to a recording of the song multiple times. This method, much like the method used in Memorization Technique 1, gives your mind time to absorb the words. It's especially effective if you listen to, then sing, the song, repeating this process several times. You can use this technique when you're driving, cleaning, or performing a variety of other tasks.

If you are more of a visual learner, you can use a variation of this technique: tape a lyric sheet to the bathroom mirror or carry the sheet with you throughout the day and read, then sing, the lyrics frequently.

The main point to be made about memorization is that it doesn't happen automatically. If you use any or all of these techniques and you put in the time, you can begin to let go of the fear of forgetting words, get your eyes off of the page and onto the audience, and sing with more confidence and passion.

Singing Instrumentalists

If you're a singer who also plays an instrument while you're performing, you face a few special challenges. I know all about this—I play keyboards, guitar, banjo, ukulele, accordion, and other instruments when I'm singing.

As a singing instrumentalist, you must learn to divide your attention so that you can focus on both playing your instrument and singing. All too often, however, we singing instrumentalists find that the mechanics and artistry of our singing, as well as our stage presence, are compromised in the process.

Here's the key thing that I've learned about successfully managing the task of singing while playing an instrument: **don't let a challenging instrumental passage steal your focus and energy from the vocal**. Learn to be OK with making mistakes on your instrument, if need be, in order to keep your energy on your singing. Remember: your voice is telling the story of the song, so it's your number one priority.

If you are performing acoustically, be sure that the volume of your instrument doesn't drown out your voice. You want to have the vocal slightly louder than the instrument at all times—remember that the voice is the most important instrument in a song that contains vocals.

If the volume of your voice is moving from a 6 to a 3 but the instrument's volume is at a steady 6, the dynamic impact of your changing vocal volume will be lost. Changes in a singer's vocal dynamics must be accompanied by equal changes in the dynamics of all of the instruments that accompany the singer. This is true whether the singer is accompanied by an acoustic guitar, a keyboard, or an entire band. Yes, it's true that if you are playing through a sound system that's being controlled by a sound technician, you can get away with a mismatch between the volume of the vocal and the volume of the instruments because the sound tech can adjust the balance as you sing. However, it's much better to make this adjustment yourself. For starters, this will make it easier for a sound technician to do his or her job. More important, you'll have a stronger connection with the audience and you'll create better dynamics if you're the one who's controlling the balance of the instruments and the vocal.

In a band situation, it's really effective to go over the dynamics of a song at rehearsal, discussing the volume that each part of the song should be performed at. Experiment—many happy accidents lead to great artistic discoveries. For example, you might try getting softer where you usually get louder and vice versa. Try changing the volume of just one word or line in a song. You can create new ways to connect to both the song and the audience.

Support can be an issue for a singer who is holding an instrument against his or her belly while performing. Many a guitar player has relayed to me the challenge of expanding to breathe correctly because the guitar is getting in the way of this action. When you're in this situation, you must allow the instrument to move with you, not against you. Hold it away from your body, expand a few times, and then slowly let the instrument rest against your belly. Continue expanding without singing just to get a feel for whether or not you need to work any differently to expand. By doing this, you can become accustomed to the feel of the instrument without allowing it to block or minimize your breathing. If your instrument has a strap, you can also try different ways of adjusting it in order to find the position that best allows you to both play the instrument and maintain efficient breathing and support.

Singing instrumentalists can face one other hurdle that other singers don't: if you play an instrument that must be mic'd, you must limit your body movement in order to stay on the mic. Consequently, you must make up for less body movement by using more facial gestures and other dynamics to tell the story of your song.

Singing for Fun as Well as for Practice

After all this information about practicing, I want to make sure to point out this important bit of advice: sing at least as much for pleasure as you do for practice. If the majority of the time you spend singing in your life involves *working* on singing, it will probably be harder for you to experience the *joy* of singing. If you primarily associate singing with work or practice, spend more time singing along with your favorite singers on the radio, singing in the shower, singing in the car, and performing. As much as I've talked about singing a song until you run into your first "snag" and working it out before you move on in the song, please balance that with singing songs all the way through just for the fun of it. The old saying is true: all work and no play make Jack and Jill very dull people indeed.

Important Points to Remember

- Become aware of whether you are predominantly a visual, auditory, or kinesthetic learner and use that knowledge to help yourself take in information efficiently.

- Become aware of whether you are a linear or holistic learner and approach learning through the path that suits you best.

- To retain more information, say your intention out loud before you practice a behavior.

- It's critical to your development as a singer that you have a safe place to practice where you can sing loudly without the fear of being overheard.

- Ideally, your practice space will contain equipment that allows you to record yourself so that you can listen to, analyze, and re-record your singing as part of your practice.

- Be very careful about who you allow to hear you practice; many well-meaning listeners may not understand the process and could end up sabotaging your progress with misguided criticism.

- Don't waste time (and run the risk of programming mistakes into your memory) by singing through the entire song every time while you're learning it. Instead, start at the beginning of the song and sing until you experience a problem; then stop and work through the problem before you move on.

- It's usually easier and more productive to sit while practicing the Vocal Power Workout exercises.

- One of the best ways to help yourself become a confident singer is to record and analyze your voice.

- By setting up in a circle, blocking the vocals, and rehearsing songs with an AA, BB approach, you can lessen the stress to your voice.

- Always work less strenuously during regular rehearsals than you would at a final pre-performance run-through, a dress rehearsal, or an actual performance. This will greatly reduce the stress that's put on your voice.

- Always warm up before singing. The vocal folds are muscles, and they work more efficiently when they're warm. Warm-ups help you to reduce the potential for muscle injury, increase your vocal range, and increase your endurance.

- By including a post-performance "cool-down" exercise as part of your routine, you will drastically improve the flexibility of your voice.

- By singing for a designated "challenge person" as part of your practice routine, you can learn valuable techniques that allow you to have a more positive experience when you feel nervous, frightened, or timid before or during a performance.

- When singing for a challenge person, focus is the key:

Remember to put your attention on telling the story of the song. Sing in the moment!

- Don't assume that you can sing in a strong-emotion situation without practicing your performance beforehand.

- If you find it impossible to control your emotions even after practicing the song several times, consider recording and playing your performance instead of singing it live.

- If you are a singing instrumentalist, you must split your attention between the mechanics and artistry of playing and the mechanics and artistry of singing. Make your voice the number one priority.

- If you play an instrument that is held against the belly (such as a guitar, a mandolin, or a banjo), practice expanding and lifting while playing to ensure that your support system works properly.

- It is critical that the dynamics of your instrument match the dynamics of your voice.

12

Own the Stage—How to Get Them Rooting for You

The bus pulls into town and the first person who gets off asks someone crossing the street, "How are the people in this town—are they friendly?" The woman asks the newcomer, "How were they in the town where you lived?" "Cold and unfriendly." "Well," she replies, "that's how you'll find the people in this town, too." The next person who gets off the bus asks the same person the same question: "How are the people in this town?" She asks again, "How were they where you lived?" "Warm and friendly." "Well, that's how you'll find the people in this town, too."

This story is a great illustration of the basic idea of stage presence: the way you come across to the audience—as warm and friendly or cold, nervous, or unfriendly—is how the audience will tend to react to you. Ultimately, it's your perceptions that dictate how much joy you experience in your performance. Let's look at the elements of stage presence that can help you get the audience to "be on your side."

Tell Me a Story

In any vocal performance, the main purpose of the singer is to tell a story. Whether they know it consciously or not, the audience members have a desire to go on an adventure with you, the singer—to be told a story. And, whether you know it consciously or not, whenever you sing, you have agreed to lead the group on this journey. Ironically, focusing *all* of your energy on mechanics can get in the way of delivering a great singing experience; no matter how hard you try, you may end up with a performance that feels liked it missed the mark. If you don't also incorporate the critical elements of artistry and stage presence, your storytelling may suffer, making it difficult for your audience to connect to you or the song. If you then mistakenly conclude that your lack of perfect mechanics created a negative singing experience, you might find yourself working even *more* on mechanics to the exclusion of artistry and stage presence—and a vicious cycle is born.

So, should you ignore the mechanics? Absolutely not. Mechanics are every bit as important as the other elements that make up a successful performance. The key to freeing your voice and singing with power, passion, and confidence is to strike the proper balance of focus on all three elements—mechanics, artistry, and stage presence. Once you do that, you'll have a very stable "three-legged stool" on which to base a great performance.

What makes for good story telling in the context of singing? First of all, you have to look like you can't wait to take your audience on a trip with you. If you appear overly nervous, the audience will pick up on it and will become nervous as well. This isn't a great way to start an adventure. If you're worried about the skill of your tour bus driver, it's hard to sit back and enjoy the scenery. (Notice, though, that I didn't say you can't *be* nervous—you just need to learn ways to not broadcast your jitters to the entire world.)

When it comes to audiences, here is an important insight:

The audience listens more with its eyes than with its ears. This may be hard to believe at first—but various studies have shown that about 90 percent of human communication is nonverbal.

This means that most of the information we give and receive is transmitted in ways that have nothing to do with the words we use. You communicate a lot of information through your facial gestures, body language, vocal mechanics (volume, vowel color, registration, and so forth), general appearance, and energy you produce. Let's look at how to get the most from these nonverbal aspects of singing in order to enhance stage presence.

Using Every Part of Your Instrument

A great technique that can help you to get in touch with all of these nonverbal singing elements is to play a recording of a song that you really love, get in front of a mirror, and lip-synch or sing along with the song. Pretend that you are onstage in front of a crowd that loves you, that you have absolutely no doubt that you are a world-class singer, and that the audience adores everything you do. Pour it on, be an actor, and notice what you're doing—the facial expressions you're using, the way your arms are moving, and so forth—and how it feels. If you can completely take on the role of a world-famous singer who's doing a marvelous job of telling the story of the song, you will know how it looks, feels, and sounds to incorporate nonverbal elements into a performance.

The next step is to sing the song on your own—either use a karaoke version or perform it a cappella (without accompaniment). Were you able to perform with the same abandon and confidence? If not, go back and sing along or lip-synch with the song—whichever lets you get more into the role of "world-class singer." Notice what you do with your hands; how you move around onstage; your facial gestures. Then make each aspect a part of your own performance as you sing the song by yourself. For example, say you choose to start the process by adding in the hand movements you were making when you were lip-synching; once you've successfully incorporated those into your performance, add in another aspect—say, facial gestures—and so on. This process may be challenging at first. You may think that your voice quality or singing skills are not developed enough for you to even pretend that you are a great singer, but that is exactly what you need to do. "Fake it until you make it."

When you develop the ability and confidence to "act," through body language and facial gestures, as if you were already an accomplished singer, you'll find that it has a huge effect on your vocal mechanics. Your voice will begin to reflect what the rest of your body is doing. I've seen and heard this happen time and time again in my studio. In general, the more you move, the better your vocal mechanics become. I've observed that it takes a lot of energy to hold your body still. When you start moving, you release this energy, and you can use it to make your voice more dynamic.

This, in turn, will help you to make the connection with the audience that is so important to telling a story well. Your listeners will start rooting for you, wanting more of what you have to offer. You'll begin to feel more confident and willing to turn yourself inside out. This is the connection that helps to create a more meaningful performance. The audience members will feed off your energy (we are all hungry for you to take us on a journey), and you will feed off theirs. Don't assume that the audience will get the ball rolling, though. It's up to you to start this energy exchange.

Let's take a closer look at specific ways that eye contact and the movement of your hands and body can have great impact on how and where you direct your energy.

Eye Contact

Eye contact is a critical element of stage presence, but it is one that many singers find very threatening. I frequently remind singers who are preparing to perform to make eye contact with the audience. More often than not, that's when the cringing and squirming usually starts. What is it about eye contact that makes us uncomfortable? I believe it has to do with the very personal connection you make when you look someone in the eye. You know that the person you are looking at might make observations, assumptions, and even judgments about you—and that you may see these things reflected in his or her eyes. You might think that the person's eyes will tell you, in an instant, that he or she is, or is not, enjoying your performance—that he or she is "with you" or not. You might get the feeling that the person doesn't like your singing, which may lead you to think that he or she doesn't like *you*. Or you may get a warm and fuzzy feeling when you make eye contact. Many singers decide that the risk of seeing rejection in an audience member's eyes is just too huge and that the safer choice would be to avoid all eye contact whatsoever.

There are two problems with this "safer" approach. The first is that you can *never* really "know" what someone is thinking or feeling about your performance. Here's an example. Years ago I was watching a guy who was sitting in the third row at one of my concerts. I quickly sized up his straightlaced appearance—from his short hair to his blue suit—and thought to myself, "He's not going to like *my* kind of music." And, the minute we made eye contact as I was singing, I knew in my heart that I'd been right. The guy obviously hated what I was doing—he had a scowl on his face, his arms were crossed high on his chest, and his body language said, "I don't like anything about you." I quickly became so emotionally invested in this guy's reaction toward me that I had hard time ignoring him, and every time I looked in his direction I felt as if I were sinking lower and lower. I thought to myself, "I'm not going over at all tonight."

After the show, Mr. I Hate Your Guts walked up to the stage. "Uh-oh," I thought, "here it comes." To my great shock, he came over to me, shook my hand, and told me that my performance had been a life-altering experience for him. It turned out that he had seen me perform before, and he told me that, on this night, I sounded better than I ever had and that my songs really connected with him. I couldn't believe it! It was a great lesson for me. In the blink of an eye, I had made an assumption about what he was thinking and feeling, concluded that he hated me, and decided that, if this guy wasn't enjoying my performance, surely nobody else in the audience was enjoying it, either. On top of all that, I'd allowed my inaccurate hallucination of what others were thinking of me to interfere with *my* enjoyment of my performance.

How could I have avoided this situation? First, I could've realized that his appearance said nothing about whether or not he would enjoy my music. Second, I could have noticed that he seemed to be unhappy—*and then let that thought go*. After all, his emotional state might not have had a single thing to do with me. He might have been feeling ill; he might have just had an argument with a friend; he might have recently lost his job. Who knows? Third, I could have realized that, even if this one person *didn't* like what I was doing, the rest of the audience might be loving it. Last, by "singing in the moment" and focusing more on what I was *giving* the audience instead of on what I perceived I was *getting* from it, I could have enjoyed my own performance regardless of how it was received.

Eye contact is a great way to help you sing in the moment. Whether they like your performance or not, people appreciate being sung *to*, not sung *at*, and eye contact helps to make this happen. It also helps you to experience "singing to give" instead of "singing to get." When you look someone in the eye while you sing, practice letting go of any attachment to what that person might be thinking or feeling.

The second problem with avoiding eye contact when you sing is that, by doing so, you're directing your energy to a place you don't want it to go. Regardless of whether you are looking down at your feet or up to the heavens, your energy follows. If you are looking at sheet music, that's where your energy goes. If you close you eyes a lot, your energy goes inward, not out to your audience, and oftentimes audiences interpret your closed eyes as you saying, "I am too afraid to look at you."

A major part of developing stage presence is realizing that, when you sing, your energy goes where your eyes go.

If you consciously or unconsciously direct your energy downward, skyward, or inward, you can create a "disconnect" between yourself and your audience. The occasional gaze at something other than the audience or decision to sing with your eyes closed can add to your performance if it's an intentional dynamics change, but these tactics only works if they are done for short periods of time.

So how can we overcome our feelings of vulnerability enough to look people in the eye? There are two keys to making this easier.

1. Don't make contact with any one person for more than a few seconds. If you do, it's likely that both you and the person you're looking at will become uncomfortable.

2. Mentally divide the room into four sections—left front, right front, left rear, and right rear. If you move your gaze among each of these sections in a slow, steady manner, everyone in the room will feel included in your performance. Even if you don't look directly into every single person's eyes, each member of your audience will still feel as though you are singing specifically to him or her.

It takes intentional practice to become skillful at making eye contact with an audience because it does move most singers out of their comfort zone. Notice what speed makes the most sense when it comes to moving your gaze and how long you can stay focused on any one area before it feels uncomfortable. Practice making eye contact with small, supportive audiences so that you can safely experience, and learn to deal with, the distraction that eye contact can sometimes create. Some singers, when they are just learning to make consistent eye contact, find it hard to stay focused, to remember lyrics, and so forth. The more you practice making eye contact, the faster your level of comfort will grow.

What to Do with Your Hands

Your hands are instrumental (yes, another pun) when it comes to telling the story of a song. If you are not playing an instrument while you are singing, you have the opportunity to use your hands to enhance your performance. Subtle movements of the hands, made at appropriate times, can greatly reinforce the meaning of the lyrics. However, poorly timed or inappropriate hand movements can reveal a lack of confidence or cause you to appear nervous, over-choreographed, or just plain phony. Knowing what to do with your hands, as well as what *not* to do, can go a long way toward singing with confidence and connecting with your audience.

I recently watched a great show featuring a funk band whose lead singer studies with me. We've worked quite a bit on stage presence because, in the past, Bob would stand in one spot on the stage while singing. His only movement would be the twitching of his hands—sometimes in rhythm to the beat, sometimes completely out of rhythm. As you can imagine, this was distracting and it made Bob look nervous.

Most of his stage presence issues were the result of his limited singing experience—he *was* nervous whenever he performed. Of course, most people feel some anxiety and nervousness when they sing, no matter how experienced they are. Part of what makes for great stage presence is the ability to hide it from the audience. Bob had worked a lot on the mechanics and artistry of his voice, but not on connecting with the audience. During our lessons, every time he twitched his hands I would gently alert him to the fact that he was doing it. Over time he became more aware of this habit and he was able to reprogram new habits.

The process of noticing bad habits and reprogramming yourself can involve practicing while watching yourself in a mirror. This is one of the best techniques you can use to figure out which body movements look good and which do not. If you have a way to record video of yourself, you can use this method as well. Early in my teaching career I would assign certain hand movements to singers as a way to both help them emphasize the lyrics and get them to do something with their hands. This often helped them to loosen up onstage, but I soon realized that the hand movements I'd prescribed didn't look natural because they'd been chosen by me, not by the singers. After that, I switched to encouraging my students to come up with their own hand movements.

I had Bob try any hand movements he could think of while watching himself in the mirror. Very quickly, he was able to judge whether a particular gesture looked corny or unnatural to him or whether it looked and "felt" right for him and his performance style. This is very important. In order for any hand (or body) movement to work, you have to sell it onstage. You have to feel comfortable with the overall look of your own movements. For some singers, this will turn out to be big, exaggerated movements. For others, it will be subtle, understated gestures. The genre and style of the song can also help you decide what types of hand movements are most appropriate.

Through mirror work and practice, Bob replaced his habit of hand twitching with some simple, elegant movements that helped to tell the stories of the songs he was singing. The improvement was radical. His confidence rose and his connection with his audience soared.

Sometimes a hand movement that is a literal interpretation of a lyric works wonders. For example, I once saw a singer make a motion as if he were swinging a baseball bat while singing "you hit a home run with my heart." For some people, this would feel and look unnatural or corny, but he made it work well. Keep in mind, though, that a little of this literal kind of movement goes a long way. I've seen singers "act out" the lyrics of entire songs, and the result was always a performance that looked over-choreographed, canned, and corny. Be careful not to overdue literal movements, and be sure to practice varying them slightly each time you use them in order to make your hand movements look spontaneous.

Let's look now at a few things *not* to do with your hands. Many singers who've had some form of classical training have been taught to clasp their hands together, hold them at the base of the rib cage, and look to the heavens during the entire song. However, both their lack of eye contact and the fact that their hands never change position make their chances of connecting with the audience extremely difficult. Maintaining any particular hand position throughout the entire song—especially one in which the hands are clutched together tightly—says "I'm nervous and I'm trying to 'hold it' together." Even if that's actually how you feel onstage, you need to develop the habit of changing your hand position so that the audience doesn't feel your nervousness. Remember: in order to make a connection, you've gotta "make a move."

If you're like some singers, you may find yourself wanting to put your hands in your pockets when you sing. This rarely works. Instead of looking casual and confident (some singers have told me that those are the emotions they were trying to get across with that movement), you usually end up looking as though either you don't know what to do with your hands or you're bored. While the old "hands in pockets" technique may have worked for a couple of the Munchkins in *The Wizard of Oz*, it probably won't work for you or me. Neither does crossing your arms. The body language of this movement says "keep out—no admittance." It doesn't exactly promote an open channel of communication between you and the audience.

So what *could* you do with your hands? Here are a few ideas.

A good default move is to place your hands at your sides and to keep them in a comfortable, relaxed state. From that position, it's relatively easy to lift one or both hands a few inches now and then in order to accent a word or a line of the song.

From the hands at your side position you can turn your inner wrists toward the audience; this opens the hands and invites the audience in. It's a great movement to have in your repertoire—it's simple and easy, and it usually looks spontaneous. Another fairly easy move, if you're using a microphone, is to reach up and grab the mic with one or both hands occasionally. Like any other movement, however, if it is the *only* movement you make, it will get stale and begin to make you look nervous. The key to creating a winning stage presence is to vary what you do.

To help them develop natural-looking hand movements, I frequently ask my students to dance to songs they enjoy. You can do this in front of a mirror in a safe setting (usually alone). Once you see what you tend to do with your hands while you're dancing, you can try making those same movements while you're singing. If the movements look and feel right to you, presto—you have some new tools to add to your repertoire. Some people feel really uncomfortable with the idea of dancing, even by themselves—but, if you start by simply moving to the music, you may be surprised by how much dancing can generate ideas for hand movements. Just remember that everyone is different and that each singer has to discover what works for him or her. I'm sure there's someone out there who actually looks and feels comfortable imitating John Travolta's signature *Saturday Night Fever* moves when he or she sings. If that person is you, great! If it isn't, keep experimenting until you find movements that look authentic and feel natural when *you* make them.

Facial Expression

Dynamics are just as important in facial expressions as they are in hand movements. If your expression never changes during a performance, you can appear bored and it's easy to lose the audience. Your songs will connect with the audience much more strongly if your face reflects what you're singing.

One day I was working in my studio with songstress McKenzie "Mackie" Paige. Mackie was focusing on making eye contact during her performance. She found it uncomfortable at first, as many singers do, but eventually she was able to scan the imaginary audience and make eye contact with various imaginary listeners. However, she was smiling the whole time she was singing a song that was filled with sadness and anger. There was a mismatch between what she was singing and what she *looked* like she was singing.

Mismatches such as this happen frequently, and they can cause the audience to disconnect from your singing. If you are aware of the specific emotions you want to feel and express when you sing a particular song, you can experiment to find the facial expressions that best support them. Once I had Mackie look in the mirror, she was able to see how her facial gestures were taking away from the effectiveness of her performance. With practice, she was able to change the default facial gestures she had always used and customize them to fit the emotions in each song she sang, becoming an even more dynamic singer.

Most singers have no idea of what they look like while they're singing. Again, mirror work can be so valuable here—and videotaping yourself as you sing can be even better than mirror work because you can observe and analyze your own habits and movements, including facial gestures, when you're not singing at the same time. Using either a mirror or a video camera, experiment with different facial expressions and find out what works for you. Again, the most critical factors are that your facial expressions support what you're singing and that you feel comfortable with how your facial movements look and feel.

Also be on the lookout for unintentional changes in your facial expressions that can occur because of your vocal mechanics. I've seen singers whose attempts to sing a bright vowel color, challenging notes, or a sustained line caused their faces to look exaggerated or downright scary. If the tendons in your neck are bulging, your eyebrows are hiked up, and your teeth are bared, chances are good that your facial expression isn't reflecting the emotion you're trying to get across (unless, of course, you're *trying* to look like the most frightening creature ever to hit the stage).

With some practice in front of a mirror or a video camera, you'll be able to quickly learn how to better synchronize your facial expressions and the emotions you want to express as you sing a song. This will go a long way toward making your performances effective.

Body Movement

The next element of stage presence to explore is your body movement—or, if you're like many singers, your lack of body movement. Nothing alerts the audience to a singer's mental state during a performance as much as body movement. I have watched many performances where a singer's voice worked well but the overall effect was flat and disconnected because he or she appeared to be stuck in cement. The word "motivation" comes from the Latin word *motivus*, which means "to move." It's hard to move your audience when you're not moving.

We've already talked about the importance of a balanced stance when it comes to support. By standing with your feet about shoulder width apart, positioning one foot just ahead of the other, and bending your knees slightly, you'll be in a great balanced position to sing from. A balanced stance is only a starting point, however, when it comes to creating a moving performance (pun alert!). Too often singers find a balanced position, only to freeze in that position for the entire performance. To an audience member, it's like watching a singing "deer in the headlights."

Here's an important principle I've discovered: *If you don't show it, they won't know it!* This is true in a couple of different ways: First, if you are nervous (or if you make a mistake) but you don't telegraph it, chances are very good that the audience won't even notice. And second, if you remain frozen in one position while you sing, the audience won't "know what you're trying to show."

The brilliant jazz pianist Earl Hines said about being onstage, "You may have holes in your shoes, but don't let the people out front know it. Shine the tops."

An easy first step to looking more natural during a performance is to shift your weight from one foot to the other. There is a huge energetic difference between this subtle movement and standing still. In reality, of course, we never stand completely still. Even when we appear to stand motionless, slight shifts in weight are constantly occurring. This is the body's instinctive way of helping to protect joints and muscles from becoming fatigued. By deliberately shifting your weight from foot to foot, you're just makes a subtle, natural movement more obvious.

At an early point in my career, I realized that I felt very uncomfortable moving while I was singing. I approached a dance teacher to help me feel and look more comfortable during performing. I didn't want to learn some type of choreographed moves—I just wanted to look good moving. She taught me to become aware of the space on the stage around me that I wasn't using. I call this space "the bubble"—and learning to use it is the next step to improving body movement.

Imagine that you're standing inside a bubble that extends an arm's length in front, behind, above, and to each side of your body. If you use more of your bubble by moving inside of it in all those directions, you can create a more dynamic connection with your audience.

You can fill your bubble in many ways. For example, you can take a step forward, backward, or to the side. You can extend one or both arms out in any direction. You can drop to one knee or bend your body into any position you can think of. By filling the bubble with movements that look and feel natural to you, you strengthen your appearance of being comfortable and "in command" while you sing. A great way to explore this is to dance to songs while looking at yourself in a mirror. You can also lip-synch to a song while making a variety of movements; keep trying different moves until you find some that fit well with the song you're listening to. You might also watch videos of your favorite singers and try out their moves in front of the mirror.

By matching the style of your body movement to the style of music you are singing, you can become a very effective "storyteller" when you perform. If your movements don't match the music, however, the result will seem confusing and disconcerting. For example, it probably won't work to use very theatrical moves that are well suited to a Broadway show tune if you're singing a folk song, and hip-hop moves performed while you sing a country song will probably raise a few eyebrows. If you aren't sure what kind of moves would work for a particular song, watch what people do while dancing to the song (or to the same style of song) and borrow whatever movements seem like a good fit to you.

You really don't need to invest in dance lessons (although some singers do find them very helpful)—you just need to figure out what looks and feels natural to you. Once you do that, it's just a matter of selecting the movements that best "match" whatever song you're singing and integrating those movements into your performance. You might find it helpful to use the lyrics of the song to create a "mental movie" that you "watch" as you sing. The visual images in your movie can help you to use more dynamic body movements as you sing—and, therefore, more effectively tell the story of the song.

Dealing with Fear

Fear is the number one reason that most people who want to sing don't. In our culture, many people are afraid of revealing themselves through their voices. Fear is also what helps our bodies to create our unconscious vocal defense mechanism. Many singers have told me that, even when they just *imagine* themselves standing up and singing for an audience, they experience a fear so strong that they feel like they're going to die. Others have mustered enough courage to stand up and sing, but the fear they experienced while performing was so overpowering that they literally did not remember anything about the performance after it was over.

I got to experience this phenomenon one night when I was performing with a rock band called Evermore. We were playing at a function held at San Diego State University and, along with being the keyboard player, I got to sing one song (this was the first time I would ever sing with a band). I became so nervous about singing that one song that it wasn't until the next set that I glanced at the song list and realized I must have already sung it. I had absolutely no memory of it!

In an extremely uncomfortable singing experience, the unconscious mind can cause the conscious mind to "go away" as a protection mechanism, just as it can during terrible trauma, sexual abuse, an automobile accident, and other such events. How can you turn this kind of fear into joy, free your voice, and allow yourself to become a confident singer? First, you must become aware of exactly what scares you when you sing (or think of singing). Then you can break down your fears about singing in order to make them more manageable. But, before we work on that, I want to tell you about a doctor who studied singing with me.

Daniel is a physician who often has shifts in the ER. During one of his lessons, I talked to him about how threatening the fear of singing is for many people. I asked him how nervous he was about performing in the upcoming Performance Night that I was presenting for my students. He replied that he had recently had a patient come into the ER in severe distress and that he'd had only a few seconds to intubate (place a tube down the patient's throat so that he could breathe) and stabilize him. One slip, and he could easily have killed the patient. Daniel put things into perspective when he said to me, "That type of situation worries me. If I screw up singing, I might be embarrassed for five seconds, but nobody dies."

I'm not telling this story to make fun of anyone's fears—they are real, and oftentimes they do feel life threatening. However, when you can step back and put singing into perspective, you can start the process of melting the fear and move into singing with power, passion, and confidence.

I have asked thousands of singers what scares them the most about performing, and I've discovered that most fears fall into three main categories:

1. **Fear of "sounding bad."** This is the most common fear, and it has to do with fears about singing a note out of tune, cracking, or being unstable in some way.

2. **Fear of not having a unique sound.** This is the second-most-common fear, and it has to do with a singer being afraid that he or she does not have a style or a voice that distinguishes that singer from every other singer.

3. **Fear of "looking bad."** This involves fears about forgetting the lyrics and panicking, stumbling on the way to the stage or performance area, and not knowing what to do with the hands or the rest of the body.

Do any or all of these sound familiar?

Each of the 3 steps that make up this book—Power, Passion, and Confidence—teaches you skills and techniques that allow you to overcome one of these three types of fears. The first step, Power—Make Friends with Your Belly, helps you to gain control of your instrument so that you can worry less about how it will sound and instead focus on telling the story of the song. The second step, Passion—Make It Your Own, gives you the information, tools, and techniques you need to create your unique style and sound by helping you to sing with dynamics and emotion. And the third step, Confidence—Make a Move, Make a Connection, helps you to learn how to "look good" by mastering the nonverbal aspects of communicating the song to your audience.

Many singers have a fear that the audience will notice—and possibly laugh at—a mistake they make while singing. Have you ever watched a singer performing and noticed something go wrong? How could you tell? More often than not, the singer telegraphed his or her "mistake" to the audience with a grimace, a shake of the head, an abrupt glance downward, or perhaps even a mumbled "argh!" (I put the word "mistake" in quotes because "mistakes" often end up giving you useful or creative ideas that otherwise wouldn't have occurred to you.) Had the singer not made such a fuss about pointing out the "mistake," you might never even have known it happened. Even a crack in the voice or a note that's not sung in tune can go by so quickly that "if you don't show it"—in other words, if you don't draw attention to it— "they won't know it."

If you want to improve your stage presence, you need to learn how to stop yourself from telegraphing any "mistakes" that you make. Here's a great exercise to help you practice this important skill:

Exercise: Learn Not to Show It So They Won't Know It

Stand in front of a mirror and visualize yourself performing in front of an audience. Now practice deliberately doing things that you would call "mistakes" while you sing. Try singing an unsupported high note, forgetting a lyric, and messing up the melody or timing. Repeat this exercise until you can make each "mistake" without telegraphing it in any way. Once you've mastered "not showing it," do the same thing in front of a safe practice audience. This could be a friend or a family member.

Brian, of my teenage students, was once preparing for a performance in which he was to sing a solo while accompanied by a backup band. He'd choreographed the solo to include a bit of audience participation—in the middle of his number, someone in the front row was to toss him a shaker (a percussion instrument), which he'd proceed to use. I asked Brian, "So, what are you going to do if you drop the shaker?" To simulate this—and to prepare him to keep his composure if it did happen—I had him practice dropping the shaker on purpose while smoothly continuing his performance. Sure enough, the shaker was tossed way off course during the actual performance and Brian wasn't able to catch it. But he was able to keep his composure just fine—without missing a beat, he just strolled over to the shaker, picked it up, and proceeded to sing the rest of the song.

It's important to create a performance atmosphere when you practice your "if you don't show it, they won't know it" skills. The more you practice these skills in a performance environment (even if you're just performing for a friend or an imaginary audience), the better prepared you'll be to handle the unexpected when you give actual performances. In addition to mastering your responses to "mistakes," you can also have a friend try to distract you while you are singing by talking, slamming doors, or making other noises. This will allow you to practice maintaining your focus while you sing no matter what's happening around you. After all, when it comes to real-live performances, distractions can, and will, occur.

One last thing: **don't confuse excitement with fear.** These two very different emotions can cause similar reactions in the body—from adrenaline rushes to butterflies in the stomach to a host of other reactions. If you experience any of these feelings, ask yourself if you're worried about performing. If you can't pinpoint any one thing that you're afraid of, chances are good that what you're actually experiencing is excitement. Don't ruin your excitement by telling yourself that you're afraid!

Exercise: Breathe Your Way to Excitement

Because they produce such similar reactions in the body, it is possible to "reprogram" yourself to move from fear to excitement. The noted German psychiatrist Fritz Perls once defined fear as "excitement without breathing." I think that is pretty accurate. Practice breathing your way from fear to excitement before a performance. Expand. Lift. Smile. Repeat.

Preparing for a Performance

The way that you prepare to sing in public can have a huge effect on whether or not the performance is a positive experience for you. Some aspects of preparation, such as memorizing lyrics, arranging songs, and practicing eye contact and hand and body movements, are best done a few days or even weeks ahead of the performance. In fact, if you try to refine these elements at the last minute, you probably won't make them that much better during the performance and you may end up making yourself nervous and unfocused. So what *should* you do on the day of a performance?

An important part of your day-of-show routine is vocal exercises. I recommend that you sing your first set of the Vocal Power Workout exercises as soon as you can after you wake up. Drink some water, begin with a few glides, and then, when you are ready, start your vocal exercises. Take your time, don't sing too hard, and don't panic if you discover noise, stiffness, or any thing else about your voice that seems less than perfect. If you're at all nervous about your performance, your voice can show it in the morning—but I've found that, if you plan your day so that you can have multiple short warm-up sessions, you can almost always get your voice to a good performance level by the time you take the stage.

Once you've completed the first set of exercises, make a note of any issues with your voice that you noticed. Wait 60 to 90 minutes, then sing your second set of Vocal Power Workout exercises. Wait another 60 to 90 minutes before you do any more warming up.

Throughout the rest of the day, whenever you can, sing one or two exercises and then let your voice rest. Your goal is to sing all of the heavy-register exercises in pure heavy register as high as possible without strain.

If your voice is stiff or noisy, start each pure heavy register exercise in balanced registration instead, and use a darker vowel color than you normally would. As your voice warms up, move toward singing those exercises in pure heavy register and toward using a vowel color that is closer to the average vowel color you'll be using when you perform.

When your voice feels like it's ready, sing one or two songs to stretch your vocal folds even more. Later in the day, sing one or two songs just as you would sing them onstage. Notice if anything about your "performance" voice is not working as well as you would like it to be. For example, you may notice that you're having some difficulty with singing high or low notes, moving easily across the register transition, and so forth—or you may notice that everything seems to be working just fine. If you discover that something is not working the way you want it to, wait a few minutes and then do exercises that will help you work through those challenges (see Appendix B).

If your performance is during the day, make sure to get up early enough to have plenty of time for this routine. If you'll be singing in the morning, give yourself as much time as you can for your routine. If you sing regularly at church, your body clock will eventually adjust. The more time you can spend warming up, the better. When you work your voice in short bursts over longer periods of time, you will stretch it out and warm it up more easily than you will if you try to cram your exercises and song practices into a short window of time.

Be very careful not to over-rehearse your songs on the day of your performance. Of course you will want to run through them once or maybe twice—but if you sing them too many times during the day, you run the risk of stiffening up your vocal folds and the songs will likely sound canned (as though you are just "phoning it in") when you actually give your performance. During your warm-ups, sing songs that you are not going to perform that day; this will ensure that your performance songs sound fresh when you do sing them.

Know Your Space

A common factor in making singers nervous before a performance is fear of the unknown. If you are performing somewhere you've never been, you won't know what to expect. What will the venue look like, sound like, and feel like? I highly recommend that you visit your performance space ahead of time, if it is at all possible, to answer these questions. This is something that people in all kinds of professions do all the time. For example, no world-class athlete would try to qualify for an Olympic event without having checked out, ahead of time, the ski slope, swimming pool, or other venue in which he or she is to perform. Top-notch attorneys also do this when they prepare for important trials: by walking through the courtroom in which they are to present or defend a case, they get a chance to "feel out" the room, hear the way their voices sound when they speak in it, and so forth. This helps them to feel more comfortable and better prepared when they begin their own "performance" before a judge or jury.

If you can, arrange to get into the venue at a time when it's empty and you can sing for a minute or two. This will help you know what to expect during your performance. Imagine scanning the audience and making eye contact with various listeners. Walk through the entire space and look at the stage from many different places in the room in order to get a feel for what the audience will be seeing and hearing. When the unknown becomes familiar, your anxiety level will drop, you will have more confidence, and you will experience more joy when you perform.

Eat Right (and Drink Right, Too)

When it comes to eating and drinking on the day of a performance, timing is very important. If you perform frequently, you may have already discovered the optimal time(s) to eat before a show. If you haven't performed much, experiment on days that you can simulate a performance. Many people find it difficult to sing on a full stomach. Some find that it's harder to lift and expand soon after eating. Others can eat whenever they want to without running into problems. For example, I can sing without noticeable difficulty right after eating. I believe this stems from years of singing on the road and only having a few minutes to eat dinner before a show. But everyone is different. Some singers *have* to eat shortly before a performance; they find that, if they allow too much time to pass between eating and singing, their blood sugar drops too far and they have difficulty keeping their focus.

The bottom line is this: you have to take steps to figure out what works for you. You can practice this whenever you want by running through a simulated performance right after a big meal. Is it OK? Is it harder? Now wait a few hours between eating and singing. Is it better? Worse? When you know what works for you, you can adjust your mealtime to suit your body's unique preferences.

The same thing goes for figuring out which foods work and don't work for you on the day of a performance. It's a good idea to write down what you eat in a food journal (see Appendix A) well in advance of a gig to find out if there are foods and beverages that negatively affect your voice.

Many books on singing generalize about what singers should and shouldn't eat and drink. The truth is, everyone is different. While sugar, caffeine, alcohol, gluten, and other foods that are often said to be "off limits" to singers can negatively affect some people, they may have no effect at all on others' ability to sing. Experiment and find out what works best for you.

Hydration is also a critical factor on the day of a show. It takes 30 to 40 minutes for water to reach the vocal folds, so start drinking early in the day. If you regularly drink lots of water your body will be used to taking in a lot of fluids. Generally speaking, the more water you drink throughout the day (within reason), the better—but keep in mind that your body needs to become used to getting increased amounts of fluid. If you suddenly decide, on the day of a performance, to drastically increase your water intake, you may find yourself needing bathroom breaks at inopportune times. The keys are figuring out what amount *you* need to drink—and when you need to drink it—for optimal singing success and making that part of your *daily* routine, not just your day-of-show routine.

Get Organized

An important part of your day-of-performance routine is organizing your day so that you have time to do everything you need to do before your performance. For example, knowing what you are going to wear and having your clothes together well ahead of time will help you avoid a last-minute wardrobe meltdown that could disrupt your focus.

Another thing that can you do to stay organized and make your day easier is to put together a performance bag that has what you need in it. Your performance bag might include charts or lyric sheets, a pen or pencil for last-minute changes to a set list or chart, an apple or some other healthy snack, contact information for performance-related personnel (bandmates, choir director, church music director, manager of the venue, and so forth), directions to the venue—anything you can think of that would help when (not if) something unexpected occurs. Be prepared for anything and your singing experiences will be more fun.

Some singers tell me that physical exercise (or even a nice walk) on the day of their performance helps take the edge off any nervousness; this can also be a good time to mentally remind yourself to move effectively when singing.

Another activity I recommend on the day of a performance is yawning. Brain-scan studies have shown that yawning is effective in reducing performance anxiety and tension in the throat. It also stimulates parts of the brain involved in creating social awareness and empathy (two qualities that are good for connecting with your audience) and memory retrieval (what were those lyrics?). If you yawn deeply 15 to 20 times at a sitting a few minutes before your performance, you can enjoy all these results. This can also help to stimulate your Bosnian Belly Breathing at the same time.

Plan to arrive early for your performance so that you won't feel rushed. This will do wonders in terms of helping you to keep your focus. Once you're at the venue, try to find a place where you can be alone for a few minutes before the performance to center yourself and do some focused breathing.

Slowly expand and lift your belly a few times as if you were singing your exercises. This can calm you down and remind your body to breathe when you start singing. You could also add in some more yawning at this point.

This is also a great time to remind yourself of both your strengths and your intentions for the performance. Your strengths could be your abilities to connect with the audience, to hit a high note in a particular song, and to put your stamp on what you sing. Whatever your strengths are, have them in your mind in advance and focus on them right before you begin to sing. Your intention could be to really "get inside" a song (or songs) and deliver your feelings to the audience. It could be to remember that you can't please everyone, which will allow you to let go of trying to be "perfect." It could just be to sing a song in public for the first time without any major mishaps. Whatever your intentions are, reviewing them before you begin to perform will help you to concentrate your energy when you sing. Keep in mind, however, that there is a difference between an *intention* and an *expectation*. Having an expectation can lead to being attached to an outcome that might or might not actually occur. Someone once said that an expectation is a premature regret, and I think that sums it up quite well. Avoid creating expectations; instead, learn to set *general* intentions when you sing—and then to be flexible enough to roll with whatever *specifically* happens.

The more you perform and become aware of what works for your voice, the more your day-of-performance routine will evolve. This leads to singing with confidence and to actually looking forward to singing in public. (Yes, this *can* be a reality for you!)

Important Points to Remember

- As a singer, your main purpose is to tell the story of the song.

- The audience "hears" more with its eyes than with its ears.

- The more you make and let your body move, the better your vocal mechanics become. There is an energy exchange between you and your audience, and it is up to you to start it.

- When you sing, your energy goes where your eyes go.

- Don't stare at one person or spot the whole time; instead, be sure that your gaze moves to each of the four sections of the room.

- Subtle movements of the hands, made at appropriate times, can really bring alive the meaning of the lyrics.

- Your hand movements must look and feel comfortable to *you* onstage. Practice making these hand movements in front of a mirror.

- Use a mirror or videotape yourself to practice making facial expressions that reflect the emotions you want to feel and express when singing.

- When it comes to facial gestures, variety is critical. As you sing, vary your facial expressions as much as is appropriate to the song.

- Nothing says "I'm nervous" to an audience like little or no body movement.

- One simple way to loosen up your body movement is to shift your weight from foot to foot.

- Most of the fears that singers experience fall into three main categories: fear of "sounding bad"; fear of not having a unique sound; and fear of "looking bad."

- Practice making—and handling—"mistakes" while simulating a performance. This will help you to reduce your fear, and it will help you to learn how to adjust for mistakes that are made while you're singing.

- Develop a performance-day preparation routine to help you sing with more confidence.

- When you prepare for a performance, remember that exercises and practice songs are best sung in short periods throughout the day. Preparation that consists of rushing through a couple of exercises and a song or two right before you hit the stage is not as effective.

- Keep a food log to help you determine what and when to eat on performance days, and be sure to start drinking plenty of water well before each performance in order to ensure that you're well hydrated.

13

Going Deeper

A few years ago the Dalai Lama visited Portland, Oregon, my hometown. The whole city was excited to host his one-week visit, and every day there were activities involving him and the few Tibetan monks that traveled with him. One day during the event, I got a phone call from a friend of mine.

"Hey, Mark, it's Jody. You've *got* to come to my house tomorrow morning. Five of the Dalai Lama's monks are staying here and I want you to help me serve them breakfast." Although the idea of meeting the monks seemed pretty cool, I wasn't crazy about becoming somebody's kitchen help so early in the morning. "Oh, I don't know, Jody; that sounds kind of . . . *early*." But my friend was not deterred. "Mark, you have to come. I served them breakfast today, and it was incredible!" I couldn't understand what the big deal was, but I promised that I would be there bright and early the next morning.

Needless to say, my experience turned out to be a memorable one. A couple of the monks were older "curmudgeon" types and weren't particularly interested in interacting with their hosts, but the four younger monks were a blast! One of them taught me a few phrases in Tibetan. Another wore a Michael Jordan basketball jersey underneath his saffron robes. Their energy—their *presence*—was both hard to describe and wonderful to be around.

I came back the next four days to serve them breakfast and to bask in the peace that surrounded them. I followed them to the public library (by this time, I had become a groupie) and I watched in awe as they worked for hours each day to create a colorful, ornate sand mandala (an intricate, circular pattern that has spiritual significance in Buddhism). Then, in an amazing display of nonattachment (so apropos to practicing singing), the monks carried their fragile artwork to the Willamette River in downtown Portland and let the wind blow it all into the water! They'd labored for days to create the beautiful piece, and then—poof! They just let it go. And they did this *every week* on their national tour!

The moment I will never forget occurred on their last day in town. The Dalai Lama was going to be speaking to thousands at downtown Portland's Pioneer Courthouse Square in a couple of hours. I had helped serve breakfast to the monks for the last time, and I watched as they ironed their robes and polished their instruments. They would be singing and playing music as part of the Dalai Lama's program. I said to one of the monks, "This is a big day, isn't it?" With a quizzical look on his face, he stared into my eyes and calmly said, "Every day is a big day." In that single, great moment, I was invited to go deeper.

So, you've learned the 3 Steps to Power, Passion and Confidence; you're singing exercises from the Vocal Power Workout (almost) every day; you're noticing that your voice is getting stronger; and you are on your way to being a more confident singer. Is that the end of the story? Not necessarily. Some of you may be satisfied with the "nuts and bolts" information we've discussed so far—and this information definitely allows you to take your singing to a level you haven't experienced before. But that is not the only level you can reach. If you want to go deeper into the process of revealing yourself through your voice, this chapter is for you.

Experiencing Your Authentic Self

In the beginning of this book I mention the idea of experiencing your authentic self through singing. I think that is the main reason we *all* want to sing (and I believe that's true even of people who say they can't or don't want to sing). I believe we all want to experience our authentic selves and connect positively with others by moving sound energy through our bodies.

What do I mean by your "authentic" self? I am referring to who you were when you got here, in all your natural glory—to who you were before all your protection circuitry developed; before you experienced being "less than" (the feeling that you aren't smart enough, talented enough, or any other kind of "enough"); before you started doubting your magnificence. Most of us had at least a little time hanging out in this space when we were kids. Some of us lasted there longer than others before Growing Up tamped down our natural tendencies to express our individuality. In that space, singing was an activity that we used to express emotion—and to have fun! A major part of freeing your voice and becoming a powerful, passionate, and confident singer is recovering the feeling you had as a little kid when you sang for the pure joy of it and had no awareness of the concept of sounding "right."

One of the most important aspects of this journey of experiencing your authentic self is the concept of grace, which I define as the ability and willingness to fully receive, appreciate, and respect the gifts bestowed upon you by the Universe, even if you feel as though you've done nothing to "earn" or "deserve" them. Your singing voice is one of these gifts. Each of us received one at birth. No one was left out of the line where they were passing out voices.

This doesn't mean that everyone is at the same place on the path to being a confident singer—it just means that, no matter what your current ability is, you have a right to be on that path just like everyone else.

Whether or not you move forward on that path is up to you. The good news is that, even if you spend only a small amount of time working on the steps outlined in this book, you *will* move forward, and the payoff can be great. There is nothing quite like singing when everything is working and sounding the way you want it to. Phil Lesh, vocalist and bass player of the Grateful Dead, once said, "It's like touching the face of God. You can't go looking for it because it's a state of grace: the best you can do is open yourself to the possibility and be ready. You have to get out of yourself, so when magic happens, the music is making itself—you're not there at all."

In my own adult life, this payoff first showed its face one night when I was performing in a small club in front of 50 or so people. As I was singing a song, I suddenly had a strange moment of clarity: I seemed to be observing the performance as if I were outside my own body—almost as though I was onstage and in the audience at the same time. During the entire song, I was able to maintain the experience of "watching" myself sing while still being very aware of the mechanics, artistry, and stage presence I was utilizing while I sang. I could tell that my singing was strongly connecting with the audience—I sounded and felt great, and I could see that the people who were listening to me felt great and were really enjoying the moment as well. The experience was exhilarating and calming all at the same time, and I remember not wanting the song to ever end. I was on cloud nine—until the song was over. Then the sensation vanished, and I was back to being in my own body up there on the stage.

"Oh, man, I want that *again*!" I thought. Fortunately, although it didn't happen again that night, I have since experienced that sensation while singing on other occasions. At some point, I began to see that this was the ultimate way to experience my authentic self—as both a singer and a transcendent observer of my singing. Nowadays, I basically do my best to get out of my own way, let what I have to say come through me, and hang on and enjoy the ride. Do I get that transcendent feeling of experiencing my authentic self every time I sing? No—but, now that I know what can happen and I have a clearer picture of what I'm aiming for, it happens more often, and singing in general is more fun and more rewarding for me. Instead of worrying about whether or not everyone will love the gift I've picked out to give them, I just give it, and I allow myself to experience the joy of knowing that I have a gift to give and someone to give it to. The rest is out of my control.

Your Gift to Give—Your Personal Mission Statement

I've mentioned that your singing is a gift that you can give to both yourself and others. I can understand this may be a hard concept for some people to grasp. If you don't yet feel that your voice sounds good or that you know how to use it well, you may feel scared to sing to anyone. You might assume that you have to wait until you are "better at it" before anyone ever hears you. You may not relate at all to the idea of giving a gift with your singing. What matters most is your intention in giving it—that you realize that you have something worth sharing and you are willing to share that something with others through your singing. If there is a song that moves you and makes you want to sing, you have a gift just waiting to be given.

I do believe that *every* person has an original story to tell. It's the song of your soul. You might think of your song—your story—as a type of personal mission statement, much like a mission statement that an organization or business might write to let the world know why it exists (but your "mission statement" is far more honest than many corporations' explanations). Your soul's unique song can help to shape the way in which you give your "vocal gift."

For example, once, when I was teaching at a fantastic music camp called the Puget Sound Guitar Workshop, one of my students shared with the class that almost all of the songs she had written and recorded were about animals—how great it was to have a pet friend, how funny dogs can be, how pets help us to experience unconditional love, and so forth. Her bond with animals was her gift—her soul's unique story—to give.

You might want to write a personal mission statement about your original story and ponder its connection to what you like to sing or would like to sing. Obviously, when you choose songs, you don't have to restrict yourself in any fashion, even if a particular song doesn't seem to "fit" with your mission statement. But this exercise will help you to get in touch with your unique way of experiencing life and how that shapes your singing. You might find that you love to sing sad or poignant songs that speak about the challenge of life. You might like to "rock out," and your story could be about "putting the pedal to the metal" as you go through life. You may be interested in singing sacred songs as a way to practice your faith, or in singing blues tunes as a way to empathize with people who are going through hard times.

As you write your mission statement, you may discover something about yourself that you didn't know before. Remember that the point of this exercise is to get in touch with your life purpose and then to make a connection between this and your general intention (or intentions) when you sing.

There are many websites that can help you write a personal mission statement. Here are three that you might want to check out. But remember—while websites such as these may be helpful in terms of being references, it is up to you to figure out what your original story—your mission statement—means in relation to your singing.

- www.timethoughts.com/goalsetting/mission-statements.htm
- www.franklincovey.com/msb/inspired/mission_statement_examples
- http://ace.nsula.edu/assets/Writing-a-Personal-Mission-Statement.pdf

Your personal mission statement is a powerful tool that can help you to become a more intentional singer. Not only will you know how you want to use vocal elements like vowel color and registration, but also, you can better connect to your purpose in singing a song in the first place.

You may find that, over time, your mission statement changes as you change. I suggest you refer to it every three or four months to remind yourself of your original story. If your mission statement needs changing, change it. Your life experience, your perceptions, and your musical taste may evolve and your mission statement may need to reflect what your focus and intentions are *now*.

Prana and Chi (Qi)—Another Way to Look at the Breath

In India it is taught that there is a basic life force called *prana*. This name could be translated as "the breath within all breath." It is another example of grace, as the gift of this force brings life to the body and is the foundation of singing. Often I hear singers say that singing is "all about the breath." The breath is obviously very important—but merely being alive is not enough to create joy when you sing. In order to receive the bliss that comes from freeing your voice and experiencing your authentic self, you have to sing from the heart and soul. This is not just about drawing a breath. It is about making art—what I've called "turning yourself inside out."

This involves trusting that you are here on this planet for a reason and that your uniqueness is worth sharing through your voice. It's about knowing that the "transcendent observer" experience can happen at any moment when you sing. In his article, "Qi: The Practice of a Life Force," noted spiritual teacher Solihin Thom speaks about a second life force that the Chinese call *chi* or *qi*. (Hawaiians call this *mana*; the Japanese name for it is *ki*.) This is different than prana—the breath makes us alive, but chi allows us to live and sing from the heart and soul. It brings us into a state of harmony, balance, and rhythm that makes us *come* alive, not just be alive.

In singing, this is the difference between a singer who merely has control over mechanics (sometimes this comes off as being "slick"—as if the singer is simply phoning in the performance) and one who brings artistry and stage presence to the performance as well. What we're after as singers is a heightened balance of mechanics, artistry, and stage presence. The Sanskrit word for this balance is *sama*, which could be translated as "the center point between effort and ease." In order to be in balance, you need both. The effort comes from belly muscles, vocal folds, and a host of other muscles working together to make the sound we call singing. The ease comes from the strength and coordination you build through repetitions of the exercises and practice songs. By combining focused intent with practice of your dynamics, you can achieve this "effortless effort" (which is called *wu wei* in Chinese).

As you become stronger and more coordinated, it will take less effort to achieve your intentions. When you experience more confidence, you won't "sweat the details" as much. You will trust that what you want to hear come out of you when you sing actually will come out—and, if it's different at all from what you'd intended it to be, you will learn to celebrate this difference.

There's a common misconception that singing is "all about relaxing." That isn't true—but neither is it true that singing is all about effort. I've mentioned that you can't sing a high note in pure heavy register without effort—but, to sing well, that effort must be balanced with an open throat and the relaxation of muscles that are not needed to make the sound. This is very important. If you completely relax your abs or vocal folds, you can't make any sound at all. But other muscles in your body should, in fact, be relaxed. If you tense muscles that are not needed to make sound (neck muscles, shoulder muscles, facial muscles, your glutes—these are just some of the muscles the body tenses in order to try to "help"), you may experience a strained, restricted, or forced sound. Singing from the center point occurs when you know the minimum amount of work it takes to make the sound you want. When you are in balance, you will experience the joy of singing. Your mind will be at peace and your body will be energized. Both prana, the breath (Bosnian Belly Breathing), and chi, the life force (singing from your heart and soul), will be active and in balance. This allows you to sing from your center point—the intersection of your spirit and your body.

Chakras and Singing

There is a significant parallel between the flow of this life force energy (chi) in the body and the path that the energy follows during singing. When you sing, the movement needed to make sound efficiently begins with an expansion of your support system. The energy created by this expansion then rises from the pelvic floor through the torso, then through the throat, and then to the mouth and resonators in the head. This is also the path that energy takes in the human body through a system of seven *chakras*, or energy centers.

The ancient study of chakras looks at the effects of moving energy in the body. Each of the seven chakras acts like a valve to regulate the flow of energy from the tailbone up the spine to the crown of the head. Those who work with their chakras tune into areas on this path where energy is blocked.

The Seven Chakras

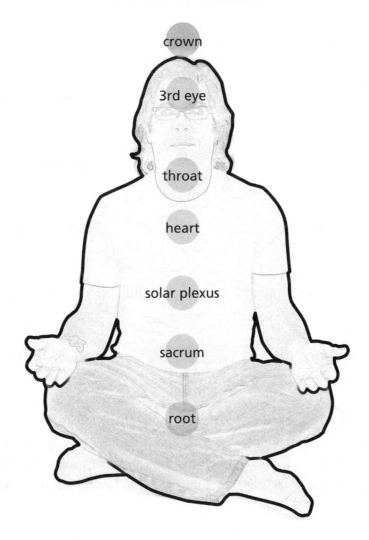

Table 4
Chakras: Blocked Versus Unblocked

Blocked Chakras	Unblocked Chakras
Root: ungrounded; disconnected	balanced power
Sacrum: breathy, unsupported sound	control of mechanics
Solar plexus: unwilling to sing with emotion	emotional, engaging performing
Heart: insincere, distant performing	compassionate, open singing
Throat: mechanical, unrevealing singing	ownership of your power
Third eye: unimaginative, "safe" approach	adventurous, "outside the box" singing
Crown: rigid, conservative performing	dynamic, emotional performing

If energy is blocked or restricted in any of the lower three chakras (the chakras near the tailbone, the sacrum, and the solar plexus), you might experience fear or nervousness and be unwilling to show your emotions. Or you may feel reluctant to be "out there" in the world. In singing, this can translate to having a breathy, unsupported sound, weakened dynamics and emotion, and a timid stage presence.

I've coached thousands of singers who have felt "butterflies" when they sing. If this feeling is strong enough, the muscles used to expand and lift can lock up, the ability to perform Bosnian Belly Breathing disappears, and good vocal mechanics become almost impossible to control. But when energy flows freely through these chakras, you'll have more balanced power and control of vocal mechanics, good use of dynamics, and a willingness to sing with an open, inviting stage presence.

When energy is blocked in the heart chakra, a person can seem insincere and distant—and, unsurprisingly, the same lack of sincerity or presence can come across in his or her singing. I've witnessed too many performances where singers clasped their hands together at their hearts (maybe they were praying they would hit all the notes?), turned their eyes to the heavens, and sang. Even if the sound of their voice was pleasant, I could feel very little from their performance. On the other hand, energy flowing freely through this chakra helps a person to have compassion. In singing, this leads to passionately telling the story of the song so that the audience feels sung *to*, not sung *at*.

I will never forget what happened to Larry, one of my students, during a Performance Night one year. He was singing to a track that had no intro— the vocal had to start right as the music did. The first time he started singing, he came in late, got nervous, was off key, and stopped after a few moments. He sheepishly asked if he could start over. The same thing happened on the second attempt. He told the audience that he couldn't do it and, with every inch of his body showing the emotional pain he felt, he started to leave the stage.

As he reached the edge of the stage, however, something in him shifted. He turned around and asked me if he could try it one more time. This time, he stopped worrying about getting it right and he just sang. His mechanics weren't perfect, but his heart was so open that he connected with every person in the audience. People leaped to their feet when he was done and gave him a standing ovation.

If the throat chakra is blocked, communication and self-expression suffer and you may be reluctant to speak your truth. Your singing would tend to be mechanical, and it would reveal little of your true self. It's important to free the energy that is blocked or restricted in this region because the throat chakra is the physical seat of your voice. Open this chakra and you open the door to safely revealing your authentic self through your voice and to safely owning your power. Some practitioners consider the throat chakra the center for healing. In his book *Meditation As Medicine*, medical pioneer Dharma Singh Khalsa, MD, quotes studies that reveal that singing and chanting can actually boost your immune system.

The next chakra is situated between your eyebrows, right at the top of the pharyngeal resonation chambers. Blocked energy here can cause you to sing "inside the box"—to do things the way you've always done them with little imagination. When this chakra is blocked, you'd tend to sing every song the same way, playing it safe. When it is open, the free flow of energy through this area will enable you to make art with your voice instead of just copying what other singers have done.

I worked for years with a singer who loved to sing karaoke. Martin would often tell me about his karaoke experiences, and I soon learned that success, to him, was all about how close he got to sounding exactly like the original singer of whatever song he was performing. This is a common occurrence in karaoke. When I suggested to him that he try putting his own stamp on a song, thereby making it his own, I could see and feel how much this scared him. It *is* safer to do what someone else has done, but you then miss out on revealing and experiencing your unique self when you sing. After some focused practice and resetting of his intentions, he was able to "wow" his audiences by creatively telling the story of the song "his way."

The last chakra is at the crown of the head. Blocked energy here can cause a person to be rigid and uninterested in exploring the mysteries of life.

This can manifest as singing that isn't able to take the listener on a journey. Free-flowing energy at the crown chakra helps a person to experience life as a mystical journey and makes for engaging performances filled with dynamics and emotion.

There is much information online, as well as in numerous books and workshops, about how to affect the chakras and energy flow in the body. Some of this work involves singing or chanting, making it a nice complement to your voice practice. I invite you to explore this area if it calls to you. It can be very helpful in freeing yourself to be yourself—and a much better singer.

As you can see, part of the journey to singing from the heart and soul involves learning where the energy is blocked as it travels on its upward path, removing the blocks, and freeing the energy to move easily. When our chakras are blocked we stay in fear; we stay small; we stay in mediocrity. We don't experience our authentic selves. The soul is expansive and yearns to experience life in greater and greater degrees. Singing allows the soul to expand. My friend Jody Stevenson, author of *Doorway to Your Destiny*, states that we are soul first, human being second. Singing from the heart and soul integrates the two.

The Yin and Yang of Singing

The Chinese concept of *yin and yang* states that there are polar opposites existing in all things. There is yin and yang present during every vocal performance. The left brain, which can be characterized as masculine energy, directs the mechanical and analytical aspects of singing. This part of us observes how the instrument is working and makes whatever adjustments are needed to produce the best sound possible. The right brain, the feminine energy side, directs the artistry and feeling of the performance. This involves the choices we make about dynamics and how much we allow our authentic selves to come through in our singing.

These masculine and feminine aspects of ourselves and our voices are present in all of the elements we use during singing. In volume, they manifest as loud and soft. In vowel color, they are dark and bright. You can sing in pure heavy or pure light register. You can make a line staccato or legato; your phrasing can be ahead of the beat or behind it. A duality exists in the voice; between the polar opposites of this duality lies a vast playground on which we can create our performances.

In order to connect with an audience, it's critical that you learn to integrate both halves of your voice. I understand that this can be uncomfortable for many singers. For example, almost everyone has one register in which they are most comfortable singing. For men, it's usually the heavy register. The heavy register equates with masculine energy: louder; stronger; more powerful. Many men find that it feels and sounds strange to sing quietly in pure light register; some describe the experience as having a feeling of being soft, weak, or out of control. For many men, the challenge, then, is to combine the feminine energy of the light register with the masculine energy of the heavy register. This creates balanced registration and a complete, or whole, voice.

For many women, singing high notes loudly in the heavy register can be very uncomfortable. Some describe the experience as sounding and feeling like yelling instead of singing. The challenge, in this case, is to integrate the masculine energy of the heavy register with the feminine energy of the light register.

Years ago, a woman came to my studio to learn how to improve the lower notes of her voice. It became immediately clear to me that she sang completely in her light register and that she had no idea how to access her heavy register. I explained the concept of registration to her and had her begin to experiment with her heavy register. She experienced an extremely strong resistance to singing out of her comfort zone. Eventually, she became so uncomfortable that she abandoned her voice study and went back to singing everything in her light register. Because she'd relied on it solely for such a long time, it had become so strong that she could use it to reach most of the notes in the songs she was singing, but she definitely sounded weak when singing notes that fell in the lower part of her range.

Both from an energy standpoint as well as a sound standpoint, it was as if she was dancing on one leg. This is difficult to do well, to say the least. Her voice was not integrated and she would never be able to move from high to low notes without sounding like she was missing something. *That something is having a whole, complete voice.*

Oftentimes in Western culture, yin and yang are mistakenly equated with good and evil. This happens in singing as well. Singers tend to place negative labels on anything that is not in their comfort zone. When I teach a singer about vowel color, he or she invariably develops an opinion that some aspect of vowel color sounds terrible. I've heard "yuck—I would never sing with a *bright* vowel color" just about as often as I've heard "singing dark sounds awful—I will never use that." Eventually, however, almost everyone comes to see that the polar opposites of each vocal element can be useful and can give them more variation in their singing.

The concept of yin and yang is, at its heart, simply about two halves fitting together to make a whole. In singing, this can involve the past and the present. When it comes to our voices, almost all of us are carrying some baggage from the past. The minute we open our mouths to sing, up come the negative thoughts: "My mom always says I can't sing." "I started too late to do something with my voice." "I don't have what it takes to be a good singer." "I remember being laughed at when I sang." But what you are experiencing as a singer now, especially after going through this book, could be the polar opposite of the beliefs or experiences of your past. By learning to acknowledge where the past beliefs came from, realizing that they no longer serve you, and embracing new skills and attitudes, you can integrate both halves—the past and present—into a whole, "I *am* a singer," you.

Remember—by accessing both the yin and yang of your voice, you can elevate yourself to being a much more confident and powerful performer.

Safely Owning Your Power

I use the phrase "owning your power" to mean acknowledging that you *have* power and making it OK to *use* your power. When you own your power you can create emotional changes in both the audience and in yourself. Be prepared to experience different emotions as you begin to work with your voice. Feelings of fear, sorrow, grief, and anger can come up as you explore singing. If you're aware of this as you start your journey or continue on it, these emotions will be easier to navigate.

Over my years of teaching, I've witnessed the whole gamut of emotions and reactions from singers. When my friend Jody Stevenson, a successful speaker and author, arrived at my studio for her first voice lesson, she was obviously anxious and agitated. She wanted to work on her voice more for speaking than for singing. When I explained to her that we were going to do a simple exercise in which she'd sing just a few notes as part of a scale, she burst into tears. She confided to me that all of the fear and grief she'd carried as a child began to surface when she attempted to sing. She had been made fun of by her family for trying to be creative, and singing tapped into that long-buried desire. It also triggered the fear and pain that she had come to associate with using her creativity.

On a similar note, my wife, Tracy, decided to heal some issues she had about singing, and she courageously agreed to take her first voice lesson with me. For eight years she had been petrified to sing a note in front of me—to the point that she would move far enough away at a birthday party that I couldn't hear her singing "Happy Birthday to You." When I asked her to sing a few notes for me during her lesson, her throat locked up, her face contorted, and she began to cry. She pleaded with me not to go on. When I asked her if she actually wanted to stop, she said no, but her fear was so strong that it took 45 minutes of gentle support to help her move to the point of being able to make a sound.

She was able to trace this to an experience she'd had in her elementary school choir. The teacher had different students sing a line from a song. After

Tracy sang, the teacher said to the rest of the class, "Do not sing like Tracy did; she sounds like a duck." Everyone laughed, and it would be years before Tracy ever dared to sing in front of anyone again. The healing began once she sang a few notes in front of me and realized that she was still alive. (I say that in all seriousness—many people feel as though they will literally die if they have to sing or speak in public.) Eventually, Tracy was able to free herself from this intense fear she had carried all her life. Now she often sings in front of groups in her teaching and facilitating profession. Being able to trace the fear to an event or comment in our past can be very helpful in the healing process.

Looking back, I can now clearly see that I got into singing and working with my voice to help heal my own pain (and here I'd always thought it was to be a "rock star" and to meet girls). I have come to an awareness that we all have opportunities and responsibilities to step up to the microphone as a lead singer in life and own our power. There are also times to step back and be a background singer when someone else is singing lead. Owning your power is one of the ways that you can share your talents and your skills and help uplift the consciousness of humanity.

Here's what I've learned as both a singer and a teacher of singers: As you explore singing, befriend your voice, no matter what emotions come up for you. Whatever your voice has to show you is the perfect piece of the puzzle for you to experience at this moment in time. If emotions come up, ride the wave, cry hard if you need to, and really feel what singing brings up for you—because, as my friend Jody says, "On the other side of pain is no pain."

Oftentimes when we start to cry, we cover our faces and restrict our breathing. *Don't block—**breathe**!* The challenge is that we all tend to breathe inefficiently in general. Even if you know to breathe, you will often *forget* to breathe in the heat of emotion. Singing could bring up repressed memories, some of which can be very strong and feel very dangerous. If you ever feel that something is coming up for you that is beyond your abilities to cope with, don't stuff it back down or think that you have to go it alone. Get some help. Find a counselor and work through it. Singing can be a catalyst to free your soul!

The Grand Prize—Sing Free Now!

You now have the tools you need to establish and use the mechanics that Nature provided you to breathe and make sound efficiently. You have the awareness to use dynamics, sing with emotion, create your own style, and put your unique stamp on everything you sing. You also have an understanding of how to use stage presence to tell the story of a song when you perform.

So, now that you know how to approach singing in a new way by using the 3 Steps to Power, Passion and Confidence, where do you go from here? I'm glad you asked!

The 3 Steps are critical in your journey to confident singing, but they are *steps*. They are not the end goal, the grand prize. They are simply tools you can use to free yourself to sing from your soul. *That* is the grand prize, and I want you to experience that with your voice.

I encourage you to achieve this goal by doing anything and everything that helps you to make singing a part of your everyday life. You can join a choir, go karaoke singing, put together a barbershop quartet, start or join a band, offer to sing at a wedding, lead a sing-along, audition for a musical—the list goes on and on. What's important is that you realize you have something to share with the world and that you look for ways to do that with your voice. The more opportunities you can find and create that allow you to sing for others, the more you will experience your authentic self and own your power, and the happier you will be. There really is nothing like the joy of singing.

When you have the power, passion, and confidence to sing your song, you not only will experience more joy in your life, but you will also inspire others to free their own voices and experience joy through singing. This is one of the great bonuses in freeing your voice—your act of courage has a ripple effect on those around you.

The path of exploring and using your voice is similar to that of learning a foreign language. You learn some vocabulary and some concepts, you begin to converse, and you start to gain confidence. If you practice daily, speaking this language begins to come automatically. The challenge with both learning a foreign language and freeing your voice is that, without opportunities to use your new skills, your confidence can begin to fade, you can get a little rusty, and it's easy to tell yourself that you "can't do it anymore." The secret to counteracting this is simply to keep "doing it." Sing every day—even if it's along with a song on the radio or in the shower. Notice how you feel when you sing. Because singing is the universal human language, you have a built-in memory of experiencing joy with your voice that goes beyond any negative experiences you may have had.

I have found that the smallest action is more powerful than the greatest intention. If you sing every day, you will make it a habit. You will not be one who *studies* singing or one who *practices* singing—you will *be* a singer. This is one of the greatest gifts you can give to yourself. My sincerest wish is that you continue experiencing the joy of singing, and I hope *Sing Free Now!* helps you on your vocal journey.

Appendix A

Grim Fairy Tales—Common Fallacies and Misconceptions

Many of you have heard sweeping generalizations tied to singing, from what you can or cannot eat to what you need to do to be a good singer—even to how you have to look in order to sing well. Let's shine the light on some of these tales once and for all.

Fairy Tale 1: "It's All About Learning to Relax"

I can't count how many times I've had new voice students tell me, during the first or second lesson, that they already know one of the major things that I'm going to tell them—that they have to learn how to relax. Here's the problem: muscles can't work when they're in a relaxed state. If your support system muscles do not tighten, they can't lift and resist and the vocal folds can't tighten enough to hold a note or make a clean sound. In order for us to make sounds that are louder than a whisper, certain muscles *have to* tense and engage.

The problem lies with all the other muscles that we tend to use to "help" in the action of singing. Often I see tendons in the neck working overtime, eyebrows reaching for the sky, jaws jutting out, shoulders lifting, heads turning, and all kinds of other muscles trying to assist in "reaching" the note. What we need is to become aware of *which* muscles have to engage in order to do the work and which muscles can relax.

The abdominal and pelvic floor muscles need to engage, the vocal folds need to engage, and the muscles that hold the upper torso stable need to engage. That is just about it. Every other muscle that tries to help is really sabotaging the process.

Fairy Tale 2: "You Either Were Born with the Ability to Sing or You Weren't—That's Just the Way It Is"

This is one of the most damaging misconceptions in existence. If you can talk, you can sing. Both activities involve the same mechanism, and that mechanism is all that's needed to be able to sing. What prevents most us from singing is fear, the actions of the defense mechanism, a lack of awareness of the mechanics involved, and a belief that we don't have what it takes to sing.

Learning to sing involves getting rid of the false beliefs that you or others have programmed into your system and returning to the state of mind that small children have when they experience the joy of making music with their voices.

Fairy Tale 3: "Some Singers Smoke and Still Sound Great, so It Must Be OK to Smoke and Sing"

Yes, smoking actually enhances good singing. OK, it really doesn't. It is true, though, that some smokers can make good recordings and can even sound good live. What we don't see and hear is how difficult it is for them to get their voices to do what they want. We aren't aware of all the problems they have dealing with the effects of smoking on their voices.

Here's the bottom line: any kind of smoke that's inhaled dries out the mucus membrane that covers the vocal folds. This leads to loss of vocal range, instability, noise in the voice, endurance issues, and a host of other problems, including reduced air capacity of the lungs. Some singers who smoke can have great performances and careers, but it is much more difficult to maintain a high level of skill for very long if you smoke. You can't smoke without paying a price for it in the end. But you already knew that.

Fairy Tale 4: "Once You Get Good Enough, Your Voice Will Always Work Perfectly"

I wish! It would be so great to have an instrument that stops fluctuating, stops having off days, and works the same way every time. This may be fairly true about a keyboard or a guitar (but even they go out of tune eventually), but it's not true about your voice. Because your instrument is a living, changing, human body, it will always have more ups and downs than other instruments. What you *will* experience as your instrument becomes stronger and more coordinated is that the problems happen less often and are easier to deal with. You will also have more experience at adjusting to challenging situations and you will have less anxiety about how your voice will work at any given moment.

If you go to a professional basketball game, you will see the players stretching, often with the assistance of a trainer. It has nothing to do with their ability—NBA players are some of the greatest athletes in the world. It has to do with muscles—they change, tighten up, and lose strength over time. This is why athletes must continue to do strength-building exercises and warm-ups. As a singer, you are an athlete, as well. You must keep your instrument in shape if you want to continue to experience the joy of singing for the rest of your life. So keep doing exercises, keep singing songs, and you will keep singing with power, passion, and confidence.

Fairy Tale 5: "Tilting the Head Back Makes It Easier to Reach High Notes, and It Looks 'Cool'"

This happens unconsciously more often than it does intentionally, but it is very common. The notes go up and the chin follows, as if that is needed to reach the notes. Not true. The higher the pitch of the note, the higher up in the resonators the sound needs to go to begin resonating. If you tilt your head upward, you'll be pinching the back of the throat—which makes it that much harder to sing the note in tune.

When you do your exercises and practice singing songs, watch yourself in a mirror and work to keep your head level (or even a couple of degrees below level). This will straighten out the back of your throat and ease your workload on higher pitches.

Fairy Tale 6: "If You're an Older Person, It's Too Late for You to Learn How to Sing"

This is a common misconception. If you're dead, it's too late. Otherwise, go for it! Age is not important—desire is. If singing calls to you, it's absolutely possible for you to learn the skills that will enable you to sing yourself "inside out." What I mean is that you will be able to take what is inside you and bring it out to the world through your voice. This is an incredible gift to yourself as well as to the rest of us. Don't make the mistake of thinking you have to be young to give this gift—you don't. I see 90-year-old golfers and tennis players enjoying themselves, and singing is no different. I watched three singers in their 80s and 90s in the Buena Vista Social Club band from Cuba who completely blew me away. The flexibility, vocal range, and beauty of their voices were astonishing. You can learn to sing better at any age.

Fairy Tale 7: "When It Comes to Singing, It's Better to Be a Large Person (Just Look at All Those Big Opera Singers!)"

I get asked about this a lot. The truth is that you *do not* have to be big to get a big sound or a good sound. Your ability to project well has to do with your understanding of support, with your strength level, and with your muscle density. I once heard a five-foot-tall, 100-pound woman literally rattle windows with the power of her voice. In fact, opera singers who have lost weight have reported more ease in creating support. Being healthy is what it's really about. Exercise and nutrition are critical to good health and to good singing.

Fairy Tale 8: "Dairy Products Hurt Your Ability to Sing Well, While Hot Tea with Lemon Helps You to Sing Better"

Another common misconception is that certain foods are good for everyone and others are bad for everyone. There are foods that *can* create problems for your instrument. Caffeine—whether it's in sodas, coffee, tea, chocolate, or any other food—can cause drying of the mucous membrane surrounding the folds. Spicy foods can trigger gastric reflux. Citrus foods can irritate the throat. Dairy products can increase mucous production. Sugar can cause energy crashes and inflammation. Alcohol can dehydrate your body as well as numb your senses to other damage you could be doing (such as singing too loudly or for too long). Gluten (a component of wheat and other grains) can cause swelling and inflammation that, in turn, can increase mucous production and lower your energy.

The important word here is *can*. Each of these foods and drinks is known to cause problems for some singers. None, however, causes problems for *every* singer. It's important to find out for yourself what, if anything, that you eat or drink causes you problems. The best way to do this is with a food journal. Every time you eat one of these potential trigger foods, write down the date, time, the specific food, and any reactions that occur. Over time you will be able to tell if any of these foods causes enough of a problem to warrant limiting your intake of it when singing.

But what about foods or beverages that can *help* your voice? Unfortunately, there's just no truth to the myth that beverages such as hot tea with lemon (or any other liquid) can—directly, anyway—affect your vocal folds. No food or beverage has that power. The epiglottis, a piece of cartilage that's almost like another tongue, closes over the windpipe whenever you swallow. This is to prevent food or liquids from going down past the vocal folds into the lungs, where it could choke you. Because of that action, food or drink can't directly touch the vocal folds. The only way they can help you at all is if they are first digested and then reach the folds through the bloodstream.

Fairy Tale 9: "If You Drink Water While You're Singing, You Will Keep Your Voice Lubricated"

If you wait to start drinking water until you start singing, you've waited too long. Water must go through the digestive tract and the bloodstream to reach your vocal folds. This can take 30 to 40 minutes or longer to happen, so start drinking water one to two hours before singing. The best way to stay hydrated is to drink water all day long. In this way, your body gets used to a constant supply of liquid. If you skimp on the water throughout the day and then try to make up for it by drinking a lot of water right before you sing, all it's likely to do is cause a bathroom interruption (maybe that's why Elvis moved around the way he did).

Fairy Tale 10: "If You Want to Be a Good Classical Singer, You Should Study with a Classical Voice Teacher; If You Want to Be a Good Jazz Singer, You Should Study with a Voice Teacher Who Specializes in Jazz" (and So On)

Voice *teachers* teach the "how to" of making sounds and using the instrument properly. Voice *coaches* are versed in the ways that songs are usually sung in a particular style. No matter what style you want to specialize in (if any), if you want to experience the joy of singing, learn the 3 Steps to Power, Passion and Confidence that are presented in this book. A good voice teacher will help you to learn the mechanics, artistry, and stage presence techniques to connect with your audience. If a teacher wants you to sing in only one style, chances are good that he or she doesn't know how to show you the options you have available to sing in all styles. Many professional opera singers have both a teacher and a coach as part of their team. For most singers, a good teacher who can teach the 3 Steps—mechanics, artistry, and stage presence—is usually all they need.

Fairy Tale 11: "Once You Get Good Enough, You Won't Be Nervous Anymore"

On the surface, this may seem true. If your voice works better, you won't have anything to worry about when you sing in front of people. The reality, though, is that almost all fear that singers experience is a result of their attachment to the goal of singing with perfect mechanics and to the hope that everyone in the audience will love their performance. Neither of these things happens on a regular basis. But, if you can learn to focus on turning yourself "inside out" and enjoying the experience, you will, indeed, have less anxiety. Your singing will then be about telling the story of the song, and mechanical perfection won't be your most important goal. Once you learn to connect with your audience and really feel what you are singing, the idea of hitting all the notes perfectly becomes far less important. When you begin to make this your goal and your experience, the nervousness will slip into the background. More than anything, you will learn to enjoy your singing even when you notice that you are nervous.

Appendix B

Troubleshooting—The Singer's Toolbox

Secrets to Quickly Adjusting Your Singing When Things Seem to Be Going Wrong

After reading and working with this book, if you are like most singers, you will probably still run into issues with your singing that you can't seem to fix (I know—you hoped that reading a book on singing would permanently solve all your issues, transforming you from croaking frog to melodious prince). This appendix will help you create a Singer's Toolbox—a set of tools to use when your voice is in trouble or won't do what you want it to.

If You Have Trouble Projecting or If Your Voice Sounds Breathy

Help your body learn to create support by lifting as vigorously as you safely can against an immovable object like a kitchen counter, an appliance, or the steering wheel of your parked car. While lifting, loudly sing a note in pure heavy register that's fairly high in your range. Notice how your abs are tensing and resisting. Now stop lifting against your immovable object, reproduce the same muscle action on your own, and sing the note again. These activities help you to train the muscles of the support system and improve your projection.

Another helpful way of making your body aware of what is needed to create support is to start to cough, stopping just before you hear the sound.

Feel the compression in the belly. Not only are you engaging the abdominal muscles, but you are also bringing the pelvic floor muscles into play. This is the muscle action that will help you to project and to eliminate unwanted breathiness.

If You Feel and Sound Tentative at the Beginning of a Song

Often there are multiple elements at play with this issue. If you are unsure of the actual first note or notes of the opening line, you may sound as though you're putting your toe in the pool instead of diving in. Before you begin to sing a song, make sure that you really know the note that the melody starts on and that you have set numbers, on a scale of 1 to 10, for the volume, vowel color, and registration. Use those target numbers for the first word or words. By sending specific instructions to your body, you will be much more likely to feel and sound confident when you begin to sing a song.

If There Is Noise in Your Voice

If your voice has been compromised at all due to illness, allergy symptoms, overuse, lack of sleep, or anything else, you may experience unwanted noise in your voice. There are three things you can do to tackle temporary noise in your voice.

First, you can change your level of support. You may need to use *less* power in order to "sing under the interference"; then, as your vocal folds warm up and stretch out, you can try turning up the power. If your voice gets noisy again, turn the power down again. If you are getting ready for a performance and you can't get your voice to "clean up" enough so that you can use the power that you are used to without experiencing noise, you will probably have to adjust the registration so that you can use less power to make a clean performance sound.

Second, you can change the vowel color. If you use a vowel color that's too bright, especially if your voice is in less-than-perfect shape, you can definitely experience noise. Sing a few exercises or a song or two using as dark a vowel color as you need to get under the interference. Then, if your voice starts to clean up, you can adjust to a brighter color.

Third, you can squeeze your cheeks together (yes, the ones in your face) to the point that they're almost touching. This creates pressure that can stabilize the folds, often causing noise to be decreased or eliminated even when changing the level of support or vowel color doesn't help. Periodically let up on the pressure and check for noise. If the noise returns, keep squeezing your cheeks until you are able to sing a clean sound without squeezing them.

If your voice is always noisy, different factors may be at play. Support is always the first element to focus on when noise is present. If you are using more power than your system can cleanly handle, noise can occur. By using less power, you can often sing under the interference, thereby avoiding the noise. You could, however, be underpowering the voice and air could be leaking between undertensed vocal folds. If lowering the power doesn't clean up the noise, try temporarily raising the power. If noise persists for more than two weeks, consider seeing an otolaryngologist.

If You Have Trouble with Singing a Note in Tune

When it comes to singing in tune, three main issues are involved: using the correct power; singing with the appropriate vowel color; and making the proper vowel pronunciation. You may need to adjust one or all of these elements, but start with power.

Determine whether you are singing above or below the pitch, then adjust the power accordingly: if you are singing under the pitch, give the note more power; if you are above the pitch, give the note less power. If you don't know whether you are singing above or below the pitch, try using more power—it is more common to be flat (under the pitch) than sharp (above the pitch). Once you have determined that you are singing the note in tune, figure out how much power you're using on a scale of 1 to 10. By setting that number and using that as your target power, you'll be more likely to sing the note in tune the next time.

If changing the power doesn't seem to help, darken the vowel color. If the note is at all high for you, the vowel color you're using may be too bright for you to hold the note in tune. A darker vowel color can often make the note easier to reach and allow you to sing in tune. Again, once the note is in tune, assign the vowel color a number on a scale of 1 to 10, with 10 being the brightest. This will give you a target to shoot for, and it will greatly up the odds of singing the note in tune the next time.

If neither of those approaches seems to work, modify the vowel that you are singing. In fact, use a pure "oo" vowel to sing the note and notice if it is in tune. If so, temporarily replace the vowel of the word you're singing with an "oo"—love becomes loov; rose becomes roose, and so forth. Once you can sing the word in tune, start moving the pronunciation of the vowel away from "oo" and back toward the correct vowel, keeping the pitch steady.

A wonderful practice tool for improving pitch is a software program called PitchPerfector (available at www.SingFreeNow.com). I use it in my own singing practices as well as with my students.

If You Have Trouble with Singing a High Note

The same three issues that are involved in singing in tune also apply to singing a high note—appropriate power, vowel color, and vowel pronunciation. If any one of those elements is out of adjustment, your high note may be shaky. You also need to be aware of three other factors that can affect your ability to sing a high note with ease. The first is the vowel that's being sung. Many singers have asked me why they can sing a high note in one song but have a hard time singing the exact same note in a different song. Almost always, the note that is giving them trouble is sung on a vowel with a naturally bright vowel color.

If you refer to Figure 1 (page 105), you will notice that there are vowels that are naturally darker or brighter. Changes in vowel color can cause difficulties in some situations. For example, you may find that it's easier to sing a note using an "o" vowel than it is to sing the same note using an "e" vowel. The "e" naturally wants to go brighter, putting more tension on the back wall of the throat and making it more difficult to hold the note steady. Your job is to match the color of the "e" vowel to that of the "o" vowel. Once you can do that, it may then be possible to brighten the "e" a little and still hold it steady.

The second factor involved in hitting a high note is the "set-up note," or the note that falls just before the high note. It is critical to sing it in a way that helps you to hit the high note that follows. If the set-up note is just a little lower than the high note, both notes will require a very similar approach in terms of power and vowel color. If you let the set-up note become too bright or if you underpower it even slightly, you will have to make too many adjustments between that note and the high note. This makes it tough to get the sound you want on the target (high) note. If you assign numbers for power and vowel color to both the set up note and the high note and you practice singing them with those intentions (settings) in mind, you will have much better results.

If the set-up note is quite a bit lower than the high note, you will have to make more radical adjustments to power and vowel color on the way up. The key is to have your intentions firmly in mind. If you have no intentions for vowel color and power in mind when you sing the notes, your body will have a much harder time singing the high note. If, however, you set your intention to move from, say, a 6 vowel color on the set-up note to a darker 4 vowel color on the high note, you'll greatly improve your chances of getting the sound you want. Eventually you won't have to micromanage the process—but, in the beginning, doing so will enable you to sing high notes much more easily.

The third factor that can affect the ease with which you can sing high notes is the position of your head. Many singers have a tendency to tilt their heads back when moving up the scale. It's as if the chin wants to follow the pitch. This pinches off the resonators and makes you have to work harder to get the note to initially resonate in the correct place. By holding your chin level with the ground or very slightly below level, you'll straighten out the pharyngeal tract and make high notes easier to sing. As a way to break the habit of tilting the head back, some singers find it helpful to occasionally bend over while practicing the line that contains the high note.

If You Have Trouble with Singing a Low Note

The same basic issues are involved in singing both high and low notes, but different adjustments are required for each. When singing a low note, you must reduce the power, but be aware that it is easy to go too far. Experiment with different power settings while singing the note until you find the one that works best; then assign it a number, on a scale of 1 to 10, so that you can find it again.

One of the main ways that singers sabotage their low notes is by either consciously or unconsciously making them "bassier"—deeper, darker, and more like a true male bass would sing them. The problem with this approach is that notes get duller and muddier as they get lower—and, if you make them "bassier," their clarity gets even worse. This makes it very difficult to project while singing a low note. Sing brighter as notes get lower to counteract the dull, muddy sound. Just as higher notes require you to modify all vowels sung on those notes to "oo," lower notes require you to modify all vowels sung on those notes to "ah," making them brighter. With practice, your body will automatically find the right combination of power, vowel color, and vowel modification to make your low notes easier to sing.

If You Are a Habitual Throat Clearer

If you constantly clear your throat, you are probably causing more problems with your voice than you are aware of. The sound made when you clear your throat is the result of the vocal folds scraping against each other, trying to rid themselves of mucous or phlegm. Oftentimes, however, throat clearing removes nothing. This can be because the phlegm is so thick that you can't dislodge it or it may be that tissue around the vocal folds is swollen, causing it to come into contact with the folds. This feels like phlegm, so you clear your throat, trying to get rid of something that isn't there. The constant scraping can cause the mucous membrane covering the vocal folds to produce even more mucous, which just adds to the problem. It's similar to using gasoline to try to put out a fire.

What can you do instead? The best idea is to do nothing, but that doesn't really work for most people. (It's like saying "don't scratch a mosquito bite" when it's itching like crazy. When you feel that something is on your vocal folds, it's almost impossible to ignore.) First, clear your throat as you normally would. If the action kicks up some phlegm that you can get rid of, great. If not, try swallowing. If that doesn't work, cough lightly (a light cough is much less traumatic to the vocal folds and will "scratch the itch"). Humming can also help to relieve the desire to forcefully or repeatedly clear the throat. You can also try taking an expectorant. This is a product that helps to thin and liquefy mucous so that coughing or throat clearing can actually move it out of the body. Be sure to drink plenty of water when taking such a product, and avoid any expectorant that also contains a decongestant or antihistamine. Both of those can dry out the vocal folds, causing flexibility and vocal range issues.

The bottom line for throat clearers is this: you need to become aware of whether or not your attempts to clear your throat are really effective. If they aren't actually helping to get rid of the "problem," stop.

If Your Voice Wobbles or Is Otherwise Unstable

If your voice is unstable, the first thing to examine is your lift. If your lift is unstable, your voice will be unstable. Lifting without proper stability is very much like rapidly changing your foot pressure on the gas pedal of your car. The car will jerk with every change. By smoothing out the lift and keeping the speed with which you lift constant through the line you are singing, you will go a long way toward helping yourself to stabilize your voice.

If you practice holding a note for a few seconds, you will soon realize that a stable voice is not defined by a lack of movement or change—on the contrary, it is created through constant micro-adjustments to both the intensity and speed of your lift that allow your voice to remain steady. The simple practice of sustaining a note for 10 seconds or more will help your body learn how to make these micro-adjustments in order to keep your voice stable.

Appendix C

Top 20 Issues That Singers Experience

Issue	Vocal Principles Involved
1. Singing in Tune	Power (Support; Resonation; Registration)
2. Projecting	Power (Support; Resonation)
3. Having a Unique Sound	Passion (Style; Dynamics)
4. Being Confident	Power; Passion; Confidence
5. Singing High Notes	Power (Support; Resonation; Registration)
6. Singing Low Notes	Power (Resonation)
7. Breathing Efficiently	Power (Bosnian Belly Breathing)
8. Maintaining Endurance	Power (Support; Strength)
9. Looking "Good" Onstage	Confidence (Eye Contact; Hand and Body Movement)
10. Remembering Lyrics	Confidence (Memory Exercises)
11. Owning a Song	Passion (Style; Dynamics; Musical Arrangement)
12. Sounding "Full," "Resonant," or "Musical"	Power (Support; Resonation; Registration)
13. Maintaining Control	Power (Support; Resonation; Registration)
14. Singing Across the "Break"	Power (Registration; Strength; Coordination)
15. Having Options	Power; Passion

16. Straining to Sing Notes   Power (Support; Strength; Registration)
17. Sounding Good When Singing High Notes   Power (Resonation)
18. Maintaining Stability While Sustaining a Note   Power (Support)
19. Beginning a Line Correctly   Power (Support); Passion (Knowing the Melody)
20. Experiencing Joy Onstage   Power; Passion; Confidence

Glossary

Artistry: the use of dynamics, emotion, and style to make singing interesting.

Arytenoid cartilage: a pair of cartilages to which the vocal folds are attached. Their rotation causes the vocal folds to open or close.

Bernoulli's principle: the principle that states that moving gas exerts less pressure than stationary gas. This principle explains why your vocals folds are closed during singing. The less power that's used, the less able your vocal folds are to be closed as a result of pressure, resulting in the folds themselves having to work to stay closed.

Bosnian Belly Breathing: a way to jump-start natural, efficient breathing. It involves expanding and lifting your belly in order to both cause and allow your diaphragm to do its job efficiently, as well as holding the rib cage in a lifted and expanded position, as if you were holding up a pair of pants that are too big.

Break: the transition between the heavy register and the light register; it's often used to describe a transition that does not sound smooth.

Breathy: a term used to describe the sound of air leaking through your glottis. When done intentionally for artistic effect, the vocal folds are relaxed to allow extra air to pass between them. Unintentional breathiness can be caused by inflammation of the vocal folds due to allergies, sickness, overuse, or inefficient mechanics.

Chakra: a Sanskrit word that means "wheel." Traditional Indian medicine describes seven chakras, or energy centers, that are aligned with the spine from the tailbone to the crown of the head and that receive and express life force energy (chi).

Chi (Qi): An ancient Chinese term that refers to the "life force" energy that runs through and around all things.

Circadian rhythm: the pattern of human biological activity in a 24-hour period.

Cricoarytenoids: a pair of muscles, located in the larynx, that help tense the vocal folds during speaking and singing.

Cricothyroids: a pair of muscles involved in controlling the length of the vocal folds, which determines pitch.

Diaphragm: a large, dome-shaped muscle that separates the thoracic cavity (where the lungs and heart are) from the abdominal cavity. Nature intends for your diaphragm to move up and down, like the plunger in a syringe, to move air in and out of the body efficiently.

Diphthong: a sound that is made up of one vowel sound gliding into a second vowel sound within a single syllable.

Dynamics: the varied use of any element of singing or performance, such as volume, vowel color, and body movement, to create interest.

Epiglottis: a flap of cartilage that closes over the windpipe to stop food and liquid from entering the lungs during swallowing.

Glide: an exercise in which "yoh" is sung, starting on the lowest note you can sing and gently sliding to the highest note you can sing, then sliding back down to the starting note. It should be sung at a 2 volume on a scale of 1 to 10.

Glottal fry: a creaky sound made when the vocal folds are relatively slack and air moves slowly between them. It can be used intentionally as an artistic effect but it can irritate the folds if used habitually.

Glottis: the space between your vocal folds. The size and shape of your glottis helps to determine the pitch that is to be sung.

Hard palate: the hard, bony part of the roof of your mouth. It ends where the soft palate begins, toward the back of your mouth.

Ideal Voice Model (IVM): a mental image of the sound of your voice working exactly as you want it to; used in analyzing the state of your voice at any given moment.

Interference: unwanted noise in the voice.

Kinesthesia: awareness of the sensations felt by your body during a certain circumstance or action.

Laryngopharynx: the lowest of the three laryngeal resonators.

Larynx: the structure in the throat that houses your vocal folds. (Commonly called the voice box.)

Legato: an Italian word that means "tied together." It indicates that notes should be sung in a smooth, connected way.

Lombard effect: the automatic reaction of the body to sing or speak louder in an attempt to be heard above background noise. Can cause fatigue to the vocal folds and loss of vocal endurance.

Mechanics: the physical techniques that are required and used to breathe and to make sound.

Melisma: the act of singing a syllable over two or more notes. (Commonly called ornamentation.)

Nasal cilia: small hair-like cells in the nostrils that filter out dust and dirt as you breathe in and that trap moisture as you breathe out, keeping the air in your nose hydrated.

Nasopharynx: the highest of the three laryngeal resonators.

Note: a term that refers to the musical steps on a scale and the letter names assigned to those steps, such as C sharp, A, and B flat. In the Solfége system, these steps are named do, re, mi, and so forth.

Onset: the moment that your vocal folds come together and create the beginning of a sound during singing. (Also called the start-up.)

Oropharynx: the middle of the three pharyngeal resonators.

Passaggio: the Italian word for "passage." In singing, it refers to the transition from one register to another.

Pelvic floor: a system of muscles between your tailbone and pubic bone that can help to create support and produce efficient Bosnian Belly Breathing. (Also called the pelvic diaphragm.)

Pharyngeal resonators: the three areas in the back of your throat that encompass the space from your vocal folds to the bridge of your nose. Along with your mouth, they are the resonation chambers for your voice.

Pitch: a term that refers to whether or not a note that is sung or played is in tune.

Prana: a Sanskrit word meaning "the breath within all breath."

Proprioception: awareness of whether your body is moving or not and where your body parts are in relation to one another.

Rectus abdominis: the large, paired abdominal muscles that lie vertically in the belly; commonly called the "six-pack" muscles.

Register transition: the movement from heavy register to light register and vice versa. (See also *Break*.)

Registration: one of the Big Three Vocal Principles; used to refer to the two distinct ways in which the muscles that tense the vocal folds can be used to make sound. The two ways of making sound are referred to as heavy register and light register (as well as "chest voice" and "head voice," lower register and upper register, and other terms). The simultaneous use of both registers is called balanced registration.

Resonation: one of the Big Three Vocal Principles; refers to your ability to change the tone of your voice by manipulating the mouth, the pharyngeal resonators, or both to change vowel color and vowel pronunciation.

Reverse ratio: the relationship between mechanics used to produce sound and some aspect of the sound that actually is produced (for example, the relationship between the power that's used to sing a high note and the volume that's produced when that note is sung).

Shoulder breathing: breathing that is performed by lifting the clavicles (collarbones) and shoulders to move air in and out of the body. It is the least efficient way to breathe.

Soft palate: the soft, fleshy part of the roof of your mouth. It can move to open and close access to the upper regions of your pharyngeal resonators.

Staccato: the Italian word for "detached." It indicates that notes should be sung with a short, choppy, or "separated" feel.

Stage presence: a term used to refer to all nonverbal aspects of a singer's performance, such as eye contact, facial gestures, and hand or body movement.

Strain: overexertion of the muscles used to create sound, causing the voice to become noisy and preventing the vocal folds from holding together; may result in discomfort.

Style: a term used to refer to the unique combination of elements you use in singing; also used to refer to singing in the manner of a particular musical genre (such as jazz, classical, rock, and so forth).

Support: the control you have over the airflow when you sing; it is created by lifting the belly and resisting against the lift.

Swallowing muscles: the muscles that move the tongue when you swallow; unintentional or inappropriate use of these muscles during singing can cause noise in the voice and can make it difficult to sing higher notes.

Tessitura: the comfort zone, or "sweet spot," of a singer's range; in a song it refers to where the pitch range of the melody most often lies, excluding the extremes of high and low.

Tone: a term that describes the character or timbre of a sound. It is what allows you to tell a piano from a flute when they are both playing the same note.

Uvula: the small projection of tissue at the back end of the soft palate.

Vocal cords: a term that's commonly used to describe the vocal folds.

Vocal defense mechanism: an unconscious system that works to protect you from embarrassing yourself, hurting yourself, or working too hard.

Vocal folds: a pair of small bands of muscle tissue, lying horizontally in your windpipe, that vibrate, causing sound to be created.

Vocal tract: the parts of your body (the throat and mouth) through which sound travels once it's created by the vibration of the vocal folds.

Voice box: a term that's commonly used to describe the larynx.

Voiceprint: the set of unique characteristics that make up each person's voice. A voiceprint is as identifiable as a fingerprint.

Vowel color: a term used to describe the particular tonal quality of a sound that is made (similar to treble and bass); vowel color ranges from ultradark to ultrabright.

Vowel integrity: a term used to refer to the purity of a vowel sound based, mainly, on how the vowel is pronounced.

Vowel modification: the act of changing any vowel's pronunciation in order to help it initially resonate in the correct place.

Wabi-sabi: as opposed to the West's view that beauty comes from perfection, wabi-sabi is the Japanese view of art and beauty, which is based on three principles: nothing is permanent; nothing is finished; and nothing is perfect.

Wu wei: the state of "effortless effort" that, in singing, describes the balance between working enough to produce sound and being efficient enough to avoid overworking. It has been translated as "action without effort."

Resources

Here are a few books, movies, and TV shows that you may find interesting.

Books

Allen, Jeffrey. *Secrets of Singing for Female Voice*. Van Nuys, CA: Alfred Music Publishing, 2005. A resource for female singers who want to better understand how the vocal instrument works. (Includes two CDs—one for "high voice" and one for "low voice.")

Allen, Jeffrey. *Secrets of Singing for Male Voice*. Miami, FL: Warner Bros. Publications, 1994. A resource for male singers who want to better understand how the vocal instrument works (Includes two CDs—one for "high voice" and one for "low voice.")

Baxter, Mark. *The Rock-N-Roll Singer's Survival Manual*. Milwaukie, WI: Hal Leonard Corporation, 1990. A maintenance guide for working singers.

Bayles, David and Ted Orland. *Art & Fear*. Santa Barbara, CA: Image Continuum Press, 2001. A how-to book on being creative in spite of your fear.

Cameron, Julia. *The Artist's Way*, 10th ed. New York: Tarcher, 2002. A guide to rediscovering the spark that makes you want to sing.

Chun-Tao Cheng, Stephen. *The Tao of Voice*. Rochester, VT: Destiny Books, 1991. A manual of vocal and physical exercises that combine Western technique with ancient Chinese practices.

Conable, Barbara and William Conable. *How to Learn the Alexander Technique*, 3rd ed. Chicago, IL: GIA Publications, 1995. A manual for singers (and others) who want to explore improving performance, ease of movement, and well-being through body alignment.

Craig, David. *On Singing Onstage*, revised ed. New York: Applause Books, 2000. This guide offers verbal and nonverbal techniques to improve stage presence.

Farhi, Donna. *The Breathing Book*. New York: Holt Paperbacks, 1996. A practical guide to expanding your awareness of the breath.

Jourdain, Robert. *Music, the Brain, and Ecstasy*. New York: Harper Perennial, 1998. An exploration of why the music you love moves you.

Karpf, Anne. *The Human Voice*. New York: Bloomsbury USA, 2006. This book offers insight into ways that your voice reveals important aspects of who you are.

Levitin, Daniel J. *The World in Six Songs*. New York: Dutton, 2008. Rock musician turned neuroscientist Levitin explains how music is a core element of human identity.

Mathieu, W. A. *The Listening Book*. Boston, MA: Shambhala, 1991. This book discusses the importance of listening (to music as well as to other sounds) as a tool for self-discovery and personal transformation.

Mithen, Steven. *The Singing Neanderthals*. Cambridge, MA: Harvard University Press, 2007. Archeologist Mithen explores how the evolution of music has affected our language and our lives.

Sacks, Oliver. *Musicophilia*, revised ed. New York: Vintage, 2008. Acclaimed neurologist Sacks shares stories of how music can alter the brain.

Stevenson, Jody. *Soul Purpose*. Portland, OR: Source Communications, 1995. A guide to rediscovering your creative genius.

Sudo, Philip Toshio. *Zen Guitar*. New York: Simon & Schuster, 1998. A student of Eastern philosophy and an avid guitar player offers insight into finding and awakening the song within each of us that makes us unique.

Vennard, William. *Singing: The Mechanism and the Technic*. New York: Carl Fischer, Inc., 1967. One of the first "bibles" of vocal physiology.

Wilson, Frank R. *Tone Deaf and All Thumbs?: An Invitation to Music Making*.

New York: Vintage Books, 1987. This book explores ways to get acquainted with your inborn ability to make music.

Wooten, Victor L. *The Music Lesson*. New York: Berkely Books, 2008. Grammy-winning musical icon Wooten discusses the magic and mystery of making music.

Movies

American Harmony. This Is Just a Test Productions, 2009. This award-winning documentary "journeys into the ultra-obsessive, zany, and heartfelt world of competitive barbershop singing." The film follows four quartets as they, along with more than 40 others, duke it out to win the International Championships of Barbershop Singing, resulting in the closest—and most controversial—victory in the organization's 70-year history. Available on DVD.

American Idol. Freemantle Media; 19 Television, 2002–. This television juggernaut, which airs on Fox, showcases previously unknown singers as they hone their skills and compete to win the hearts of at-home voters in the world's most popular singing competition. Past seasons available on DVD.

Buena Vista Social Club. Road Movies Filmproduktion, 1999. Directed by renowned filmmaker Wim Wenders, this documentary showcases an aging group of Cuban singers whose "vitality and passion belie their years" and whose return to the stage results in worldwide recognition and acclaim. Available on DVD.

Christmas Choir, The. Hallmark Channel, 2008. Based on a true story, this is a heartwarming tale of a group of 10 homeless men who came together, created a choir, and discovered the joy of singing. Available on DVD.

Glee. Ryan Murphy Productions, 2009–. This television show, which airs on Fox, follows a talented group of misfit high school singers as they struggle to win a national championship while dealing with the pressures of teenage life. Past seasons available on DVD.

Little Voice. Miramax Films, 1998. An inspirational and poignant film about a painfully shy young woman who discovers how the power of her singing voice can change her life. Available on DVD.

Once. Fox Searchlight, 2006. Two singer-songwriters meet in Dublin, fall in love, and find success as they write and record songs that tell the story of their relationship. Available on DVD.

Sister Act. Touchstone Pictures, 1992. Whoopi Goldberg hides from a gangster boyfriend who's out to murder her—and, in the process, turns a convent's insecure choir into "swingin', singin' sisters" who find not only their vocal harmony, but also the confidence to claim their place in the community and the church. Available on DVD.

Songcatcher. ErgoArts; Rigas Entertainment, 2000. A wonderful drama in which a brilliant musicologist ventures into the most isolated areas of the Appalachian Mountains to learn about the history of Appalachian songs and the singers who preserve them. Available on DVD.

Young@Heart. Fox Searchlight, 2007. This uplifting, highly entertaining documentary follows a chorus of senior citizens who cover songs by Sonic Youth, Talking Heads, Jimi Hendrix, and other rock and alternative musicians. Available on DVD.

The King's Speech. See Saw Films, 2010. A heartwarming film about finding your voice. George reluctantly becomes king of England when his brother abdicates the throne. Because of his serious stammer, George works with an unorthodox speech therapist and discovers how to own his power. Available on DVD.